LES PRIX NOBEL

EN 1976

STOCKHOLM 1977
IMPRIMERIE ROYALE P. A. NORSTEDT & SÖNER

La présente série de publications est éditée par ordre des corporations chargées de décerner les Prix Nobel.

COMITÉ DE RÉDACTION :

MM. les professeurs K. Siegbahn, G. Hägg et B. Uvnäs, M. A. Österling, docteur ès lettres, et M. le directeur T. Greve ainsi que M. le baron S. Ramel, directeur général de la Fondation Nobel.

RÉDACTEUR :

Dr W. Odelberg, conservateur en chef de la Bibliothèque de l'Académie Royale des Sciences.

Conformément à une décision du Comité de rédaction des Prix Nobel, les discours introductifs ne sont présentés qu'en une seule langue depuis l'année 1972. On a également procédé à certaines simplifications rédactionnelles. Ainsi, les reproductions des médailles, qui ne doivent jamais changer, ont figuré pour la dernière fois dans la publication de 1971 à l'exception de celle de la médaille attribuée par l'Académie Royale des Sciences qui porte l'effigie d'Alfred Nobel et qui orne la feuille du titre. Enfin, on a joint les biographies aux conférences des lauréats.

ISBN 91-970072-6-9

Copyright © by the Nobel Foundation 1977
This book or any part thereof must not be reproduced in any form without the written permission of the Nobel Foundation.

Norstedts Tryckeri
Stockholm 1977
773528

TABLE DES MATIÈRES

INSTITUTIONS NOBEL

LA FONDATION NOBEL est l'organisation à laquelle a été confiée la fortune léguée par Alfred Nobel dans l'intention de faire décerner un prix au plus méritant dans chacun des cinq domaines suivants : la physique, la chimie, la physiologie ou la médecine, la littérature et la paix. La Fondation constitue l'organe administratif du grand ensemble Nobel. La tâche essentielle qui incombe à son Conseil d'Administration est de gérer les fonds et d'autres biens de la Fondation. Les institutions chargées de l'attribution des prix et mentionnées ci-dessous élisent des mandataires qui, à leur tour, élisent les membres du Conseil d'Administration à l'exception du président et du vice-président. Malgré le caractère privé de la Fondation, ces derniers sont désignés par le Roi en Conseil.

en Suède :
L'ACADÉMIE ROYALE DES SCIENCES — pour les prix de physique et de chimie ;

L'INSTITUT ROYAL CAROLIN (les professeurs en titre de sa Faculté de Médecine) — pour le prix de physiologie ou de médecine; et

L'ACADÉMIE SUÉDOISE — pour le prix de littérature.
(Les noms des membres de ces institutions figurent à l'annuaire officiel de l'État suédois *Sveriges Statskalender*).

en Norvège :
LE COMITÉ NOBEL NORVÉGIEN composé des membres suivants :
Mme Aase Lionæs, présidente du Odelsting, présidente du Comité; M. Egil Aarvik, président du Lagting, vice-président; M. John Sanness, professeur d'université; M. Trygve Haugeland, directeur; M. Sjur Lindebrække, directeur et M. Egil Toreng, éditeur.
Suppléants : M. Francis Sejersted, professeur et Mme Else Germeten.

Les institutions suédoises constituent des *Comités Nobel* spéciaux chargés de préparer des rapports et de formuler des propositions en vue de la désignation des lauréats.

En Norvège, les travaux préparatoires correspondants sont confiés par l'institution qui décerne le prix de la paix, le Comité Nobel Norvégien, à son président secondé du secrétaire du Comité et de trois experts dans les domaines du droit international, de l'histoire politique et des sciences économiques.

Les candidatures transmises par les personnes habilitées par règlements spéciaux à présenter des propositions sont étudiées par les organes préparatoires compétents, et des rapports motivés soumis aux institutions chargées de décerner les prix. Ces institutions prennent ensuite leurs décisions qui sont irrévocables. De tradition, toutes les délibérations et recommandations des comités sont secrètes.

En 1976, les Comités Nobel suédois chargés de préparer les affaires étaient composés des membres suivants:

pour la physique :
MM. L. HULTHÉN, professeur de physique mathématique à l'École Polytechnique Supérieure de Stockholm, *président du Comité;* B. EDLÉN, professeur de physique à l'Université de Lund; P. O. LÖWDIN, professeur de chimie quantique à l'Université d'Upsal; S. LUNDQVIST, professeur de physique mathématique à l'École Polytechnique Supérieure Chalmers de Gothembourg; S. JOHANSSON, professeur de physique atomique, recteur de l'Université de Lund; *secrétaire du Comité:* M. B. NAGEL, professeur de physique mathématique à l'École Polytechnique Supérieure de Stockholm.

pour la chimie :
MM. A. FREDGA, anc. professeur de chimie organique à l'Université d'Upsal, *président du Comité;* G. HÄGG, anc. professeur de chimie inorganique à l'Université d'Upsal; B. MALMSTRÖM, professeur de biochimie à l'Univeristé de Gothembourg; G. BERGSON, professeur de chimie organique à l'Université d'Upsal; S. CLAESSON, professeur de chimie physique à l'Université d'Upsal; *secrétaire du Comité:* M. A. MAGNÉLI, professeur de chimie minérale à l'Université de Stockholm.

pour la physiologie ou la médecine :
MM. R. LUFT, professeur de médecine, *président du Comité;* B. PERNOW, professeur de chimie clinique, *vice-président du Comité;* A. ENGSTRÖM, professeur de biophysique; E. NORRBY, professeur de virologie; B. UVNÄS, professeur de pharmacologie; *membres adjoints:* R. BLOMSTRAND, professeur de chimie clinique; U. BORELL, professeur d'obstétrique et de gynécologie; G. KLEIN, professeur de biologie tumorale; J. LINDSTEN, professeur adjoint de génétique médicale; G. MÖLLER, professeur adjoint de biologie immunisée; G. NYLANDER, professeur de chirurgie; S. ORRENIUS professeur de médecine légale; D. OTTOSON, professeur de physiologie; N.-R. RINGERTZ, professeur adjoint de biologie cellulaire; R. ZETTERSTRÖM, professeur de pédiatrie; *secrétaire du Comité:* M. B. GUSTAFSSON, professeur de recherches de symbiose médicale; (tous de l'Institut Carolin de Stockholm).

pour la littérature :

MM. K. R. GIEROW, docteur ès lettres, secrétaire perpétuel de l'Académie suédoise, *président du Comité;* A. J. ÖSTERLING, docteur ès lettres; L. GYLLENSTEN, professeur; A. LUNDKVIST, docteur ès lettres; J. EDFELT, docteur ès lettres; *secrétaire du Comité:* M. A. RYBERG, licencié ès lettres, conservateur en chef de la Bibliothèque Nobel de l'Académie suédoise.

Prix Nobel de la Paix :

En 1976, le groupe norvégien chargé d'assister la présidente du Comité Nobel dans la même tâche préparatoire se composait des membres suivants ;

MM. TIM GREVE, directeur de l'Institut Nobel Norvégien, *secrétaire du Comité;* P. MUNTHE, professeur de sciences économiques à l'Université d'Oslo; A. SCHOU, ancien directeur de l'Institut Nobel Norvégien; J. SVERDRUP, professeur d'histoire à l'Université d'Oslo.

ATTRIBUTION DES PRIX

L'ACADÉMIE ROYALE DES SCIENCES
a décidé, le 18 octobre 1976, d'attribuer la moitié du Prix Nobel de Physique à

BURTON RICHTER
de l'Université de Stanford, Californie, États-Unis

et à

SAMUEL C. C. TING
de Massachusetts Institute of Technology, Cambridge, Mass., États-Unis

pour leurs éminents travaux dans la découverte d'une particule élémentaire lourde de type nouveau.

A cette même date, l'Académie a décidé d'attribuer le Prix Nobel de Chimie à

WILLIAM N. LIPSCOMB
de l'Université de Harvard, Cambridge, Mass., États-Unis

pour ses travaux sur la structure des boranes et les problèmes posés par celle-ci en ce qui concerne la nature de la liaison chimique.

LA FACULTÉ DE MÉDECINE DE L'INSTITUT ROYAL CAROLIN
a décidé, le 14 octobre 1976, d'attribuer le Prix Nobel de Physiologie ou de Médecine en commun à

BARUCH S. BLUMBERG
de l'Institute for cancer research, Philadelphia, Pa., États-Unis

et à

D. CARLETON GAJDUSEK
des National Institutes of Health, Bethesda, Maryland, États-Unis

pour leurs découvertes sur des nouveaux mécanismes de la genèse et la diffusion de maladies infectieuses.

L'ACADÉMIE SUÉDOISE
a décidé, le 21 octobre 1976, d'attribuer le Prix Nobel de Littérature à

SAUL BELLOW
des États-Unis

pour la compréhension humaine et la subtile analyse de la culture contemporaine réunies en son œuvre.

LE COMITÉ NOBEL NORVÉGIEN
communiqua, le 15 octobre, sa décision de ne pas décerner le prix de la paix pour 1976. Conformément à l'article 5 du Statut de la Fondation Nobel, le montant du prix pour 1976 sera réservé pour 1977.
Le nombre de propositions statutaires de candidatures aux différents prix Nobel en 1975 s'est monté

en physique, à 128
en chimie, à 127
en physiologie ou médecine, à 217
en littérature, à 135
pour la paix, à 204.

CÉRÉMONIES NOBEL

REMISE DES PRIX A STOCKHOLM

Les prix de physique, de chimie, de physiologie ou de médecine, de littérature et le prix de sciences économiques institué en mémoire d'Alfred Nobel furent remis aux lauréats au cours d'un programme traditionnel établi par les institutions qui décernent ces prix et par le Conseil d'Administration de la Fondation Nobel. L'organisation de la fête avait été confiée au directeur général de la Fondation, M. le baron Stig Ramel. La cérémonie solennelle se déroula dans la grande salle du Palais des Concerts.

Parmi les invités on remarquait les lauréats de l'année MM. Richter, Ting, Lipscomb, Blumberg, Gajdusek, Bellow et Friedman (*prix de sciences économiques en mémoire d'Alfred Nobel*) et les membres de leurs familles, ainsi que certains lauréats des années précédentes: MM. Theorell (1955), Granit (1967), et von Euler (1970).

De nombreux représentants du Gouvernement, dont Son Excellence M. Fälldin, Premier Ministre, les Chefs de Mission et d'autres membres du corps diplomatique honoraient la cérémonie de leur présence. En dehors des organisations Nobel en Suède, différentes académics, diverses sociétés savantes et littéraires, l'université, la famille Nobel, le monde des arts, de l'industrie et de la presse s'étaient aussi fait représenter. L'assemblée comptait en outre de hauts fonctionnaires civils et militaires.

A 16 heures et demie, S. M. le ROI, S. M. la REINE, Leurs Altesses Royales, le Prince Bertil, duc de Halland et la Princesse Lilian entrèrent dans la salle, salués par l'hymne royal. Puis la cérémonie se déroula conformément au programme reproduit à la page suivante.

A la fin de chaque discours, prononcé par l'orateur chargé de présenter l'œuvre récompensée, S. M. le Roi remit au lauréat le *diplôme*, la *médaille* et un *document* indiquant le montant du prix.

PROGRAMME

« Trumpet Voluntary » .... *Jeremiah Clarke*

Les Lauréats prennent leurs places sur l'estrade

Discours du *Professeur Sune Bergström*, Président du Conseil d'Administration de la Fondation Nobel

Prologue de « West Side Story » .... *Leonard Bernstein*

Remise du Prix Nobel de Physique 1976 à MM. Burton Richter et Samuel C. C. Ting, après une allocution du *Professeur Gösta Ekspong*

Remise du Prix Nobel de Chimie 1976 à M. William N. Lipscomb, après une allocution du *Professeur Gunnar Hägg*

From « The Tender Land » .... *Aaron Copland*

Remise du Prix Nobel de Physiologie ou de Médecine 1976 à MM. Baruch S. Blumberg et D. Carleton Gajdusek, après une allocution du *Professeur Erling Norrby*

2ᵉ mouvement de « Orphée en ville » ....*Hilding Rosenberg*

Remise du Prix Nobel de Littérature 1976 à M. Saul Bellow, après une allocution du *Docteur Karl Ragnar Gierow*

Finale de « Orphée en ville » ....*Hilding Rosenberg*

Remise du Prix de Sciences Économiques 1976, institué par la Banque de Suède à la mémoire d'Alfred Nobel, à M. Milton Friedman, après une allocution du *Professeur Erik Lundberg*

L'Hymne National suédois : « Du gamla, du fria »

Musique exécutée par des membres de l'Orchestre
Philharmonique de Stockholm
sous la direction de *M. Sten Frykberg*

HÄLSNINGSTAL

Av ordföranden i Nobelstiftelsens styrelse professor SUNE BERGSTRÖM
(Traduction en anglais page 16)

Eders Majestäter, Eders Kungliga Högheter, Mina Damer och Herrar,
På Nobelstiftelsen vägnar hälsar jag Er alla välkomna till årets prisutdelning.

The Foundation takes great pleasure in welcoming the laureates of 1976—you are all citizens of the United States—by birth or by choice—a coincidence not totally unexpected in view of the strength and vitality of science and culture in your country—but still probably a unique coincidence.

Det är nu 75 år sedan de första Nobelprisen utdelades. Fördelningen av prisen i fysik, kemi och medicin mellan olika länder speglar på ett intressant sätt förändringarna i forskningsaktiviteten i världen under dessa år.

En återblick på utvecklingen kan också ha sitt speciella intresse i år, då alla de i Sverige utdelade prisen liksom även ekonomipriset "till Alfred Nobels minne" tilldelats amerikanska medborgare.

Detta förhållande har givit upphov till en mängd presskommentarer världen runt — utöver de vanliga — från att Nobelstiftelsen uppenbarligen ville deltaga i firandet av USA:s tvåhundraårsjubileum till att den nya svenska regeringen på detta sätt avsåg att göra en politisk manifestation.

En kort översikt av Nobelstiftelsens organisation och arbetssätt kan därför vara motiverad.

Pristagarna utses av de s. k. prisgrupperna: Vetenskapsakademien, Karolinska institutets medicinska fakultet, Svenska Akademien och Norska Stortingets Nobelkommittée. Prisgrupperna tillsätter även Nobelstiftelsens femton fullmäktige. Dessa utser i sin tur stiftelsens styrelse så när som på ordföranden och ytterligare en ledamot, som utses av regeringen.

Varje prisgrupp är sålunda i sitt arbete helt suverän och oberoende av såväl stiftelsens styrelse som av regeringen.

Styrelsen har däremot ansvaret för den ekonomiska förvaltningen av stiftelsens tillgångar som nu har ett dagsvärde på omkring 170 millioner kronor.

Avkastningen skall täcka prisen liksom kostnaderna för det omfattande utredningsarbetet inom prisgrupperna och deras Nobelkommittéer av alla de prisförslag som kommer in.

Behöriga förslagställare är bl. a. alla professorer i Skandinavien inom respektive prisområden, tidigare pristagare samt medlemmar av ett stort antal akademier och universitet världen runt varierande år från år. Därigenom säkerställes bredd och oväld i förslagen.

Låt oss nu ett ögonblick blicka tillbaka på fördelningen av prisen genom åren.

Till en början dominerade européerna stort bland pristagarna.

Under de första 25 åren utdelades 84 pris av vilka endast fyra gick till

Amerika. Under trettiotalet började antalet amerikanska pristagare öka och under de senaste 25 åren har 100 pris utdelats av vilka inte mindre än 48 helt eller delvis gått till amerikanska medborgare.

Under efterkrigstiden har varje år, med två undantag, minst ett pris gått till USA och fyra gånger har samtliga ett års tre pris inom fysik, kemi och medicin gått till USA. Ur ren sannolikhetssynpunkt är det därför inte helt oväntat att därutöver även litteraturpriset — som 8 gånger under de senaste 50 åren gått till amerikanska författare — och ekonomipriset "till Nobels minne" något sådant år skulle gå till USA, som nu skett i år.

Den kraftiga dominansen av den amerikanska forskningen speciellt efter det sista världskriget har givetvis flera orsaker utöver verkningarna av de två stora krigens härjningar och deras olika politiska följdverkningar, som kraftigt hämmat utvecklingen i Europa.

Redan på 30-talets mitt började USA:s regering och kongress att inse forskningens betydelse för den ekonomiska utvecklingen och ökade kraftigt stödet till sådan verksamhet inom de federala myndigheterna.

Genombrottet kom under andra världskriget genom de stora framgångarna för det militärt initierade, omfattande forsknings- och utvecklingsarbetet inom bl. a. atom-, radar- och antibioticaområdena. Under de två första decennierna efter kriget ledde dessa erfarenheter till en exempellös expansion inom den civila forskningssektorn i USA genom National Science Foundation och National Institutes of Health.

Dessa satsningar har på ett kvartssekel gjort den amerikanska forskningen dominerande inom många områden.

Förutom dessa ekonomiska grundförutsättningar är det emellertid även andra förhållanden som spelat en stor roll för snabbheten i denna expansion och som kanske är av speciellt intresse för européer. Universiteten världen runt utvidgades kraftigt under 40- och 50-talen. Till en början skedde detta mångenstädes — inte minst i Europa — med bibehållande av hävdvunna hierarkiska och stela former.

Inom USA karakteriserades utvecklingen inom universitetsforskningen i stället av en dynamisk öppenhet under former som skulle kunna karakteriseras mer som en forskarnas demokrati — många besökare vid amerikanska institutioner och vetenskapliga kongresser efter kriget slogs av med vilken naturlig självklarhet professorer och doktorander kunde föra vetenskapliga diskussioner som likställda och hur unga forskare redan tidigt fick eget ansvar för självständiga forskningsprojekt inom de stora institutionerna.

Ytterligare en faktor av betydelse i USA har helt enkelt varit landets storlek och den därav möjliga stora rörligheten — den unge forskaren kan lätt nå den forskningsgrupp eller miljö som passar honom — motsvarande rörlighet som tidigare funnits mellan nationerna i Europa var samtidigt nästan lamslagen.

Dessa förhållanden, tillsammans med USA:s liberala invandringspolitik, har också resulterat i att många forskare funnit en fristad och goda arbetsförhållanden i USA antingen de måst lämna sitt hemland på grund av politiska förföljelser eller av brist på förståelse eller resurser för sitt arbete.

14

Flera pris har gått till sådana nyblivna amerikaner som tecken på den förstärkning denna immigration inneburit.

Den amerikanska dominansen torde nu ha nått sitt maximum eftersom vi de närmaste decennierna kan vänta att andra regioner ökar sin forsknings- och utvecklingspotential. Som en indikation kan man se att en av fysikpristagarna utfört en väsentlig del av sitt arbete i CERN — det europeiska atomforskningscentret i Genève.

Utvecklingen har visat hur snabbt forskningspotentialen i ett industriland kan byggas ut.

Det gäller nu att ta vara på dessa erfarenheter för att påskynda den utvecklingen i världen som helhet — något som måste ske inom FN-systemets ram bl. a. genom stöd till det nybildade FN-universitetets och världshälsoorganisationens program för forskarutbildning och forskning inom u-landsområdet.

Nobel själv har i olika sammanhang betonat att han inte avsåg prisen som hedersbetygelser för någon person. De var bidrag för att underlätta för nyskapande forskare och författare att fortsätta sin verksamhet. Nobelstiftelsen är alltså det första sant internationella forskningsrådet och i prissammanhang gäller därför att skilja på sak och person.

All kunskap kan missbrukas vilket inte minst Nobel fick erfara. Detta får inte tas till intäkt för tvångsåtgärder för att hämma arbetet på att öka våra kunskaper. Därigenom begränsas bara utbudet av alternativ och nya möjligheter att förbättra förhållandena i samhällen och kulturer av olika typer.

Men i dag firar vi vad pristagarna åstadkommit genom inträngande analys och åratal av hängivet och outtröttligt arbete — av hävd sker detta i solenna former men i en glad fest med gäster från världens alla hörn och med den ungdom som vi ställer så stora förhoppningar på.

OPENING ADDRESS

By the President of the Nobel Foundation, Professor SUNE BERGSTRÖM
Translation from the Swedish text

Your Majesties, Your Royal Highnesses, Ladies and Gentlemen,
On behalf of the Nobel Foundation I should like to bid all of you welcome to this year's prize presentation ceremony.

The Foundation takes great pleasure in welcoming the laureates of 1976—you are all citizens of the United States—by birth or by choice—a coincidence not totally unexpected in view of the strength and vitality of science and culture in your country—but still probably a unique coincidence.

It is now seventy-five years since the first Nobel prizes were awarded. The distribution of the physics, chemistry and medicine prizes between different countries provides an interesting reflection of the changes undergone by international research activity during this period.

A retrospect can be all the more interesting this year, with all the prizes, including the Economics Prize "in memory of Alfred Nobel" having been awarded to citizens of the United States.

This occurrence has given rise to a great deal o press comment all over the world, over and above the normal publicity. Some writers, for example, have inferred a desire on the part of the Nobel Foundation to participate in the US bicentenary celebrations, while others believe that they can discern a political manifestation by the new Swedish Government.

Let us therefore begin with a brief outline of the organization and working methods of the Nobel Foundation.

The laureates are selected by the "prize groups", namely the Royal Academy of Sciences, the Medical Faculty of the Karolinska Institute, the Swedish Academy and the Nobel committee of the Norwegian Parliament. The prize groups nominate a total of fifteen Trustees, who in turn appoint the members of the Board of the Foundation with the exception of the chairman and vice chairman, who are appointed by the Swedish government.

Thus each prize group is completely sovereign and independent both of the Board of the Foundation and of the Government in the discharge of its duties.

The Board is responsible for the financial administration of the Foundation's assets, which are currently valued at approximately 170 mill. Swedish Crowns.

The revenue thus obtained has to finance the prizes and also the extensive investigations done by the prize groups and their committees, which have to consider all the nominations received.

All Scandinavian professors in these fields, former laureates and a host of universities and academies from all over the world are invited each year to send in nominations, thus ensuring a wide and impartial selection of candidates.

Let us look back for a moment on the distribution of the prizes throughout the years.

During the first few decades, Europeans bulked very large among the prizewinners.

Only four of the eighty-four prizes awarded during the first twenty-five years went to America. The number of American laureates began to increase during the 1930s, and no less than forty-eight out of a total of one hundred prizes in the last twenty-five years have wholly or partly been awarded to American citizens.

During the post-war period, at least one prize has gone to the USA every year, with only two exceptions. On four occasions already, the USA has taken all three prizes in physics, chemistry and medicine. In terms of sheer probability, therefore, it is hardly surprising that the prize for literature—already awarded to American writers eight times in the past 50 years—and the economics prize "in memory of Nobel", should also go to the USA together with the scientific prizes, as they have done this year.

There are of course many reasons for the heavy predominance of American research specially after the last world war, apart from the ravages of the two world wars and their various political consequences, which have greatly inhibited developments in Europe.

Even in the mid-1930s the American government had begun to realize the importance of research to economic development, and the Congress therefore substantially increased the support given to such activities within the Federal authorities.

The principal breakthrough came during the Second World War, with the great successes from research and development work sponsored by the defence establishment resulting in the atomic bomb, radar, antibiotics, etc. During the first two decades of the post-war years, the experience thus accumulated, led to an unprecedented expansion of the civilian research sector in the USA through the National Science Foundation and especially through the National Institutes of Health.

Within a quarter of a century these efforts have put America in the vanguard of research in many sectors.

But apart from these basic economic prerequisites, there are other actors which have greatly contributed towards the rapidity of America's expansion in the research sector and which are perhaps of particular interest to Europeans. Universities all over the world expanded rapidly during the 1940s and 1950s. In many places, and not least in the European countries, this expansion took place with the retention of traditional hierarchic and inflexible structures.

In the USA, on the other hand, the growth of university research was characterized by a dynamic openness in forms which might be characterized as a democracy of research workers. Many visitors to American institutions and scientific congresses after the war were struck by the natural way in which professors and students could conduct scientific discussions on a basis of equality and also by the practice of making young researchers responsible at an

17

early stage in their careers for independent research projects within the big institutions.

The second important factor in the USA has, quite simply, been the size of the country and the great mobility thus afforded—it is easy for the young scientist to reach the group or environment that suits him—especially at a time when the mobility which had previously existed in these respects between the European countries was almost completely suppressed.

All these factors taken together with liberal immigration laws has made the USA a haven for many scientists who have left their country of origin for political reasons or for lack of support or suitable conditions for scientific work.

Several prizes have been awarded to such "new" Americans, which testifies to the reeinforcing effect of immigration in the USA.

The American predominance has now presumably attained its apogee, and during the next few decades it is to be expected that other industrialized countries will increase their research and development potential. An indication in this direction can be seen in the fact that one of the physics laureates did a great deal of his research work at Cern—the European atomic research centre in Geneva.

Events have shown how quickly the research potential of an industrial country can be expanded. Our problem today concerns the best way of using this experience to accelerate the development of research potential in the world as a whole. This can only be done under the aegis of the United Nations, e. g. by supporting the wider scheme of research training and research in developing countries sponsored by the recently established UN University and by the World Health Organization.

Nobel himself emphasized in various connections that he did not intend the prizes as mere decorations. Instead their purpose was to make it easier for creative researchers and writers to carry on with their work.

Thus the Nobel Foundation is the first truly international research council, and one should therefore distinguish between causes and persons where the award of prizes is concerned. All knowledge can be abused, as Nobel of all people was able to see. This must not be taken as a pretext for coercive measures to impede the advancement of knowledge, measures which would only serve to limit our range of options and our new opportunities of improving conditions in different societies and cultures.

But today we celebrate what the laureates have achieved as a result of penetrating analysis and years of dedicated and untiring labour. By tradition this celebration is couched in solemn forms but in a mood of glad festivity with guests from every corner of the world and together with the young people on whom we pin such high hopes.

THE NOBEL PRIZE FOR PHYSICS

Speech by professor GÖSTA EKSPONG of the Royal Academy of Sciences
Translation from the Swedish text

Your Majesties, Your Royal Highnesses, Ladies and Gentlemen,
By decision of the Royal Swedish Academy of Sciences, this year's Nobel
Prize for physics has been awarded to Professor Burton Richter and to Professor Samuel Ting for their pioneering work in the discovery of a heavy
elementary particle of a new kind.

This discovery has opened new vistas and given rise to great activity in all
laboratories around the world where resources are available. It brings with it
the promise of a deeper understanding of all matter and of several of its
fundamental forces.

Elementary particles are very small compared to our human dimensions.
They are smaller than viruses and molecules and atoms, even smaller than
the tiny nucleus of most atoms. They are of great importance when it comes
to understanding the basic structure and the basic forces of the material
world. In some cases they can even be of importance to society. A basic
philosophy is that the material units on any level of subdivision derive their
properties from the levels below.

Seventy years ago the first elementary particle was involved in a Nobel
Prize. This was at a time when no valid picture of atoms had been formulated.
In his Nobel lecture in 1906, J. J. Thompson spoke about his discovery of
the electron as one of the bricks of which atoms are built up. Today we know
that the electron plays a decisive role in many sciences and technologies and
through them in many walks of life—it binds together the molecules of our
own bodies, it carries the electricity which makes our lamps shine and it
literally draws up the pictures on the TV-screens.

Fourty years ago Carl David Andersson was awarded a Nobel Prize for the
discovery of the positron—which is the antiparticle to the electron. In the
presentation of the award in 1936, it was mentioned that twins of one electron
and one positron could be born out of the energy coming from radiation. The
reverse can also happen. If the two opposite types of particle meet they can
disappear and the energy, which can never be destroyed, shows up as radiation. Only in recent years has this description been enriched through
experiments at higher energies, where, among many researchers, both Richter
and Ting have contributed.

It is with these two particles that the Nobel laureates Ting and Richter
have again experimented in most successful ways. Ting discovered the new
particle when he investigated how twins of one electron and one positron are
born at very high energies. Richter arranged for electrons and positrons to
meet in head-on collisions and the new particle appeared when conditions

were exactly right. Both have carried out their researches at laboratories with large particle accelerators and other heavy equipment, which take the place of microscopes when it comes to investigating the smallest structures of matter. Ting and his team of researchers from Massachusetts Institute of Technology set up their cleverly designed apparatus at the Brookhaven National Laboratory on Long Island. Richter and his teams from Stanford and Berkeley built their sophisticated instrumentation complex at the Stanford Linear Accelerator Center in California. In the two different laboratories and with very different methods both found almost simultaneously a clear signal that a new, heavy particle was involved—born in violent collisions and dying shortly afterwards. The letter J was chosen as name at Brookhaven, the greek letter ψ (psi) at Stanford.

The multitude of elementary particles can be beautifully grouped together in families with well-defined boundaries. Missing members have been found in many cases, in some cases they still remain to be found. All seem to derive their properties from a deeper level of subdivision where only a few building bricks, called quarks, are required.

The unique thing about the J-ψ particle is that it does not belong to any of the families as they were known before 1974. Further particles have been discovered resembling the J-ψ one. The reappraisal of particle family structures now required has already begun in terms of a new dimension, corresponding to the new fourth quark already suggested in other contexts.

Most of the recently found particles of normal type can be described as hills of varying height and width in the energy landscape of the physicists, not too unlike pictures of the mounds, barrows and pyramids which the archeologists take an interest in. In the landscape of particles the new J-ψ surprised physicists by being more than twice as heavy as any comparable particle and yet a thousand times more narrow. One can perhaps better imagine the surprise of an explorer in the jungle if he suddenly were to discover a new pyramid, twice as heavy as the largest one in Tikal and yet a thousand times narrower and thus higher. After checking and rechecking that he is not the victim of an optical illusion he would certainly claim that such a remarkable mausoleum must entail the existence of a hidden culture.

Professor Richter, Professor Ting,

I have compared you to explorers of almost unknown territory in which you have discovered new startling structures. Like many great explorers you have had with you teams of skilful people. I would like you to convey to them our congratulations upon these admirable achievements. Your own unrelenting efforts in the field of electron-positron research over a large number of years and your visions have been of outstanding importance and have now culminated in the dramatic discovery of the J-ψ particle. You have greatly influenced and enriched your research field: the physics of elementary particles after November 1974 is recognized to be different from what it was before.

I have the pleasure and the honour on behalf of the Academy to extend to you our warmest congratulations and I now invite you to receive your prizes from the hands of His Majesty the King.

THE NOBEL PRIZE FOR CHEMISTRY

Speech by Professor GUNNAR HÄGG of the Royal Academy of Sciences
Translation from the Swedish text

Your Majesties, Your Royal Highnesses, Ladies and Gentlemen,
This year's Nobel Prize for Chemistry has been awarded to Professor William Lipscomb for his studies on the structure of boranes illuminating problems of chemical bonding.

A couple of days after the announcement of the chemistry Prize, a Swedish newspaper carried a cartoon by a wellknown Swedish cartoonist showing an elderly couple in front of their TV. The legend ran: "Can you remember ever having seen a borane, Gustav?" This question is quite proper, indeed. Gustav and his wife certainly had never seen a borane. Boranes do not exist in nature and can hardly be found in other places than chemical laboratories.

The name borane is the collective term for compounds of hydrogen with boron, the latter element forming part of among other things boric acid and borax. A great number of boranes and related compounds are known, and it is this whole group of substances which has been studied by Lipscomb. In the eighties of the last century it was understood that such compounds exist in the gas mixture that is formed when alloys between boron and certain metals are decomposed by acids. But it was only from about 1912 that the German chemist Alfred Stock succeeded in producing some pure boranes.

The structures and bonding conditions of boranes remained, however, unknown until about 1950, and it is not without reason that they have been considered problematical. The experimental study of the boranes has been very difficult. They are in most cases unstable and chemically aggressive and must, therefore, as a rule be investigated at very low temperatures. But it was still more serious that their structure and bonding conditions were essentially different from what was known for other compounds. Stock had found borane molecules that, for example, consisted of in one case two boron and six hydrogen atoms and in another case ten boron and fourteen hydrogen atoms. But when the object was to determine how these atoms are bound to each other, i.e. the appearance of the molecule, and also the nature of the bonds which keep the atoms together within the molecule, one was left in the dark for many years. One might suppose that these bonds were similar to those between the atoms in the hydrogen compounds of carbon, for instance in the hydrocarbons in liquefied petroleum gas. In these, the bond between two neighbouring atoms usually involves two electrons, an electron pair. However, boron does not have as many bonding electrons as carbon and, therefore, all the bonds cannot be of this type. A new type of bond, where two electrons co-operate in binding *three* atoms together, and which thus can master this electron deficiency, was proposed in 1949 but it was not until the researches of Lipscomb from 1954 and onwards that the problems of borane chemistry could begin to be solved satisfactorily.

Lipscomb has attacked these problems through skilful calculations of the possible combinations within the molecules of conceivable bond types and he has together with his collaborators determined the geometrical appearance of the molecules, above all using X-ray methods. But he has proceeded much farther than that in illuminating the binding conditions in detail through advanced theoretical computations. Thus it became possible to predict the stability of the molecules and their reactions under varying conditions. This has contributed to a marked development of preparative borane chemistry. These studies by Lipscomb have not only been applied to the proper, electrically neutral, borane molecules but also to charged molecules, i.e. ions, as well as other molecules related to the boranes.

It is rare that a single investigator builds up, almost from the beginning, the knowledge of a large subject field. William Lipscomb has achieved this. Through his theories and his experimental studies he has completely governed the vigorous growth which has characterized borane chemistry during the last two decades and which has given rise to a systematics of great importance for future development.

Professor Lipscomb,

You have attacked in an exemplary way the very difficult problems within an earlier practically unknown field of chemistry. You have worked on a broad front using both experimental and theoretical methods and the success of your efforts is shown by the fact that your results and your views have governed the recent development of borane chemistry.

In recognition of your services to science the Royal Swedish Academy of Sciences decided to award you this year's Nobel Prize for Chemistry. To me has been granted the privilege of conveying to you the most hearty congratulations of the Academy and of requesting you to receive your prize from the hands of his Majesty the King.

THE NOBEL PRIZE FOR PHYSIOLOGY OR MEDICINE

Speech by Professor ERLING NORRBY of the Caroline Institute
Translation from the Swedish text

Your Majesties, Your Royal Highnesses, Ladies and Gentlemen,
An occasional encounter with infectious agents is part of our daily life. The smallest among these infectious agents are called viruses. In spite of their small size viruses may cause many different types of infections. When the virus of common cold comes into contact with our respiratory tract, certain well known symptoms appear after a few days. However, the body can defend itself against the attack by the virus. Under normal conditions we recover after a few days of illness.

Occasionally infections occur which take a completely different course. The Nobel prize winners of this year have described mechanisms involved in such infections. They have studied diseases of two different kinds.

Baruch Blumberg investigated, in the beginning of 1960, the inheritance of specific blood proteins. In connection with this, he discovered a new protein. Eventually it was shown that Blumberg, like the princes of Serendip, had found something completely different from the types of substance he was looking for. The protein he had discovered was not a part of normal body constituents but instead a virus causing jaundice.

It has been known since 1940 that there are two different forms of virus-induced jaundice. One form of the disease is transmitted as an intestinal infection whereas the other form is propagated primarily by blood trans-mission. The virus discovered by Blumberg caused the latter form of the disease. After exposure to this virus, disease of the liver may appear after 3—4 months. Normally symptoms of the disease wane after a few weeks. However, in certain individuals the body lacks the capacity to eliminate the virus infection, which therefore persists throughout life. Such a persistent infection occurs in about one out of 1000 persons in an industrialized society and altogether in more than 100 million individuals around the world. Individuals who carry this kind of persistent infection represent the source of further virus transmission. Due to Blumberg's discovery it is possible today to identify these individuals. Such a person, for example, should not become a blood donor. New possibilities for prevention of this type of jaundice have also become available. A vaccine is currently beeing tested.

Carleton Gajdusek studied in the end of 1950 a remarkable disease in a neo-lithic people living in the highlands of New Guinea. The disease, named Kuru, involved a progressive destruction of the brain, which eventually resulted in death. Kuru lacks the regular signs of an infectious disease, e.g. fever and inflammation. In spite of this Gajdusek showed that the disease was caused by an infectious agent which in chimpanzees gave a disease identical with

Kuru in man. It took 1 1/2—3 years before the first symptoms appeared in infected animals. By this discovery it was made possible to clarify the origin of the disease Kuru.

Amongst the people suffering from this affection about 3000 of 35,000 persons have died of the disease during a study period of 20 years. Transmission of the disease occurred in connection with a mourning ceremony at which dead relatives were cannibalized. This form of funeral ceremony ceased in 1959 and as a consequence Kuru no longer occurs among children born after that year. However, cases of Kuru still appear among adults. This implies that the infectious agent may remain in a dormant stage in the organism for many decades prior to appearance of disease.

However, the Karolinska Institutet has not awarded the Nobel prize of this year to Gajdusek for his demonstration of the danger of cannibalism. The importance of his discovery of the origin of the Kuru disease lies in the identification of a new class of human diseases caused by unique infectious agents. The fact that Kuru, which lacks the classic signs of infections, still is caused by a contageous agent implies that we must investigate whether certain other diseases may not also arise in a similar way. An unusual form of presenile dementia of wide dissemination also has been shown by Gajdusek to be caused by an infectious agent.

Our normal defence mechanisms appear not to protect us against infectious agents of this kind. Further these infectious agents display a much greater resistence against destruction by e.g. boiling and irradiation than regular viruses. Thus, we are dealing with a completely different type of infectious agents the exact nature of which still remains to be demonstrated.

Baruch Blumberg and Carleton Gajdusek. You have made discoveries giving us new views on mechanisms of infectious diseases. The impact of your conceptual reformulations is wide. New directions have been given for future research. On behalf of the Karolinska Institutet, I wish to convey to you our warmest congratulations and I now ask you to receive your Nobel prizes from the hands of His Majesty the King.

THE NOBEL PRIZE FOR LITERATURE

Speech by KARL RAGNAR GIEROW of the Swedish Academy
Translation from the Swedish text

Your Majesties, Your Royal Highnesses, Ladies and Gentlemen,

When Saul Bellow published his first book, the time had come for a change of climate and generation in American narrative art. The so-called hardboiled style, with its virile air and choppy prose, had now slackened into an everyday routine, which was pounded out automatically; its rigid paucity of words left not only much unsaid but also most of it unfelt, unexperienced. Bellow's first work, *Dangling Man* (1944), was one of the signs portending that something else was at hand.

In Bellow's case emancipation from the previous ideal style took place in two stages. In the first he reached back to the kind of perception that had found its already classic guides in Maupassant, Henry James and Flaubert perhaps most of all. The masters he followed expressed themselves as restrainedly as those he turned his back on. But the emphasis was elsewhere. What gave a story its interest was not the dramatic, sometimes violent action but the light it shed over the protagonist's inner self. With that outlook the novel's heroes and heroines could be regarded, seen through and exposed, but not glorified. The anti-hero of the present was already on the way, and Bellow became one of those who took care of him.

Dangling Man, the man without a foothold, was thus a significant watchword to Bellow's writing and has to no small extent remained so. He pursued the line in his next novel, *The Victim* (1947) and, years later, with mature mastery in *Seize the Day* (1956). With its exemplary command of subject and form the last-mentioned novel has received the accolade as one of the classic works of our time.

But with the third story in this stylistically coherent suite, it is as if Bellow had turned back in order at last to complete something which he himself had already passed. With his second stage, the decisive step, he had already left this school behind him, whose disciplined form and enclosed structure gave no play to the resources of exuberant ideas, flashing irony, hilarious comedy and discerning compassion which he also knew he possessed and whose scope he must try out. The result was something quite new, Bellow's own mixture of rich picaresque novel and subtle analysis of our culture, of entertaining adventure, drastic and tragic episodes in quick succession, interspersed with philosophic conversation with the reader—that too very entertaining—all developed by a commentator with a witty tongue and penetrating insight into the outer and inner complications that drive us to act or prevent us from acting and that can be called the dilemma of our age.

First in the new phase came *The Adventures of Augie March* (1953). The very wording of the title points straight to the picaresque, and the connexion is perhaps most strongly in evidence in this novel. But here Bellow had found his style, and the tone recurs in the following series of novels that form the bulk of his work: *Henderson the Rain King* (1959), *Herzog* (1964), *Mr Sammler's Planet* (1970) and *Humboldt's Gift* (1975). The structure is apparently loose-jointed but for this very reason gives the author ample opportunity for descriptions of different societies; they have a rare vigour and stringency and a swarm of colourful, clearly defined characters against a background of carefully observed and depicted settings, whether it is the magnificent facades of Manhattan in front of the backyards of the slums and semi-slums, Chicago's impenetrable jungle of resourceful buisinessmen intimately intertwined with obliging criminal gangs, or the more literal jungle, in the depths of Africa, where the novel Henderson the Rain King, the writer's most imaginative expedition, takes place. In a nutshell they are all stories on the move and, like the first book, are about a man with no foothold. But (and it is important to add this) a man who keeps on *trying to find* a foothold during his wanderings in our tottering world.

Even a few minutes' sketch of Bellow's many-sided writings should indicate where that foothold lies. It cannot be pointed out, as none of his protagonists reaches it. But during their escapades they are all on the run, not *from* something but *towards* something, a goal somewhere which will give them what they lack—firm ground under their feet. "I want, I want, I want!" Henderson exclaims, and sets off for an unknown continent. What his demands are he does not know; what he demands is to find out, and his own desire is the unknown continent. "A worth-while fate", Augie March calls his goal. And Herzog, the restless seeker after truth, for his part tries out one phrasing after the other of what he means by "a worth-while fate". At one point he says confidently that "the realm of facts and that of value are not eternally separated". The words are uttered in passing but are worth dwelling on, and if we think of them as coming from Bellow himself they are essential. Giving value a place side by side with palpable facts is, as regards literature, a definite departure from realism. As a philosophy it is a protest against the determinism that must make man unaccountable for his actions as well as inert or hostile to life, since it prevents him from feeling, choosing and acting himself. The awareness of a value, on the other hand, gives man freedom, thereby responsibility, thereby a desire for action and a faith in the future. That is why Bellow, never one to look through rose-coloured spectacles, is at heart an optimist. It is the light of that conviction which makes the facets of his writing sparkle. His "anti-heroes" are victims of constant disappointment, born to defeat without end, and Bellow (it cannot be over-emphasized) loves and is able to transform the fate they find worth-while into superb comedies. But they triumph nonetheless, they are heroes nonetheless, since they never give up the realm of values in which man becomes human. And, as Augie March says, anyone can become alive to this fact at any moment, however unfortunate he may be, "if he will be quiet and wait it out".

The realm of facts and that of value—the very combination of words is reminiscent of a work by the philosopher Wolfgang Köhler, professor first at Göttingen, then at Berlin, finally at Princeton, to which he fled from the nazis. Köhler's book is called *The Place of Value in a World of Facts* and lent its name to an international Nobel symposium in Stockholm some years ago, at which a lecture was given by E. H. Gombrich, disciple and younger friend of Köhler. He told of the latter's last night in Berlin, before the flight could be carried out. Köhler spent the slow hours with like-minded friends, and while they waited, wondering if a patrol would clamp up the stairs at the last moment and pound on the door with rifle butts, they played chamber music. "Such is", Gombrich remarked, "the place of value in a world of facts".

The threatened position of value between obtrusive realities has not escaped Bellow; that is what he is always writing about. But he does not think that either mankind's conduct or the explosive development of the sciences betoken a world catastrophe. He is an optimist-in-spite-of-all, and thus also an opposition leader of human kindness. Truth must out, of course. But it is not always hostile. Facing the truth is not necessarily the same as braving death. "There may be truths on the side of life", he has said. "There may be some truths which are, after all, our friends in the universe."

In an interview once Bellow described something of what happens when he writes. Most of us, he supposed, have a primitive prompter or commentator within, who from earliest years has been telling us what the real world is. He himself has such a commentator in him; he has to prepare the ground for him and take notice of what he says. One is put in mind of another man who went out into the highways and byways with his questions, taking notice of his inner voice: Socrates and his daemon. This introspective listening demands seclusion. As Bellow himself puts it, "art has something to do with the achievement of stillness in the midst of chaos. A stillness which characterizes prayer, too, and the eye of the storm." This was what prevailed when Köhler played chamber music on his last night in Berlin while, aware of imminent disaster, "being quiet and waiting it out". It is there that the value and dignity of life and mankind have their sole haven, ever storm-lashed, and it is from that stillness that Saul Bellow's work, borne on the whirlwind of disquiet, derives its inspiration and strength.

Dear Mr Bellow, it is my task and my great pleasure to convey to you the warm congratulations of the Swedish Academy and to ask you to receive from the hands of His Majesty the King the Nobel prize for literature of the year 1976.

BANQUET NOBEL A STOCKHOLM

Après la remise solennelle des prix, une brillante société se réunit dans la Salle dorée de l'Hôtel de Ville. Parmi les personnes présentes on remarquait tout particulièrement:

SA MAJESTÉ le ROI

SA MAJESTÉ la REINE

Leurs Altesses Royales

le Prince Bertil, duc de Halland et la Princesse Lilian.

Ensuite:

Les lauréats de l'année MM. Richter, Ting, Lipscomb, Blumberg, Gajdusek, Bellow et Friedman (*prix de sciences économiques en mémoire d'Alfred Nobel*), et les lauréats des années précédentes déjà nommés.

Étaient également présents des membres du Gouvernement et du Parlement ainsi que les Chefs de Mission diplomatique des pays des lauréats, et un très grand nombre de savants, de hauts fonctionnaires suédois et d'autres personnalités de marque.

Le Président de la Fondation invita l'assistance à porter un toast en l'honneur de Sa Majesté le Roi. Les convives se levèrent pour porter ce toast, qui fut suivi de fanfares et de l'hymne royal suédois. Quelques instants plus tard, Sa Majesté proposa un toast silencieux à la mémoire du grand donateur et philanthrope Alfred Nobel.

DISCOURS DES LAURÉATS

Saul Bellow

Your Majesties, Your Royal Highnesses, Ladies and Gentlemen,

There are not many things on which the world agrees but everyone I think acknowledges the importance of a Nobel Prize. I myself take most seriously the Nobel Committee's recognition of the highest excellence in several fields and I accept the honor of this award with profound gratitude.

I have no very distinct sense of personal achievement. I loved books and I wrote some. For some reason they were taken seriously. I am glad of that, of course. No one can bear to be ignored. I would, however, have been satisfied with a smaller measure of attention and praise. For when I am praised on all sides I worry a bit. I remember the scriptural warning, "Woe unto you when all men shall speak well of you." Universal agreement seems to open the door to dismissal. We know how often our contemporaries are mistaken. They are not invariably wrong, but it is not at all a bad idea to remember that they can't confer immortality on you. Immortality—a chilling thought. I feel that I have scarcely begun to master my trade.

But I need not worry too much that all men will speak well of me. The civilized community agrees that there is no higher distinction than the Nobel Prize but it agrees on little else, so I need not fear that the doom of universal approval is hanging over me. When I publish a book I am often soundly walloped by reviewers—a disagreeable but necessary corrective to self inflation.

When the Committe's choice was announced and the press rushed at me (a terrifying phenomenon!) and asked how I felt about winning the Nobel Prize in literature, I said that the child in me (for despite appearances there is a child within) was delighted, the adult skeptical. Tonight is the child's night entirely. On Sunday I will have some earnest things to say from the pulpit. Sunday is the best day for dark reflections but the child's claim to this Friday night will not be disputed.

Baruch S. Blumberg
Your Majesties, Your Royal Highnesses, Ladies and Gentlemen:

My colleague and friend, Carleton Gajdusek, and I wish to thank the Nobel Committee for their gracious and generous hospitality. We have a special debt for I believe the size of our respective parties has established a record for the numbers invited, and I must therefore apologize to those who could not attend because of this.

The large number is a reflection, in part, of the size of our families, and for this it is difficult to provide further comment. In another part it is due to the large number of people who have worked with us to accomplish our research: microbiologists, physicians, anthropologists, chemists, field workers. In clinical research, which is honored by our awards, many workers are needed since it encompasses many disciplines, and since the sensitivities and medical needs of our subjects must be attended to as part of any observations made. The ethics of human concerns are indivisibly bound with scientific observations; human values and science cannot be separated.

Nor can basic and applied research be readily separated, for, as we have learned from our own research, apparently esoteric observations made in distant and different cultures can lead to the prevention of disease and the preservation of life.

There is an additional reward which occasionally is granted to scientists, a reward sometimes shared by artists, writers and others. We may sometimes be offered a glimpse of the wonderful order of nature which defines and guides all of our lives.

William N. Lipscomb
Your Majesties, Your Royal Highnesses, Ladies and Gentlemen,

The award this year of the Nobel Prize in chemistry for research in pure inorganic chemistry is an important event. It is a reminder that we know even now considerably less about most of the chemical elements than we know of the chemistry of carbon or the chemistry of processes underlying life itself. It is also a reminder that the inorganic area characterized by these

29

other elements is now being incorporated into organic chemistry and bio-chemistry.

On this occasion in which intellectual achievement is given its highest recognition, those of us who are being honored should remind ourselves that we are tall only because we stand on the shoulders of others: those who have gone before us showing the way, those who worked with us as our colleagues, those who supported our research giving us funds, and those who have honored us, including you, most of all.

Finally, I take special recognition of the truly international nature of science. As a personal note, I take pleasure in recalling the remarkable association that I have had with many other research groups in different countries throughout the world.

Samuel C. C. Ting

国王，皇后陛下，皇族们，各位朋友：

得到诺贝尔奖，是一个科学家最大的荣誉。我是在旧中国长大的。因此想借这个机会向在发展国家的青年们强调实验工作的重要性。

中国有一句古话：「劳心者治人，劳力者治于人。」这种落后的思想，对在发展国家的青年们有很大的害处。由于这种思想，很多在发展国家的学生们都倾向于理论的研究，而避免实验工作。

事实上，自然科学理论不能离开实验的基础、特别，物理学是从实验产生的。

我希望由于我这次得奖，能够唤起在发展国家的学生们的兴趣，而注意实验工作的重要性。

Translation

Your Majesties, Your Royal Highnesses, Ladies and Gentlemen,

Professor Burton Richter and I wish to thank the Nobel Foundation and the Royal Academy of Sciences for the great honor which has been conferred on us.

Having grown up in the old China, I would like to take this opportunity to emphasize to young students from developing nations the importance of experimental work.

There is an ancient Chinese saying "He who labours with his mind rules over he who labours with his hand". This kind of backward idea is very harmful to youngsters from developing countries. Partly because of this type of concept, many students from these countries are inclined towards theo-retical studies and avoid experimental work.

In reality, a theory in natural science cannot be without experimental foundations; physics, in particular, comes from experimental work.

I hope that awarding the Nobel Prize to me will awaken the interest of students from the developing nations so that they will realize the importance of experimental work.

Milton Friedman
Your Majesties, Your Royal Highnesses, Ladies and Gentlemen,

It is a great honour and privilege for me to be here tonight, sharing in the reflected glory from my distinguished colleagues, not only the six fellow members of the class of 1976, but the many more who, over the past 76 years, have made the term Nobel Laureate the highest mark of distinction to which a scholar can aspire.

My science is a late-comer, the Prize in Economic Sciences in Memory of Alfred Nobel having been established only in 1968 by the Central Bank of Sweden to celebrate its tercentenary. That circumstance does, I admit, leave me with something of a conflict of interest. As some of you may know, my monetary studies have led me to the conclusion that central banks could profitably be replaced by computers geared to provide a steady rate of growth in the quantity of money. Fortunately for me personally, and for a select group of fellow economists, that conclusion has had no practical impact . . . else there would been no Central Bank of Sweden to have established the award I am honoured to receive. Should I draw the moral that sometimes to fail is to succeed? Whether I do or not, I suspect some economists may.

Delighted as I am with the award, I must confess that the past eight weeks have impressed on me that not only is there no free lunch, there is no free prize. It is a tribute to the world-wide repute of the Nobel awards that the announcement of an award converts its recipient into an instant expert on all and sundry, and unleashes hordes of ravenous newsmen and photographers from journals and T.V. stations around the world. I myself have been asked my opinion on everything from a cure for the common cold to the market value of a letter signed by John F. Kennedy. Needless to say, the attention is flattering, but also corrupting. Somehow, we badly need an antidote for both the inflated attention granted a Nobel Laureate in areas outside his competence and the inflated ego each of us is in so much danger of acquiring. My own field suggests one obvious antidote: competition through the establishment of many more such awards. But a product that has been so successful is not easy to displace. Hence, I suspect that our inflated egos are safe for a good long time to come.

I am deeply grateful to you not only for the honor you have conferred on me, but equally for your unfailing Swedish hospitality and friendship.

Les organisations *d'étudiants de Stockholm* vinrent présenter leur hommage aux lauréats. Le président de l'Association Centrale des Étudiants de Stockholm. M. Lars Wijkman, leur adressa ces paroles:

Your Majesties, Your Royal Highnesses, Nobel Laureates, Ladies and Gentlemen:

It is a great honour for us, the Students of Stockholm, to be able to extend today our tribute to you, who have been chosen from among the authors and scientists of the world to receive the Nobel Prize within your respective fields. It is my belief that the youth of the world will wish to join us in our tribute.

Youth is not often known to admire or give thanks to its elders. On the contrary, the young—students as well as others—are all too often believed to seek change only for its own sake, rebellion for the sake of rebellion, protest in order to tear down what has existed before—with no regard for its values. But although this may hold true for some, it is not true for the vast majority of young people.

To most of us you stand not as representatives of an outmoded order, but as individuals engaged in the eternal quest for truth, and thus, not as symbols of that which must be replaced, but as symbols of what must at all costs be preserved: the quest for knowledge, the vision of what greatness is possible to men when they choose to follow only their conscience and their own dreams.

As man is a being of self-made wealth, so he is a being of selfmade spirit. But even though no political system, nor any laws or decrees, can shackle the spirit of a free man, yet they can and do restrict his rights of speech, of action, and of research. As we look around us at the world today, we see vast and silent desolation: nations and whole continents where no speech nor action is possible, save by the whim and grace of those who have set themselves up as omnipotent rulers of men.

Yet it is difficult, indeed impossible, to believe that any people should will itself to enforced silence, to stagnation, or to slavery. And those few voices reaching us from abroad act only to strengthen this belief, for they call on us not to follow their example, but to liberate them from their shackles. And one way in which we are able to do so is by preserving our own freedom, and by demonstrating that freedom is both moral and profitable, spritually as well as materially.

In a free country, men have the right to choose their own paths and to set their visions before those of others. You are such men who have placed your own truths before the wishes of other men, and in so doing you have created new wealth both in matter and in spirit. You have thereby enriched all other men beyond measure. That this could be possible is due only to the freedom you have held, not as a gift from your peers, but as a human right. That this should be so is a belief which must be shared by all decent men.

Nobel Laureates,

Let this, then, be the tribute which we willingly bestow upon you and to which you are entitled: that you have let no man be your master nor held any as your serf; that you have been led by no light save that of your own vision; that your actions have been guided always by a single tenet—that of truth; that accomplishment has been your only goal; and that by living and working according to these principles, you have demonstrated better in action than any others have in words the supreme value of human liberty.

For this, we honour and respect you, and we extend to you our warmest congratulations and our most sincere wishes for the future.

D. Carleton Gajdusek

Your Majesties, Your Royal Highnesses, Ladies and Gentlemen, and Specifically,

Fellow Students!—if I may be granted by you the privilege of calling myself and the other Prize Winners and Prize Givers students, like yourselves! Yet, I warn you that if you do not grant me the privilege you may doom yourselves to a disillusioned maturity and lonely old age as the next generation follows your example.

Here in Sweden we seem to find ourselves back in an old traditional culture, as in the South Pacific, where youth and so-called maturity and old age can still share a complex ritual of initiation or investiture without reciprocal condemnations. Your participation in these tribal rites tonight seems to signify your willingness to take part in the cultural experiment we call our civilization without trying to deny your heritage. You would not yet admit, I hope, the infallibility of its beliefs, goals, and methods.

You make me aware of how thoroughly we here have shared a privileged nurture not granted to most of the world's populations: a leisure, and a plenty, a freedom, an education, and a cultural tradition which encourages and permits us to play the game of the quest for truth and the satisfaction of our curiosity on a grand scale.

May yours be the generation that brings the possibility of playing this magnificent game to all mankind. Yet, may you share with me the sense of uneasiness about our ability to maintain the delicate social order which such pursuits of the truth require without destroying the wonderful human diversity of form, language, and culture still present in the world in this Century. The very truths our successful quests unfold lead to changes that tend to reduce the Community of Man to one frighteningly homogeneous cosmopolitan World Culture, which may deny us even the possibility of imagining the repertoire of the cultural alternatives open to Man.

We must leave to you the wise use of the arts and sciences which will disseminate their benefits to all peoples. May you accomplish this without bringing to extinction the many cultural varieties in the Condition of Man on which his happiness, his search for beauty, and even his survival may depend.

INSIGNES NOBEL
ET
MONTANT DU PRIX

Conformément aux statuts de la Fondation Nobel les lauréats ont reçu un *diplôme*, une médaille d'or et un *document* indiquant le *montant du prix*.

Le montant de chacun des prix Nobel décernés en 1976 s'élève à 681 000 couronnes suédoises.

La somme disponible à répartir entre les lauréats varie selon les revenus annuels nets du fonds principal de la Fondation Nobel. En 1901, la première fois que les prix furent distribués, chacun d'entre eux se montait à 150 000 couronnes suédoises.

Les diplômes présentés aux lauréats en physique, MM. B. Richter et S. C. C. Ting, ainsi que le diplôme présenté au lauréat en chimie, M. W. N. Lipscomb, sont exécutés par M. Tage Hedqvist, artiste peintre et conservateur en chef de la Galerie Thiel, Stockholm. Le diplôme présenté au lauréat en littérature, M. S. Bellow, est exécuté par l'artiste peintre suédois Gunnar Brusewitz.

Les diplômes présentés aux lauréats en physiologie ou médecine, MM. B. S. Blumberg et D. C. Gajdusek, ne portent pour motif qu'une effigie de la médaille Nobel.

Commentaires aux images des diplômes des prix exécutés par Tage Hedqvist :

Burton Richter
Le motif décrit comment la rencontre de la matière et de l'anti-matière fait naître la particule lourde PSI.

Samuel C. C. Ting
Derrière la ligne d'horizon de New York, se dissimule la courbe qui représente la formation de la particule J.

William N. Lipscomb
L'image illustre l'une des jonctions d'atomes particulière aux boranes.

Commentaires aux images du diplôme du prix exécuté par Gunnar Brusewitz :

Saul Bellow
Le fond de l'image synthétise la grande ville américaine en suggérant des détails de la silhouette gratte-ciel de Chicago au travers des voiles de vapeurs

d'essence et de fumées qui contribuent à donner de la densité à l'atmosphère de la cité.

Les noms de quelques personnages des romans de Bellow fulgurent, plus ou moins fragmentés, en traits de néon que reflète l'asphalte de la rue.

A gauche se dressent les échafaudages que le gangster Cantabile allait obliger Citrine à gravir dans une scène dramatique de « Humboldt's Gift ». A droite : la Mercédès brutalisée dont le rôle dans cette œuvre est loin d'être insignifiant.

Le visage qu'on devine au fond pourrait être celui de Citrine ou celui de Herzog ou encore celui de Bellow — cet auteur qui se dit vivre sous les sortilèges de l'Amérique, et qui voue à Chicago une ardente tendresse mi-haine mi-amour.

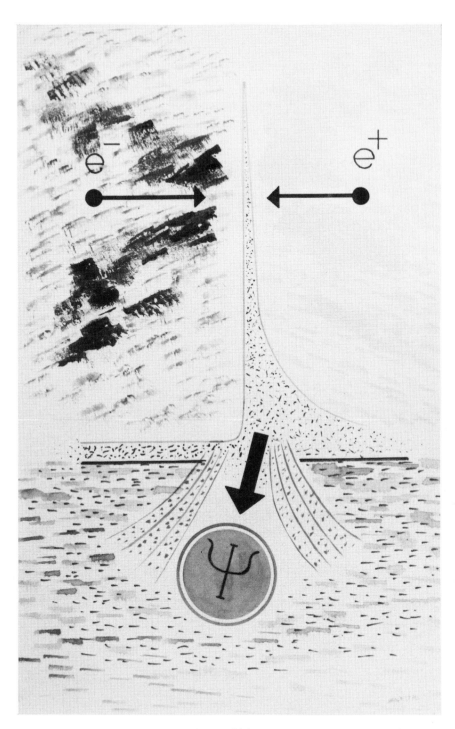

Burton Richter

Samuel C. C. Ting

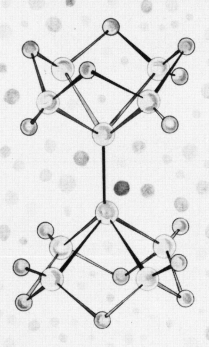

$B_{10}H_{16}$

William N. Libscomb, Jr.

Saul Bellow

Burton Richter

BURTON RICHTER

I was born on 22 March 1931 in New York, the elder child of Abraham and Fanny Richter. In 1948 I entered the Massachusetts Institute of Technology, undecided between studies of chemistry and physics, but my first year convinced me that physics was more interesting to me. The most influential teacher in my undergraduate years was Professor Francis Friedman, who opened my eyes to the beauty of physics.

In the summer following my junior year, I began work with Professor Francis Bitter in MIT's magnet laboratory. During that summer I had my introduction to the electron-positron system, working part-time with Professor Martin Deutsch, who was conducting his classical positronium experiments using a large magnet in Bitter's laboratory. Under Bitter's direction, I completed my senior thesis on the quadratic Zeeman effect in hydrogen.

I entered graduate school at MIT in 1952, continuing to work with Bitter and his group. During my first year as a graduate student, we worked on a measurement of the isotope shift and hyperfine structure of mercury isotopes. My job was to make the relatively short-lived mercury-197 isotope by using the MIT cyclotron to bombard gold with a deuteron beam. By the end of the year I found myself more interested in the nuclear and particle-physics problems to which I had been exposed and in the accelerator I had used, than in the main theme of the experiment. I arranged to spend six months at the Brookhaven National Laboratory's 3-GeV proton accelerator to see if particle physics was really what I wanted to do. It was, and I returned to the MIT synchrotron laboratory. This small machine was a magnificent training ground for students, for not only did we have to design and build the apparatus required for our experiments, but we also had to help maintain and operate the accelerator. My Ph. D. thesis was completed on the photo-production of pi-mesons from hydrogen, under the direction of Dr. L. S. Osborne, in 1956.

During my years at the synchrotron laboratory, I had become interested in the theory of quantum electrodynamics and had decided that what I would most like to do after completing my dissertation work was to probe the short-distance behavior of the electromagnetic interaction. So I sought a job at Stanford's High-Energy Physics Laboratory where there was a 700-MeV electron linear accelerator. My first experiment there, the study of electron-positron pairs by gamma-rays, established that quantum electrodynamics was correct to distances as small as about 10^{-13} cm.

In 1960, I married Laurose Becker. We have 2 children, Elizabeth, born in 1961, and Matthew, born in 1963.

In 1957, G. K. O'Neill of Princeton had proposed building a colliding beam machine that would use the HEPL linac as an injector, and allow electron-electron scattering to be studied at a center-of-mass energy ten times larger than my pair experiment. I joined O'Neill and with W. C. Barber and B. Gittelman we began to build the first colliding beam device. It took us about six years to make the beams behave properly. In 1965, after we had finally made a very complicated accelerator work and had built the needed experimental apparatus, the experiment was carried out, with the result that the validity of quantum electrodynamics was extended down to less than 10^{-11} cm.

Even before the ring at HEPL was operating, I had begun to think about a high-energy electron-positron colliding-beam machine and what one could do with it. In particular, I wanted to study the structure of the strongly interacting particles. I had moved to SLAC in 1963, and with the encouragement of W. K. H. Panofsky, the SLAC Director, I set up a group to make a final design of a high-energy electron-positron machine. We completed a preliminary design in 1964 and in 1965 submitted a request for funds to the Atomic Energy Commission. That was the begginning of a long struggle to obtain funding for the device, during which I made some excursions into other experiments. My group designed and built part of the large magnetic spectrometer complex at SLAC and used it to do a series of pi- and K-meson photoproduction experiments. Throughout this time, however, I kept pushing for the storage ring and kept the design group alive. Finally, in 1970, we received funds to begin building the storage ring (now called SPEAR) as well as a large magnetic detector that we had designed for the first set of experiments. In 1973 the experiments finally began, and the results were all that I had hoped for.

I spent the academic year 1975—76 on sabbatical leave at CERN, Geneva. During that year I began an experiment at the ISR, the CERN 30-GeV proton storage rings, and began the design of a 200-GeV center-of-mass electron-positron storage ring. Such a machine will be so large that it will probably require an international effort to construct it, but I think it will be necessary for the understanding of the weak interaction and its relation to the electromagnetic interaction.

Writing this brief biography had made me realize what a long love affair I have had with the electron. Like most love affairs, it has had its ups and downs, but for me the joys have far outweighed the frustrations.

FROM THE PSI TO CHARM—THE EXPERIMENTS OF 1975 AND 1976

Nobel Lecture, December 11, 1976

by

BURTON RICHTER

Stanford University, Stanford, California, USA

1. INTRODUCTION

Exactly 25 months ago the announcement of the ψ/J particle by Professor Ting's and my groups [1, 2] burst on the community of particle physicists. Nothing so strange and completely unexpected had happened in particle physics for many years. Ten days later my group found the second of the ψ's, [3] and the sense of excitment in the community intensified. The long awaited discovery of *anything* which would give a clue to the proper direction in which to move in understanding the elementary particles loosed a flood of theoretical papers that washed over the journals in the next year.

The experiments that I and my colleagues carried through in the two years after the discovery of the ψ have, I believe, selected from all the competing explanations the one that is probably correct. It is these experiments that I wish to describe. The rapid progress is a consequence of the power of the electron-positron colliding-beam technique, and so I also want to describe this technique and tell something of my involvement in it.

2. COLLIDING BEAMS

I completed my graduate studies at M.I.T. in 1956, and in the Fall of that year I took a position at the High-Energy Physics Laboratory (HEPL) at Stanford University. My main research interest at that time was in exploring the high-momentum-transfer or short-distance behavior of quantum electrodynamics (QED). My original plan for a QED experiment had been to use the 700-MeV electron linac at HEPL in a study of electron-electron scattering. Within a short time, however, I came to realize that a different experiment would be both technically simpler to carry out and would also probe QED more deeply (though somewhat differently). During my first year at HEPL I did this latter experiment, which involved the photoproduction of electron-positron pairs in which one of the members of the pair emerged at a large angle. This experiment succeeded in establishing the validity of QED down to distances of about 10^{-13} cm.

2.1 *The Stanford-Princeton Electron-Electron Storage Rings*

In 1957 the idea of an electron-electron scattering experiment came alive again, although in a much different form. This happened when G. K. O'Neill of Princeton University informally proposed the construction at HEPL of a figure 8-shaped set of rings capable of storing counter-rotating beams of electrons at energies up to 500 meV for each beam. In this plan the HEPL linac was to act as the injector for the rings, and the circulating electron beams would collide in the common straight section between the two rings. O'Neill's aim was not only to demonstrate the feasibility of colliding electron beams, but also to carry out electron-electron scattering at an energy that could significantly extend the range of validity of QED.

The potential of such an e^-e^-, colliding-beam experiment, with its total center-of-mass energy of 1000 MeV, was much greater than the ~ 50 MeV that would have been available to test QED in my original e^-e^- scattering idea. Thus when O'Neill asked me to join in this work, I accepted enthusiastically and became an accelerator builder as well as an experimenter. With two other collaborators, W. C. Barber and B. Gittelman, we set out in 1958 to build the first large storage ring, and we hoped to have our first experimental results in perhaps three years. These results were not in fact forthcoming until seven years later, for there was much to learn about the behavior of beams in storage rings; but what we learned during that long and often frustrating time opened up a new field of particle physics research. [4]

2.2 *A Moment of Realization*

Let me digress here for a moment to recount a formative experience. In 1959, as the work on the HEPL rings progressed, I was also trying to learn something about how to calculate cross sections in QED under the tutelage of Stanford theorist J. D. Bjorken. One of the problems Bjorken gave me was to calculate the cross section for the production of a pair of point-like particles having zero spin (bosons) in electron-positron annihilation. I carried out this calculation, but I was troubled by the fact that no point-like bosons were known to exist. The only spin-zero bosons I knew about were pions, and the strong interactions to which these particles were subject gave them a finite size. I realized that the structure function of the particle would have to enter into the cross section to account for this finite size. The structure function for the pion could be measured in an experiment in which e^+e^- annihilation resulted in the production of pion pairs. Further, the structures of any of the family of strongly interacting particles (hadrons) could be determined by measuring their production cross sections in e^+e^- annihilation. It's certain that many people had realized all this before, but it came as a revelation to me at that time, and it headed me firmly on the course that eventually led to this platform.

2.3 *The Electron-Positron Annihilation Process*

This connection between e^+e^- annihilation and hadrons is worth a brief elaboration here, since it is central to the experimental results I shall describe later. The method by which new particles are created in electron-positron collisions is a particularly simple one that I have always naively pictured in the following way. The unique annihilation process can occur only in the collision between a particle and its antiparticle. The process proceeds in two steps:
1. The particle and antiparticle coalesce, and all the attributes that give them their identities cancel. For a brief instant there is created a tiny

46

electromagnetic fireball of enormous energy density and precisely defined quantum numbers: $J^{PC} = 1^{--}$; all others cancel out to zero.

2. The energy within the fireball then rematerializes into *any* combination of newly created particles that satisfies two criteria: (a) the total mass of the created particles is less than or equal to the total energy of the fireball; (b) the overall quantum numbers of the created particles are the same as those of the fireball. There is no restriction on the individual particles that comprise the final state, only on their sum.

The formation of the fireball or virtual-photon intermediate state in e^+e^- annihilation is described in QED, a theory whose predictions have so far been confirmed by every experimental test. Since we therefore understand Step 1, the creation of the fireball, we are in a sense using the known e^+e^- annihilation process to probe the unknown hadrons that are produced in Step 2 of the process. Our ignorance is thus limited to the structure of the final-state hadrons and to the final-state interactions that occur when particles are created close together. And while that is a great deal of ignorance, it is much less than that of any other particle-production process. In addition, the quantum numbers of the final state in e^+e^- annihilation are simple enough so that we can hope to calculate them from our theoretical models. This is in sharp contrast, for example, to high-energy hadron-hadron collisions, in which very many different angular-momentum states may be involved and thus must be calculated.

2.4 *The SPEAR Electron-Positron Storage Ring*

In 1961, while work on the e^-e^- rings at HEPL continued, I began with D. Ritson of Stanford some preliminary design on a larger e^+e^- storage ring. In 1963 I moved from HEPL to the Stanford Linear Accelerator Center (SLAC), and set up a small group to carry out the final design of the e^+e^- ring. The design energy chosen was 3 GeV (each beam). A preliminary proposal for this colliding-beam machine was completed in 1964, and in 1965 a full, formal proposal was submitted to the U.S. Atomic Energy Commission (now ERDA).

There followed a period of about five years before any funding for this proposed project could be obtained. During this time, other groups became convinced of the research potential of the e^+e^- colliding-beam technique, and several other projects began construction. We watched this other activity enviously, worked at refining our own design, and tried to appropriate any good ideas the others had come up with. Finally, in 1970, funds were made available for a reduced version of our project, now called "SPEAR", and we all fell to and managed to get it built in record time—some 21 months from the start of construction to the first beam collisions [5].

The SPEAR storage ring is located in a part of the large experimental area at the end of the 3-kilometer-long SLAC linac. The facility is shown schematically in Fig. 1. Short pulses of positrons, then electrons, are injected from the SLAC accelerator through alternate legs of the Y-shaped magnetic injection channel into the SPEAR ring. The stored beams actually consist of only a single short bunch of each kind of particle, and the bunches colllide

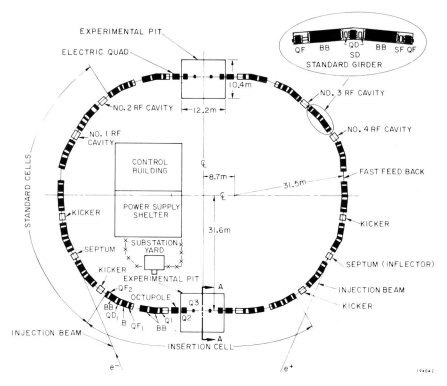

1. Schematic of the SPEAR storage ring.

only at the mid-points of the two straight interaction areas on opposite sides of the machine. Special focusing magnets are used to give the beams a small cross-sectional area at these two interaction points. The time required to fill the ring with electrons and positrons is typically 15—30 minutes, while the data-taking periods between successive fillings are about 2 hours. To achieve this long lifetime, it is necessary to hold a pressure of about 5×10^{-9} torr in the vacuum chamber. The center-of-mass (c.m.) energy of the colliding e^+e^- system can be varied from 2.6 to 8 GeV. The radiofrequency power required to compensate for synchrotron radiation losses rises to 300 kilowatts at the maximum operating energy. The volume within which the e^+e^- collisions occur is small and well-defined $(\sigma_x \times \sigma_y \times \sigma_z = 0.1 \times 0.01 \times 5 \text{ cm}^3)$, which is a great convenience for detection.

2.5 *The Mark I Magnetic Detector*

While SPEAR was being designed, we were also thinking about the kind of experimental apparatus that would be needed to carry out the physics. In the 1965 SPEAR proposal, we had described two different kinds of detectors: the first, a non-magnetic detector that would have looked only at particle multiplicities and angular distributions, with some rather crude particle-identification capability; the second, a magnetic detector that could add accurate momentum measurement to these other capabilities. When the early results in 1969, from the ADONE storage ring at Frascati, Italy, indicated

48

that hadrons were being produced more copiously than expected, I decided that it would be very important to learn more about the final states than could be done with the non-magnetic detector.

Confronted thus with the enlarged task of building not only the SPEAR facility itself but also a large and complex magnetic detector, I began to face up to the fact that my group at SLAC had bitten off more than it could reasonably chew, and began to search out possible collaborators. We were soon joined by the groups of M. Perl, of SLAC; and W. Chinowsky, G. Goldhaber and G. Trilling of the University of California's Lawrence Radiation Laboratory (LBL). This added manpower included physicists, graduate students, engineers, programmers and technicians. My group was responsible for the construction of SPEAR and for the inner core of the magnetic detector, while our collaborators built much of the particle-identification apparatus and also did most of the programming work that was necessary to find tracks and reconstruct events.

This collaborative effort results in the Mark I magnetic detector, shown schematically in Fig. 2. The Mark I magnet produces a solenoidal field, coaxial with the beams, of about 4 kilogauss throughout a field volume of about 20 cubic meters. Particles moving radially outward from the beam-interaction point pass successively through the following elements: the beam vacuum pipe; a trigger counter; 16 concentric cylinders of magnetostrictive wire spark chambers that provide tracking information for momentum measurements; a cylindrical array of 48 scintillators that act as both trigger and time-of-flight counters; the one-radiation-length thick aluminium magnet coil; a cylindrical array of 24 lead-scintillator shower counters that provide

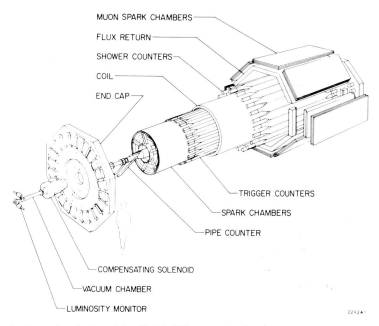

2. An exploded view of the SLAG-LBL magnetic detector.

electron identification; the 20-cm-thick iron flux-return plates of the magnet; and finally an additional array of plane spark chambers used to separate muons from hadrons.

The Mark I magnetic detector was ready to begin taking data in February 1973. During the fall of 1977 it will be replaced at SPEAR by a generally similar device, the Mark II, that will incorporate a number of important improvements. During its career, however, the Mark I has produced a remarkable amount of spectacular physics [6].

3. EARLY EXPERIMENTAL RESULTS

I would like to set the stage for the description of the journey from the ψ's to charm by briefly reviewing here the situation that existed just before the discovery of the new particles. The main international conference in high-energy physics during 1974 was held in July in London. I presented a talk at the London Conference [7] in which I tried to summarize what had been learned up until that time about the production of hadrons in e^+e^- annihilation. This information, shown in Fig. 3, will require a little bit of explanation.

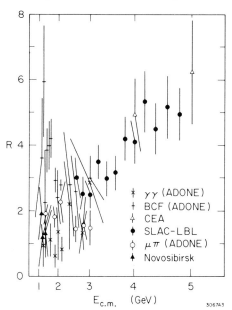

3. The ratio R as of July 1974.

3.1. *The Hadron/Muon-Pair Ratio*

Measurements of the process $e^+e^- \to$ hadrons can be presented straight-forwardly in a graph which plots the hadron-production cross section against the c.m. energy of the colliding e^+e^- system. For reasons that I shall explain later, it has become common practice to replace the hadron-production cross section in such graphs by the following ratio:

$$R = \frac{\text{cross section for } e^+e^- \to \text{hadrons}}{\text{cross section for } e^+e^- \to \mu^+\mu^-}. \tag{1}$$

50

It is that ratio R that is plotted vs. c.m. energy in Fig. 3. Historically, the earliest measurements of R were made at the ADONE ring at Frascati; these occupy the lower-energy region of the graph, and they indicate values of R ranging from less than 1 to about 6. These were followed by two important measurements of R made at the storage ring that had been created by rebuilding the Cambridge Electron Accelerator (CEA) at Harvard; the CEA measurements gave an R value of about 5 at $E_{c.\,m.}$ of 4 GeV, and $R \simeq 6$ at 5 GeV. The early experimental results from the SLAC-LBL experiment at SPEAR filled in some of the gap between the ADONE and CEA results, and between the two CEA points, in a consistent manner; that is, the SPEAR data appear to join smoothly onto both the lower and higher energy data from ADONE and from CEA. With the exception of the experimental points at the very lowest energies, the general picture conveyed by Fig. 3 is that the value of R seems to rise smoothly from perhaps 2 to 6 as $E_{c.m.}$ increases from about 2 to 5 GeV.

3.2. The Theoretical Predictions

During the same London Conference in 1974, J. Ellis of CERN [8] undertook the complementary task of summarizing the process $e^+e^- \rightarrow$ hadrons from a theoretical point of view. Once again, the predictions of many different theories could most conveniently be expressed in terms of the hadron/muon-pair ratio R rather than directly as hadron-production cross sections. The most widely accepted theory of the hadrons at that time gave the prediction that $R = 2$; but there were many theories. Let me illustrate this by reproducing here, as Table I, the compilation of R predictions that Ellis included in his London Talk. As this table shows, these predictions of the hadron/muon-pair ratio ranged upward from 0.36 to ∞, with many a stop along the way.

I included this table to emphasize the situation that prevailed in the Summer of 1974—vast confusion. The cause of the confusion lay in the paucity of e^+e^- data and the lack of experimental clues to the proper direction from elsewhere in particle physics. The clue lay just around the next corner, but that corner itself appeared as a totally unexpected turn in the road.

Table I. Table of Values of R from the Talk by J. Ellis at the 1974 London Conference [8] (references in table from Ellis's talk)

Value	Model	
0.36	Bethe-Salpeter bound quarks	Bohm et al., Ref .42
2/3	Gell-Mann-Zweig quarks	
0.69	Generalized vector meson dominance	Renard, Ref. 49
~1	Composite quarks	Raitio, Ref. 43
10/9	Gell-Mann-Zweig with charm	Glashow et al., Ref. 31
2	Colored quarks	
2.5 to 3	Generalized vector meson dominance	Greco, Ref. 30
2 to 5	Generalized vector meson dominance	Sakurai, Gounaris, Ref. 47

3—1/3	Colored charmed quarks	Glashow *et al.*, Ref. 31
4	Han-Nambu quarks	Han and Nambu, Ref. 32
5.7±0.9	Trace anomaly and ρ dominance	Terazawa, Ref. 27
5.8+3.2 −3.5	Trace anomaly and ε dominance	Orito *et al.*, Ref. 25
6	Han-Nambu with charm	Han and Nambu, Ref. 32
6.69 to 7.77	Broken scale invariance	Choudhury, Ref. 18
8	Tati quarks	Han and Nambu, Ref. 32
8±2	Trace anomaly, and ε dominance	Eliezer, Ref. 26
9	Gravitational cut-off, Universality	Parisi, Ref. 40
9	Broken scale invariance	Nachtmann, Ref. 39
16	$Su_{12} \times SU_2$)	
	) gauge models	Fritzsch & Minkowski,
35—1/3	$SU_{16} \times SU_{16}$)	Ref. 34
~5000	High Z quarks)	
	)	Yock, Ref. 73
70,383	Schwinger's quarks)	
∞	∞ of partons	Cabibbo and Karl, Ref. 9
		Matveev and Tolkachev,
		Ref. 35
		Rozenblit, Ref. 36

4. THE PSI PARTICLES

4.1. *Widths of the Psi Resonances*

Figure 4 shows the cross section for hadron production at SPEAR on a scale where all of the data can be plotted on a single graph. This figure is clearly dominated by the giant resonance peaks of the ψ and the ψ'. The extreme

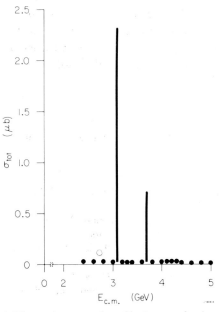

4. The total cross section of hadron production *vs.* center-of-mass energy.

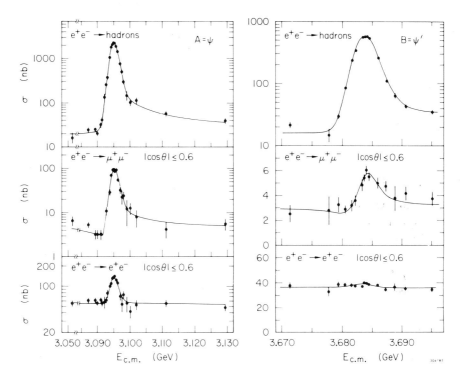

5. Hadron, $\mu^+\mu^-$ and e^+e^- pair production cross section in the regions of the ψ and ψ'. The curves are fits to the data using the energy spread in the colliding beams as the determinant of the widths.

narrowness of the peaks implies that these two states are very long-lived, which is the principal reason why they could not be accounted for by the previously successful model of hadronic structure. In Fig. 5 we show the ψ and ψ' peaks on a greatly expanded energy scale, and also as they are measured for three different decay modes: ψ, $\psi' \rightarrow$ hadrons; ψ, $\psi' \rightarrow \mu^+\mu^-$; and ψ, $\psi' \rightarrow e^+e^-$. In this figure the ψ and ψ' peaks can be seen to have experimental widths of about 2 MeV and 3 MeV, respectively. These observed widths are just about what would be expected from the intrinsic spread in energies that exists within the positron and electron beams *alone*, which means that the true widths of the two states must be very much narrower. The true widths can be determined accurately from the areas that are included under the peaks in Fig. 5 and are given by the following expression:

$$\int \sigma_i \, dE = \frac{6\pi^2}{M^2} B_e B_i \, \Gamma \tag{2}$$

where σ_i is the cross section to produce final state i, B_i is the branching fraction to that state, B_e is the branching fraction to e^+e^-, M is the mass of the state, and Γ is its total width. The analysis is somewhat complicated by radiative corrections but can be done, with the result that [9]

$$\Gamma_\psi = 69 \pm 13 \text{ keV} \tag{3}$$
$$\Gamma_{\psi'} = 225 \pm 56 \text{ keV}$$

The widths that would be expected if the psi particles were conventional hadrons are about 20% of their masses. Thus the new states are several thousand times narrower than those expected on the basis of the conventional model.

4.2. Psi Quantum Numbers

The quantum numbers of the new psi states were expected to be $J^{PC} = 1^{--}$ because of their direct production in e^+e^- annihilation and also because of the equal decay rates to e^+e^- and $\mu^+\mu^-$. In so new a phenomenon, however, anything can go, and so that assumption needed to be confirmed. In particular, one of the tentative explanations of the psi particles was that they might be related to the hypothetical intermediate vector boson, a particle that had long been posited as the carrier of the weak force. Such an identification would permit the psi's to be a mixture of $J^{PC} = 1^{--}$ and 1^{+-}. These quantum numbers can be studied by looking for an interference effect between on- and off-peak production of muon pairs, since the latter is known to be pure 1^{--}. If the new particles were also 1^{--}, then an interference should occur and produce two recognizable effects: a small dip in the cross section below the peak, and an apparent shift in the position of the peak relative to that observed in the hadron channels. In addition, any admixture of 1^{+-} could be expected to show up as a forward/backward asymmetry in the observed angular distribution.

This analysis was carried out as soon as there were sufficient data available for the purpose. The postulated interference effect was in fact observed, as shown in Fig. 6, while no angular asymmetry was seen [8, 9]. Thus both of the psi states were firmly established as $J^{PC} = 1^{--}$.

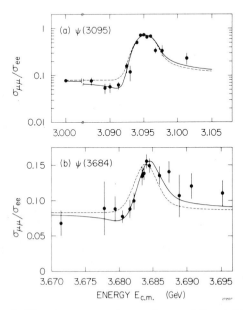

6. The $\mu^+\mu^-$ cross sections at the ψ and the ψ'. The solid curves show the results expected if both states are $J^{PC} = 1^{--}$ and hence interfere with the non-resonant $\mu^+\mu^-$ production. The dashed curves assume no interference.

4.3. *Psi Decay Modes*

We also studied the many decay modes of the ψ and ψ'. In these studies it was important to distinguish between direct and "second-order" decay processes, a point that is illustrated in Fig. 7. This figure shows the following processes:

$$
\begin{aligned}
&\text{(a)}\quad e^+e^- \rightarrow \gamma \rightarrow \psi \rightarrow \text{hadrons} & \text{(direct decay)} \\
&\text{(b)}\quad e^+e^- \rightarrow \gamma \rightarrow \psi \rightarrow \gamma \rightarrow \text{hadrons} & \left.\begin{array}{l}\text{(second-order electro-}\\ \text{magnetic decay)}\end{array}\right\} \\
&\text{(c)}\quad e^+e^- \rightarrow \gamma \rightarrow \psi \rightarrow \gamma \rightarrow \mu^+\mu^-
\end{aligned}
\qquad (4)
$$

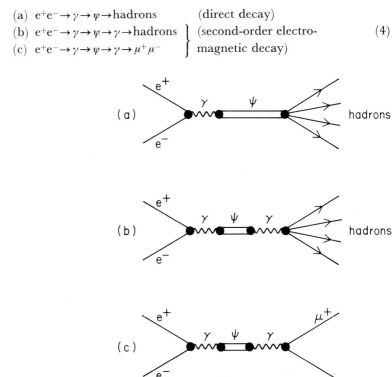

7. Feynman diagrams for ψ production and (a) direct decay to hadrons, (b) second-order electromagnetic decay to hadrons, and (c) second-order electromagnetic decay to $\mu^+\mu^-$.

In processes (b) and (c), hadrons and muon-pairs are produced by virtual photons in exactly the same way that they are produced at off-resonance energies. If the observed hadrons were produced *only* through second-order electromagnetic decay, then the hadron/muon-pair production ratio, R, would be the same on-resonance as off. This is decidedly not the case. Since R is much larger on-resonance than off, both ψ and ψ' do have direct hadronic decays.

More branching fractions for specific hadronic channels have been measured for the ψ and ψ' than for any other particles. Most of these are of interest only to the specialist, but a few have told us a good deal about the psi particles. Since the second-order electromagnetic decays also complicate these analyses, we must again make on- and off-resonance comparisons between muon-pair production and the production of specific hadronic final states. In Fig. 8 we show such a comparison plotted against the number of pions observed in the final state [10]. Even numbers of pions observed are consistent with what is

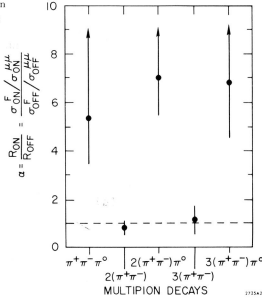

8. The ratio of the ratios of hadron to $\mu^+\mu^-$ production on and off the ψ resonance vs. the number of π mesons in the final state.

expected from second-order electromagnetic decays, while the observed odd-pion decays are much enhanced. The ψ decays appear, from these data, to be governed by a certain selection rule (G-parity conservation) that is known to govern only the behavior of hadrons, thus indicating that the ψ itself is a hadron.

There are certain specific decay modes that, if observed, provide definite evidence on the isospin of the psi particles. Such modes are

$$\psi \text{ or } \psi' \to \pi^+\pi^-\pi^0\ \Lambda\overline{\Lambda},\ \text{p}\overline{\text{p}}. \tag{5}$$

Each of these decay modes has in fact been seen, thus establishing $I^G J^{PC} = 0^- 1^{--}$ for both particles.

4.4. Search for Other Narrow Resonances

By operating the SPEAR storage ring in a "scanning" mode, we have been able to carry out a systematic search for any other very narrow, psi-like resonances that may exist. In this scanning mode, the ring is filled and set to the initial energy for the scan; data are taken for a minute or two; the ring energy is increased by about an MeV; data are taken again; and so forth. Figure 9 shows these scan data from c.m. energies of about 3.2 to 8 GeV [11, 12]. No statistically significant peaks (other than the ψ' that was found in our first scan) were observed in this search, but this needs two qualifications. The first is that the sensitivity of the search extends down to a limit on possible resonances that have a cross section $\times$ width of about 5% to 10% of that of the ψ. The second qualification is that the particular method of search is sensitive only to extremely narrow resonances like the ψ and ψ'; other, much broader resonances have been found at SPEAR, and we shall soon see how these apparently much different states fit into the picture.

56

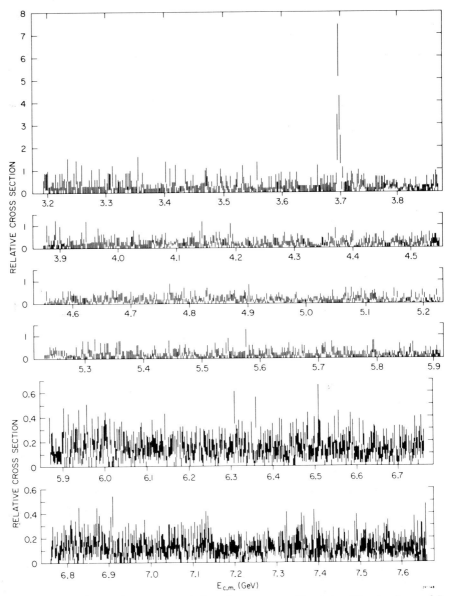

9. The fine-scan data from our search for other narrow ψ-like states. The signal near 3.7 GeV is the ψ'.

5. THE INTERMEDIATE STATES

5.1. *Radiative Transitions*

There are other new states, related to the ψ and ψ' but not directly produced in e⁺e⁻ annihilation, which are observed among the decay products of the two psi particles. More specifically, these new states are produced when either ψ or ψ' decays through the emission of a gamma-ray:

$$\psi \text{ or } \psi' \rightarrow \gamma + \text{intermediate state} \tag{6}$$

57

At least four (perhaps five) distinct intermediate states produced in this way have been observed experimentally.

The first such observation was made by an international collaboration working at the DORIS e$^+$e$^-$ storage ring at the DESY laboratory in Hamburg [13]. This state was named P$_c$, and its mass was found to be about 3500 MeV. This same group [14] in collaboration with another group working at DESY later found some evidence for another possible state, which they called X, at about 1800 MeV [15]. At SPEAR, the SLAC-LBL group has identified states with masses of about 3415, 3450 and 3550 MeV, and has also confirmed the existence of the DESY 3500-MeV state. We have used the name χ to distinguish the state intermediate in mass between the $\psi(3095)$ and the $\psi'(3684)$. To summarize these new states:

$$\begin{aligned}
\psi'(3684) &\rightarrow \gamma + \chi(3550) \\
\psi'(3684) &\rightarrow \gamma + \chi(3500) \text{ or } P_c \\
\psi'(3684) &\rightarrow \gamma + \chi(3555) \\
\psi'(3684) &\rightarrow \gamma + \chi(3415) \\
\psi\;(3095) &\rightarrow \gamma + X(2800) \text{ (not yet firmly established)}
\end{aligned} \qquad (7)$$

5.2. Three Methods of Search

The three methods we have used at SPEAR to search for these intermediate states are indicated schematically in Fig. 10. To begin with, the storage ring is operated at the center-of-mass energy of 3684 MeV that is required for resonant production of the ψ'. In the first search method, Fig. 10(a), ψ' decays to the intermediate state then decays to the ψ through γ-ray emission; and finally the ψ decays, for example, into $\mu^+\mu^-$. The muon-pair is detected along with one or both of the γ-ray photons. This was the method used at DESY to find the 3500-MeV state and also by our group at SLAC to confirm this state [16]. In our apparatus at SPEAR, it will occasionally happen that one of the two γ-ray photons converts into an e$^+$e$^-$ pair before entering the tracking region of the detector. This allows the energy of the converting γ-ray to be

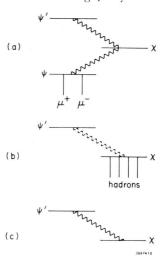

10. Schematics of the three methods of searching for narrow intermediate states.

measured very accurately, and this information can be combined with the measured momenta of the final $\mu^+\mu^-$ pair to make a two-fold ambiguous determination of the mass of the intermediate state. The ambiguity arises from the uncertainty in knowing whether the first or the second gamma-rays in the decay cascade have been detected. It can be resolved by accumulating enough events to determine which assumption results in the narrower mass peak. (The peak associated with the second γ-rays will be Doppler broadened because these photons are emitted from moving sources.) Figure 11 shows the alternate low- and high-mass solutions for a sample of our data [17]. There appears to be clear evidence for states at about 3.45, 3.5 and 3.55 GeV.

The second search method we have used, Fig. 10(b), involves measuring the momenta of the final-state hadrons and reconstructing the mass of the intermediate state [18]. Figure 12 shows two cases in which the effective mass of the final-state hadrons recoils against a missing mass of zero (that is, a γ-ray). In the case where 4 pions are detected, peaks are seen at about 3.4, 3.5 and 3.55 GeV. In contrast, the 2-pion *or* 2-kaon case shows only one clear peak at 3.4 GeV, with perhaps a hint of something at 3.55 GeV. The appearance of the 2-pion or 2-kaon decay modes indicates that the quantum numbers of the states in question must be either 0^{++} or 2^{++}.

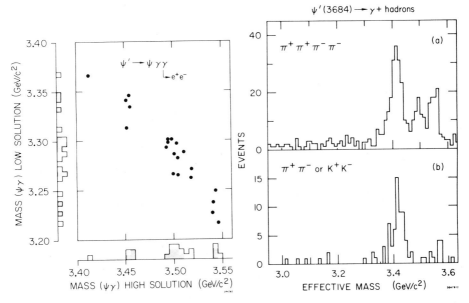

11. The high-resolution $\psi\!-\!\gamma$ mass data. The clustering indicates at least 3 intermediate states.

12. The invariant mass of the indicated hadron final states that appear with a γ-ray in ψ' decay. The data show three distinct intermediate states, one of which is not seen in the previous figure.

In the third method of search, Fig. 10(c), only a single γ-ray is detected. The presence of a monoenergetic γ-ray line would signal a radiative transition directly to a specific intermediate state. In our apparatus, this method is difficult to apply because of the severe background problems, but we were able to identify the direct γ-ray transition to the 3.4 GeV state [17]. A different experimental group working at SPEAR (a collaboration among the Universities of Maryland, Princeton, Pavia, Stanford and UC-San Diego) was able to make use of a more refined detection system to observe several of these radiative transitions and to measure the ψ′ branching franctions of those states [19].

To summarize, these studies have led to the addition of four (the 2800-MeV state is still marginal) new intermediate state, all with charge-conjugation $C = +1$, to the original ψ and ψ′ particles.

6. TOTAL CROSS SECTION AND BROADER STATES

6.1. *Total Cross Section*
So far our discussion of the process e⁺e⁻→hadrons has been concerned largely with the two psi particles, which are created directly in e⁺e⁻ annihilation, and with the intermediate states, which are not directly created but rather appear only in the decay products of the ψ and ψ′. It is now time to turn our attention to the larger picture of hadron production to see what else can be learned.

Figure 4 presented the total cross section for e⁺e⁻→hadrons over the full range of c.m. energies accessible to SPEAR. This figure was dominated by the ψ and ψ′ resonance peaks, and very little else about the possible structure of the cross section outside of these peaks was observable. We now remedy this situation in Fig. 13, which shows the hadron/muon-pair ratio R, with the dominating ψ and ψ′ resonance peaks removed, including their radiative tails.

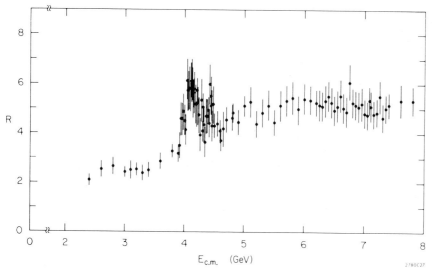

13. The ratio R with the ψ and ψ′ deleted (including their radiative tails).

We can characterize the data in the following way. Below about 3.8 GeV, R lies on a roughly constant plateau at a value of $\simeq 2.5$; there is a complex transition region between about 3.8 and perhaps 5 GeV in which there is considerable structure; and above about 5.5 GeV, R once again lies on a roughly constant plateau at a value of $\simeq 5.2$ GeV.

6.2. Broader (Psi?) States

The transition region is shown on a much expanded energy scale in Fig. 14. This figure clearly shows that there seem to be several individual resonant states superposed on the rising background curve that connects the lower and upper plateau regions [20]. One state stands out quite clearly at a mass of 3.95 GeV, and another at about 4.4 GeV. The region near 4.1 GeV is remarkably complex and is probably composed of two or more overlapping states; more data will certainly be required to try to sort this out.

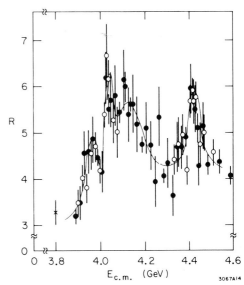

14. An expanded view of R in the transition region around 4 GeV.

The properties of the several states within the transition region are very difficult to determine with any precision. One obvious problem is that these resonances sit on a rapidly rising background whose exact shape is presently neither clear experimentally nor calculable theoretically. Since these new states are, like the ψ's, produced directly in e^+e^- annihilation, they all have $J^{PC} = 1^{--}$ and can therefore interfere with each other, thus distorting the classical resonance shape that would normally be expected from a new particle. Additional shape-distortion might be expected because new particle-production thresholds are almost certainly opening up in the transition region between the lower and upper plateaus. While precise properties can't be given for the new states, we can get some rough numbers from the data. The 3.95-GeV state (ψ'') has a width of about 40—50 MeV. The 4.4-GeV state (ψ'''') seems to be about 30-MeV wide. The 4.1-GeV region (temporarily called ψ''') seems to consist of at least two peaks: one at 4.03 GeV, which is 10—20 MeV wide, and a broad enhancement at 4.1 GeV, about 100-MeV wide.

The widths of all of these states are much greater than the intrinsic energy spread in the e^+e^- beams, and very much greater than the widths of the ψ and ψ'. The suspicion remains, however, that they may still be correctly identified as members of the psi sequence, and that the vast apparent differences between their widths and those of the ψ and ψ' may result simply from the fact that the higher mass states can undergo rapid hadronic decay through new channels that have opened up above the 3684-MeV mass of the ψ'. As with most of the questions in the transition region, this matter will require a good deal more experimental study before it is resolved. In the meantime, however, we shall tentatively add the three or four new psi-like states shown above to the growing list of members of the "psion" family.

7. AN EXCURSION INTO THEORY

Up to this point, we have been cataloguing new particles without much worrying about what it all means. Granting full status to even the several doubtful states, we have a total of 11 new particles. These are grouped together in Fig. 15 in a kind of energy-level diagram, which also includes principal decay modes.

The system shown in Fig. 15, with its radiative transitions, looks remarkably like the energy-level diagram of a simple atom, in fact like the simplest of all "atoms"-positronium, the bound state of an electron and a positron. Although the mass scale for this new positronium is much larger than that of the old, the observed states of the new system can be placed in a one-to-one correspondence with the levels expected for a bound fermion-antifermion system such as e^+e^-. Table II shows these predicted levels together with the most probable assignments of the new particles to the appropriate levels. To gain some insight into the origins of the new positronium system, let's now turn to some specific theoretical models.

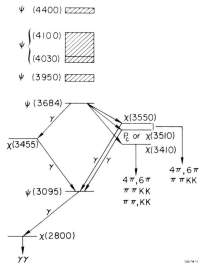

15. An energy-level diagram of the new particles. The many observed decay modes of the psi family have been omitted.

Table II. Some of the low lying bound states of a fermion-antifermion system together with an assignment of the new particle to states with appropriate quantum numbers.

State	L	S	J^{PC}	Particle
1^3S_1	0	1	1^-	ψ
2^3S_1	0	1	1^{--}	ψ'
3^3S_1	0	1	1^{--}	ψ'''
1^3D_1	2	1	1^{--}	ψ''
2^3D_1	2	1	1^{--}	ψ''''
1^1S_0	0	0	0^{-+}	X
2^1S_0	0	0	0^{-+}	$\chi(3.45)$
1^3P_0	1	1	0^{++}	$\chi(3.4)$
1^3P_1	1	1	1^{++}	$\chi(3.5)$
1^3P_2	1	1	2^{++}	$\chi(3.55)$

7.1. The 3-Quark Model

Some 25 years ago, when only three kinds of hadrons were known (proton, neutron and pi-meson), these particles were universally regarded as simple, indivisible, *elementary* objects. In those days the central task in hadron physics was the effort to understand the strong nuclear force between protons and neutrons in terms of pi-meson exchange. But as the family of hadrons grew steadily larger (they are now numbered in the hundreds), it became increasingly difficult to conceive of them *all* as elementary. In 1963, M. Gell-Mann and G. Zweig independently proposed a solution to this dilema—that *none* of the hadrons was elementary, but rather that all were complex structures in themselves and were built up from different combinations of only three fundamental entities called quarks. These quarks were assumed to carry the familiar 1/2 unit of spin of fermions, but also to have such unfamiliar properties as fractional electric charge and baryon number. A brief listing of the 3 quarks and 3 antiquarks and their properties is given in Table III.

Table III. Properties of the 3 Quarks and 3 Antiquarks

Quarks				Antiquarks			
Symbol	Charge	Baryon Number	Strange-ness	Symbol	Charge	Baryon Number	Strange-ness
u	2/3	1/3	0	$\bar{u}$	−2/3	−1/3	0
d	−1/3	1/3	0	$\bar{d}$	1/3	−1/3	0
s	−1/3	1/3	1	$\bar{s}$	1/3	−1/3	−1

According to this 3-quark model, all mesons were made up of one quark and one antiquark; all baryons, of three quarks; and all antibaryons, of three antiquarks. The quark compositions of some of the better known hadrons are shown here as examples:

$$\pi^+ = u\bar{d}, \; K^+ = u\bar{s}, \; p = uud, \; \bar{n} = \bar{d}\bar{d}\bar{u}. \tag{8}$$

Prior to 1974, all of the known hadrons could be accommodated within this basic scheme. Three of the possible meson combinations of quark-antiquark (u$\bar{u}$, d$\bar{d}$, s$\bar{s}$) could have the same quantum numbers as the photon, and hence could be produced abundantly in e⁺e⁻ annihilation. These three predicted states had all infact been found; they were the familiar $\varrho(760)$, $\omega(780)$ and $\varphi(1005)$ vector mesons.

7.2. *R in the Quark Model*
The quark model postulated a somewhat different mechanism for the process e⁺e⁻→hadrons than that previously described. For comparison,

Customary View	Quark Model Hypothesis
e⁺e⁻→γ→hadrons	e⁺e⁻→γ→q$\bar{q}$→hadrons

where q$\bar{q}$ means any quark-antiquark pair. The quark-model hypothesis is shown schematically in Fig. 16. In this picture the virtual photon intermediate state creates a q$\bar{q}$ pair, which then in turn "clothe" themselves with additional q$\bar{q}$ pairs to form the hadrons that are observed in the final state.

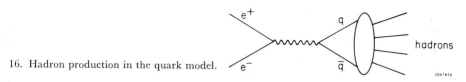

16. Hadron production in the quark model.

Since the quarks are assumed to be elementary, point-like fermions and thus similar to electrons and muons in their electromagnetic properties, it was possible to predict the ratio that should exist between the producton cross sections for quark pairs and muon pairs:

$$\frac{\sigma_{q\bar{q}}}{\sigma_{\mu^+\mu^-}} = q_i^2 \tag{10}$$

where q_i is simply the quark's electric charge. Of course, quarks were supposed to have half-integral spin and fractional charge in the final state, while all hadrons have integral charge and some hadrons have integral spin. In a breathtaking bit of daring it was assumed that the "final-state" interactions between quarks that were necessary to eliminate fractional charge and half-integral spin would have no effect on the basic production cross section. With this assumption the ratio of hadron production to muon-pair production becomes simply

$$R = \sum_{u,d,s} q_i^2. \tag{11}$$

As developed up to 1974, the quark model actually included 3 triplets of quarks, rather than simply 3 quarks, so that with this 3×3 model the hadron/muon-pair ration, R, would be

$$R = (3[2/3)^2+(-1/3)^2+(-1/3)^2]) = 2. \tag{12}$$

This beautiful model had great simplicity and explanatory power, but it could not accommodate the ψ and ψ' particles. Nor could it account for the two plateaus that were observed in the measured values of R. The model allowed for excited states of $u\bar{u}$, $d\bar{d}$ and $s\bar{s}$, but the required widths were typically some 20% of the mass of the excited state—more than 1000 times broader than the observed widths of the ψ and ψ'. Before that time there had been a number of suggested modifications or additions to the basic 3-quark scheme. I shall not describe these proposed revisions here except for the one specific model which seems now to best fit the experimental facts.

7.3. *A Fourth Quark*

The first publications of a theory based on 4 rather than 3 basic quarks go all the way back to 1964 [21], only a year or so after the original Gell-Mann/ Zweig 3-quark scheme. The motivation at that time was more esthetic than practical, and these models gradually expired for want of an experimental fact that called for more than a 3-quark explanation. In 1970, Glashow, Iliopolous and Maiani [22] breathed life back into the 4-quark model in an elegant paper that dealt with the *weak* rather than the strong interactions. In this work the fourth quark—which had earlier been christened by Glashow the "charmed" quark (c)— was used to explain the non-occurrence of certain weak decays of strange particles in a very simple and straight-forward way. The new c quark was assumed to have a charge of $+2/3$, like the u qark, and also to carry $+1$ unit of a previously unknown quantum number called charm, which was conserved in both the strong and electromagnetic inter-actions but not in the weak interactions. The c and $\bar{c}$ quarks were also re-quired to have masses somewhat larger than the effective mass of the 3 original quarks, and it was clear that they should be able to combine with the older quarks and antiquarks to form many new kinds of "charmed" hadrons [23].

7.4. *"Charmonium"*

The 4-quark theoretical model became much more compelling with the discovery of the psi particles. This model postulates that the ψ is the lowest mass $c\bar{c}$ system which has the quantum numbers of the photon. The ψ's long life is explained by the fact that the decay of the ψ into ordinary hadrons requires the conversion of *both* c and $\bar{c}$ into other quarks and antiquarks. The positronium-like energy-level states of the psions discussed earlier are also well accounted for by the $c\bar{c}$ system; indeed, 5 specific intermediate states were predicted by Applequist *et al.* [24], and by Eichten *et al.* [25], before they were actually discovered. It was the close analogy with positronium that led Applequist and Politzer to christen the new $c\bar{c}$ system *charmonium*, a name that has caught on.

The 4-quark model also requires two plateaus on R. Above the threshold for charmed-hadron production, the $R = 2$ calculation made above must be modified by the addition of the fourth quark's charge, which results in a prediction of $R = 10/3$ (not enough, but in the right direction). The broad psi-like states at 3.95, 4.1, and 4.4 GeV are accounted for by postulating that the mass of the lightest charmed particle is less than half the mass of the ψ'' (3950) but more than half the mass of the very narrow $\psi'(3684)$, which means that ψ'' can decay strongly to charmed-particle pairs, but ψ' cannot.

To summarize briefly, the 4-quark model of the hadrons seemed to account in at least a qualitative fashion for all of the main experimental information that had been gathered about the psions, and by the early part of 1976 the consensus for charm had become quite strong. The $c\bar{c}$ system of charmonium had provided indirect but persuasive evidence for a fourth, charmed quark, but there remained one very obvious and critically important open question. The particles formed by the $c\bar{c}$ system are not in themselves charmed particles, since charm and anticharm cancel out to zero. But it is necessary to the theory that particles which exhibit charm exist ($c\bar{u}$, $c\bar{d}$, etc.). What was needed, then, was simply the direct experimental observation of charmed particles, and the question was: Where were they [26]?

8. THE DISCOVERY OF CHARM

8.1. *What are We Looking For?*
By early 1976 a great deal had been learned about the properties that the sought-after charmed particles must have. As an example, it was clear that the mass of the lightest of these particles, the charmed D meson, had to fall within the range

$$1843 < m_D < 1900 \text{ MeV}. \tag{13}$$

The lower limit was arrived at by noting once again that the $\psi'(3684)$ was very narrow and therefore could not decay into charmed particles, and also that the upper limit had to be consistent with the begining of the rise of R from its lower to its upper plateau. Since the principal decay product of the c quark was assumed for compelling reasons to be the s quark, then the decay products of charmed particles must preferentially contain strange particles such as the K mesons. The charmed D mesons, for example, could confidently be expected to have the following identifiable decay modes:

$$D^\circ \to K^- \pi^+ \tag{14}$$
$$D^\circ \to K^- \pi^+ \pi^- \pi^+$$
$$D^+ \to K^- \pi^+ \pi^+$$

A further point was that, since the charmed quark would decay only through the weak interactions, one might reasonably expect to see evidence of parity violation in the decays of the D mesons.

At SPEAR our collaboration had looked for such charm signatures in the limited data taken before the psi discoveries, but without success. As the post-psi data accumulated throughout 1975, it was evident that we should have another go at it, with particular emphasis on the results obtained at energies close to the expected charm threshold, where the simplest charmed mesons would be produced without serious masking effects from extraneous background. Since I spent the academic year 1975—76 on sabbatical leave at CERN, this chapter of the charmed-particle story belongs to my collaborators.

8.2. *The Charmed Meson*

With the advantages of a much larger data sample and an improvement in the method of distinguishing between pi- and K-mesons in the Mark I detector, a renewed search for charmed particles was begun in 1976. Positive results were not long in coming. The first resonance to turn up in the analysis was one in the mass distribution of the twoparticle system $K^+\pi^+$ in multiparticle events [27]. The evidence for this is shown in Fig. 17. This was the first direct indication of what might be the D meson, for the mass of 1865 MeV was in just the right region. If it was the D°, then presumably the production process was:

$$e^+e^- \rightarrow D°\bar{D}° + X \tag{15}$$

where X represents any other particles. The D° or $\bar{D}°$ would subsequently decay into the observed $K^+\pi^-$ or $K^-\pi^+$ some fraction of the time—the data indicated a branching fraction of about 2% for this charged two-body mode.

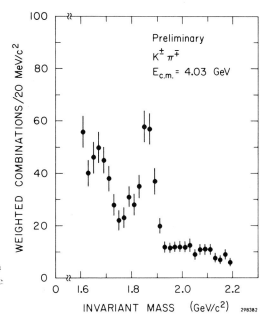

17. The invariant mass distribution of the $K^+\pi^+$ system in multiparticle final states. The peak at a mass of 1865 MeV is the D° meson.

The branching fraction was a little low compared to the charm-model predictions, but not alarmingly so. The measured width of the resonance was consistent with the resolution of our apparatus, which in this case was determined by the momentum resolution of the detector rather than by the more precise energy resolution of the circulating beams. The measured upper bound on the full width was about 40 MeV; the actual value could well be much smaller, as a weak-interaction decay of the D meson would require.

Continuing analysis of the data yielded two more persuasive findings. The first was a resonance in $K^+\pi^-\pi^+\pi^-$ or $K^-\pi^+\pi^-\pi^+$, which appears to be an alternate decay mode of the D° since the mass is also 1865 MeV. The second

67

was the discovery of the charged companions [28] of the D°, which were observed at the slightly larger mass of 1875 MeV in the following decay channels:

$$D^+ \rightarrow K^- \pi^+ \pi^+ \tag{16}$$
$$D^+ \rightarrow K^+ \pi^- \pi^-$$

The data for the charged D states are shown in Fig. 18. It is important to note that these states are *not* observed in three-body decay when the pions are oppositely charged:

$$D^+ \rightarrow K^+ \pi^- \pi^+ \tag{17}$$
$$D^- \rightarrow K^- \pi^+ \pi^-$$

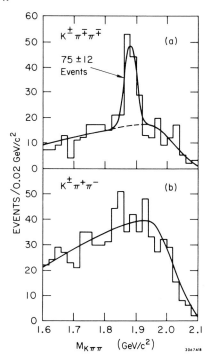

18. The invariant mass distribution of the Kππ system. The D± appears in the plot (a) with same-sign pions and not in the plot (b) with opposite-sign pions.

This is precisely what is required by the charmed-quark model. In addition to the clear identification of both neutral and charged D mesons, an excited state [29] of this meson (D*) has also turned up and has been seen to decay to the ground state by both strong and electromagnetic interactions:

$$D^* \rightarrow D + \pi \tag{18}$$
$$D^* \rightarrow D + \gamma$$

Since we have several times mentioned the possibility that the psi-like states having masses above that of the $\psi'(3684)$ may be much broader than ψ and ψ' because they are able to decay strongly into charmed-particle pairs, it is interesting to note that this speculation has now been confirmed in the case of the $\psi'''(4030)$. It now appears, in fact, that the following are the principal decay modes of this particle:

$$\psi'''(4030) \rightarrow D°\overline{D}*$$
$$\rightarrow D*\overline{D}°$$ (19)
$$\rightarrow D*\overline{D}*$$

As a final bit of evidence in support of the charmed-meson interpretation of the experimental data, the predicted parity violation in D decay has also been observed. In the decay process $D° \rightarrow K^+\pi^-$, the K and π each have spin-0 and odd intrinsic parity. This means that any spin possessed by the $D°$ must show up as orbital angular momentum in the $K\pi$ system, and thus that the parity of the $D°$ must be given by

$$P = (-1)^J$$ (20)

where $\widetilde{J}$ is the spin of the $D°$. An analysis of the 3-body decay data, $D^\pm \rightarrow$ $\rightarrow K^-\pi^+\pi^+$ or $K^+\pi^-\pi^-$, showed that the parity cannot be the same as that given above, and therefore that parity must be violated in D-meson decay [30].

The experimental data that have been described here are strikingly consistent with the predictions of the 4-quark or charm theory of the hadrons, and there is little doubt that charmed particles have now in fact been found. In addition to these charmed mesons uncovered at SPEAR, there has been recent information from Fermilab that a collaborative group working there under Wonyong Lee has now discovered the first of the charmed baryons [31] actually an antibaryon designed Λ_c to identify it as the charmed counterpart of the Λ.

9. OBSERVATION OF JETS

While this topic is not directly connected with the new particles, it does have a direct bearing on the validity of the quark model. As I noted earlier, the picture of e^+e^- annihilation that is derived from the quark model indicates that the final-state hadrons do not come directly from the virtual-photon intermediate state, but rather from the quark-antiquark pair that is first created from the electromagnetic fireball and subsequently forms the final hadrons. These hadrons are produced with low transverse momenta with respect to the $q\bar{q}$ direction, and as illustrated in Fig. 19, if the energy is sufficiently high, form two collimated jets of particles whose axes lie along the original $q\bar{q}$ direction.

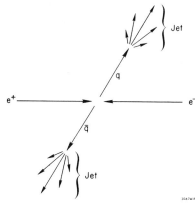

19. Jet production in the quark model.

At SPEAR we have analyzed our highest-energy data [32] by determining for each event those particular axes that minimize the transverse momentum relative to those axes for all of the observed particles. This method of analysis leads to the definition of a quantity we have called "sphericity," which is related to the quadrupole moment of the particle distribution in momentum space. The more jet-like event, the lower the sphericity. Figure 20 shows the data compared to the jet model and to an "isotropic" model with no jet-like characteristics. As the energy increases, the events do become more jet-like as required. The result was excellent agreement, not only in the general sense but also in the finding that the angular distribution of the jet axes was consistent with the $1+\cos^2\vartheta$ distribution that is expected if the jets originate from parent particles of spin-1/2.

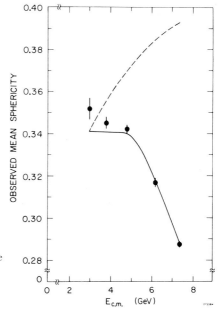

20. The mean sphericity of multihadron events *vs.* center-of-mass energy. The solid curve is that expected of the jet model, while the dashed curve is that expected from an isotropic phase-space model.

In addition, under certain operating conditions the beams in the SPEAR storage ring become polarized, with the electron spin parallel and the positron spin antiparallel to the ring's magnetic bending field. In this polarized condition an azimuthal asymmetry in particle production can appear with respect to the direction of the beams. Jets measured under these conditions also displayed the azimuthal asymmetry that is expected of spin-1/2 particles.

Further, the individual hadrons within the jets also displayed this asymmetry [33]. It will be evident that the greater the momentum of a single hadron, the closer that hadron must lie to the original direction defined by the quark. By looking at pion production in detail, we were able to determine that as the pion momentum approached the maximum value possible for the particular machine energy, so did the azimuthal asymmetry approach the maximum possible asymmetry expected for spin-1/2 particles. This point is illustrated in Fig. 21.

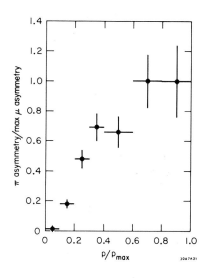

21. The azimuthal asymmetry parameter for pions normalized to the asymmetry in μ-pair production *vs.* the fractional pion momentum.

I find it quite remarkable that a collection of hadrons, each of which has integral spin, should display all of the angular-distribution characteristics that are expected for the production of a pair of spin-1/2 particles. Such behavior is possible without assuming the existence of quarks (the final-state helicity must be one along the direction of the particle or jet), but any other explanation seems difficult and cumbersome. In my view the observations of these jet phenomena in e^+e^- annihilation constitute one of the very strongest pieces of evidence for believing that there really is a substructure to the hadrons.

10. CONCLUSIONS AND QUESTIONS

The electron-positron colliding-beam experiments of the past two years have, I believe, settled the question of the significance of the psi particles. The charmonium family, the two plateaus in R, the wide resonances above charm threshold, the charmed particles themselves, the evidence for the weak decays of the charmed particles and the existence of jets—all these support most strongly the ideas of the quark model of hadron substructure and the 4-quark version of that model. To me, one of the most remarkable features of the quark model is that it correctly explains a great deal of data on strongly interacting particles with the most simple-minded of calculations. The charmonium spectrum, for example, is calculated with the nonrelativistic Schrödinger equation using a simple potential. The two plateaus in R and jet structure are explained by assuming that the final-state interactions of strongly interacting particles can be ignored. Why it is all so simple, while at the same time the quarks themselves appear confined to hadrons and are never seen in the free state, is one of the central questions of strong-interaction physics.

We already know, however, that the 4-quark model cannot be the complete story. The colliding-beam experiments are not entirely consistent with this model. The high energy plateau value of R is about 5.1 rather than 3-1/3 as demanded by the charm model. While $R = 3$-1/3 is only reached in the theory at very high energies, the difference between 3-1/3 and 5.1 are too large to be explained easily. At the same time, there is evidence in our data for a class of events (the μ-e events) which are not easily explained within the framework of 4-quarks and 4 leptons (e$^-$, v_e, μ^-, v_μ) and which may require an expansion of the lepton family and/or the quark family. These inconsistencies immediately bring up the question of how many quarks and leptons there are.

There are two schools of thought on this question. One school says that the quark system is complete or nearly complete—while there may be a few more quarks to be found, there are a small number of indivisible elements, among which are the present four, and all of the strongly interacting particles are built out of these elementary and indivisible components. The other school says that the quarks themselves are probably built from something still smaller, and that we shall go on forever finding smaller and smaller entities each inside the next larger group.

These and other questions on particle structure may be answered by the next generation of e$^+$e$^-$ colliding-beam machines now being built at DESY and SLAC which will reach 35 to 40 GeV in the center-of-mass system. Experiments on these machines will begin in 4 to 5 years and should tell us promptly about the existence of new plateaus in R, new "oniums", or new leptons.

An even more fundamental set of questions, which I find more interesting than the number of quarks, will probably not be answered by experiments at any accelerator now in construction. These questions have to do with the possibility of a unified picture of the forces of nature: gravity, the weak interaction, the electromagnetic interaction, and the strong interaction. Weinberg [34] and Salam [35] have made the first models of a unified weak and electromagnetic interaction theory. Attempts have been made at a unified picture of the weak, electromagnetic and strong interactions—more primitive than the Weinberg/Salam model, for the problem is more difficult, but still a beginning. The experimental information required to establish these unified pictures will almost certainly require still higher energies: several hundred GeV in the center-of-mass and again, I believe, in the e$^+$e$^-$ system. If any of these unified pictures is correct at very high energies, then our only correct field theory, quantum electrondynamics, will necessarily have to break down, and I will have come full circle back to the first experiment I wanted to do as an independent researcher [36].

REFERENCES

1. J. J. Aubert *et al.*, Phys. Rev. Lett. *33*, 1404 (1974).

2. J.-E. Augustin *et al.*, Phys. Rev. Lett. *33*, 1406 (1974).

3. G. S. Abrams *et al.*, Phys. Rev. Lett. *33*, 1453 (1974).

4. The early development of the colliding beams technique was an international effort. The two groups who, in those early days suffered with us through the discovery and conquest of what at times seemed to be an endless series of beam instabilities and technological problems, were those of F. Amman at Frascati and G. I. Budker at Novosibirsk.

5. The success of the SPEAR project is in large measure due to J. Rees who was then my deputy, and to M. Allen, A. M. Boyarski, W. Davies-White, N. Dean, G. E. Fischer, J. Harris, J. Jurow, L. Karvonen, M. J. Lee, R. McConnell, R. Melen, P. Morton, A. Sabersky, M. Sands, R. Scholl and J. Voss.

6. The physicists of the SLAC/LBL group who were responsible for building the detector and for the experiments I will discuss are S. M. Alam, J.-E. Augustin, A. M. Boyarski, M. Breidenbach, F. Bulos, J. M. Dorfan, G. J. Feldman, G. E. Fischer, D. Fryberger, G. Hanson, J. A. Jaros, B. Jean-Marie, R. R. Larsen, D. Lüke, V. Lüth, H. L. Lynch, C. C. Morehouse, J. M. Paterson, M. L. Perl, I. Peruzzi, M. Piccolo, T. P. Pun, P. Rapidis, B. Richter, R. H. Schindler, R. F. Schwitters, J. Siegrist, W. Tanenbaum, and F. Vannucci from SLAC; and G. S. Abrams, D. Briggs, W. C. Carithers, W. Chinowsky, R. G. DeVoe, C. E. Friedberg, G. Goldhaber, R. J. Hollebeek, A. D. Johnson, J. A. Kadyk, A. Litke, B. Lulu, R. J. Madaras, H. K. Nguyen, F. Pierre, B. Sadoulet, G. H. Trilling, J. S. Whitaker, J. Wiss, and J. E. Zipse from LBL.

7. B. Richter, *Proceedings of the XVII International Conference on High Energy Physics*, London (1974).

8. J. Ellis, *Ibid.*

9. A. M. Boyarski *et al.*, Phys. Rev. Lett. *34*, 1357 (1975); V. Lüth *et al.*, Phys. Rev. Lett. *35*, 1124 (1975).

10. B. Jean-Marie *et al.*, Phys. Rev. Lett. *36*, 291 (1976).

11. A. M. Boyarski *et al.*, Phys. Rev. Lett. *34*, 762 (1975).

12. Review paper by R. Schwitters, *Proceedings of the 1975 International Symposium on Lepton and Photon Interactions, Stanford University* (1975).

13. W. Braunschweig *et al.*, Phys. Lett. *57B*, 407 (1975).

14. B. H. Wiik, *Proceedings of the 1975 Symposium on Lepton and Photon Interactions*, Stanford University (1975).

15. J. Heintze, *Ibid.*

16. W. Tanenbaum *et al.*, Phys. Rev. Lett. 35, 1323 (1975).

17. S. Whitaker *et al.*, to be published in Phys. Rev. Lett.

18. G. H. Trilling, LBL Report 5535 and *Proceedings of the SLAC Summer Institute on Particle Physics*, Stanford (1976).

19. D. H. Badtke *et al.*, paper submitted to the *XVIII International Conference on High Energy Physics, Tbilisi, USSR* (1976).

20. J. Siegrist *et al.*, Phys. Rev. Lett. *36*, 700 (1976).

21. D. Amati *et al.*, Phys. Lett *11*, 190 (1964);
    J. D. Bjorken and S. L. Glashow, Phys. Lett. *11*, 255 (1964);
    Z. Maki and Y. Chnuki, Prog. Theor. Phys. *32*, 144 (1964);
    Y. Hara, Phys. Rev. *134B*, 701 (1964).

22. S. L. Glashow, J. Iliopolous, and L. Maiani, Phys. Rev. *D2*, 1285 (1970).

23. An excellent review of the status of the charm model at the end of 1974 is that of M. K. Gaillard, B. Lee, and J. L. Rosner, Rev. Mod. Phys. *47*, 277 (1975).

24. T. Applequist *et al.*, Phys. Rev. Lett. 34, 365 (1975).
25. E. Eichten *et al.*, Phys. Rev. Lett. 34, 369 (1975).
26. One possible example of the production of a charmed baryon has been reported by E. G. Cazzoli *et al.*, Phys. Rev. Lett. *34*, 1125 (1975).
27. G. Goldhaber *et al.*, Phys. Rev. Lett. *37*, 255 (1976).
28. I. Peruzzi *et al.* Phys. Rev. Lett. *37*, 569 (1976).
29. Papers on the D* decays and ψ''' decays are in preparation by the SLAC/LBL Group.
30. Strictly speaking, this argument is not airtight. If the D$^+$ is not in the same isotopic doublet as the D$^\circ$, the comparison of D$^+$ and D$^\circ$ decay gives no information on parity violation. The close values of the masses of D$^+$ and D$^\circ$, however, make it very probable that they are related.
31. B. Knapp *et al.*, Phys. Rev. Lett. *37*, 822 (1976).
32. G. Hanson *et al.*, Phys. Rev. Lett. *35* 1609 (1975).
33. R. F. Schwitters *et al.*, Phys. Rev. Lett. *35*, 1320 (1975).
34. S. Weinberg, Phys. Rev. Lett. *19*, 1264 (1967).
35. A. Salam, *Proceedings of the 8th Nobel Symposium* (Almquist Wiksells, Stockholm, 1968).
36. I want to acknowledge here those who have been most important in helping me on my circular path in particle physics and whom I have not previously mentioned. They are L. S. Osborne, my thesis adviser; E. Courant and A. Sessler, who helped me understand the mysteries of the behavior of beams in storage rings; S. Drell and J. D. Bjorken, who have been my guides to theoretical physics; M. Sands, who helped me design the storage ring and whose encouragement helped keep me going in the frustrating years of waiting for the funds to build it; W. K. H. Panofsky, who was Director of HEPL and is Director of SLAC, without whose support and desire to see "good physics" done there would be no SPEAR; and Laurose Richter—wife, friend and adviser.

Samuel C. C. Ting

SAMUEL CHAO CHUNG TING

I was born on 27 January 1936 in Ann Arbor, Michigan, the first of three children of Kuan Hai Ting, a professor of engineering, and Tsun-Ying Wang, a professor of psychology. My parents had hoped that I would be born in China, but as I was born prematurely while they were visiting the United States, by accident of birth I became an American citizen. Two months after my birth we returned to China. Owing to wartime conditions I did not have a traditional education until I was twelve. Nevertheless, my parents were always associated with universities, and I thus had the opportunity of meeting the many accomplished scholars who often visited us. Perhaps because of this early influence I have always had the desire to be associated with university life.

Since both my parents were working, I was brought up by my maternal grandmother. My maternal grandfather lost his life during the first Chinese Revolution. After that, at the age of thirty-three, my grandmother decided to go to school, became a teacher, and brought my mother up alone. When I was young I often heard stories from my mother and grandmother recalling the difficult lives they had during that turbulent period and the efforts they made to provide my mother with a good education. Both of them were daring, original, and determined people, and they have left an indelible impression on me.

When I was twenty years old I decided to return to the United States for a better education. My parents' friend, G. G. Brown, Dean of the School of Engineering, University of Michigan, told my parents I would be welcome to stay with him and his family. At that time I knew very little English and had no idea of the cost of living in the United States. In China, I had read that many American students go through college on their own resources. I informed my parents that I would do likewise. I arrived at the Detroit airport on 6 September 1956 with $100, which at the time seemed more than adequate. I was somewhat frightened, did not know anyone, and communication was difficult.

Since I depended on scholarships for my education, I had to work very hard to keep them. Somehow, I managed to obtain degrees in both mathematics and physics from the University of Michigan in three years, and completed my Ph.D. degree in physics under Drs. L. W. Jones and M. L. Perl in 1962.

I went to the European Organization for Nuclear Research (CERN) as a Ford Foundation Fellow. There I had the good fortune to work with Giuseppe Cocconi at the Proton Synchrotron, and I learned a lot of physics from him. He always had a simple way of viewing a complicated problem, did experiments with great care, and impressed me deeply.

In the spring of 1965 I returned to the United States to teach at Columbia University. In those years the Columbia Physics Department was a very stimulating place, and I had the opportunity of watching people such as L. Lederman, T. D. Lee, I. I. Rabi, M. Schwarts, J. Steinberger, C. S. Wu, and others. They all had their own individual style and extremely good taste in physics. I benefitted greatly from my short stay at Columbia.

In my second year at Columbia there was an experiment done at the Cambridge Electron Accelerator on electron-positron pair production by photon collision with a nuclear target. It seemed to show a violation of quantum electrodynamics. I studied this experiment in detail and decided to duplicate it. I contacted G. Weber and W. Jentschke of the Deutsches Elektronen-Synchrotron (DESY) about the possibility of doing a pair production experiment at Hamburg. They were very enthusiastic and encouraged me to begin right away. In March 1966 I took leave from Columbia University to perform this experiment in Hamburg. Since that time I have devoted all my efforts to the physics of electron or muon pairs, investigating quantum electrodynamics, production and decay of photon-like particles, and searching for new particles which decay to electron or muon pairs. These types of experiments are characterized by the need for a high-intensity incident flux, for high rejection against a large number of unwanted background events, and at the same time the need for a detector with good mass resolution.

In order to search for new particles at a higher mass, I brought my group back to the United States in 1971 and started an experiment at Brookhaven National Laboratory. In the fall of 1974 we found evidence of a new, totally unpredicted, heavy particle—the J particle. Since then a whole family of new particles has been found.

In 1969 I joined the Physics Department of the Massachusetts Institute of Technology (MIT). In recent years it has been my privilege to be associated with M. Deutsch, A. G. Hill, W. Jentschke, E. Lohrmann, G. Weber, and V. Weisskopf. All have strongly supported me. In addition, I have enjoyed working with many very outstanding young physicists such as U. Becker, M. Chen, E. Coleman, R. Marshall, and A. J. S. Smith.

I married Kay Louise Kuhne in 1960. She is an architect. We have two daughters: Jeanne M., born in 1964, and Amy M., born in 1965.

I received the Ernest Orlando Lawrence Award of 1976. I am a member of the American Physical Society, the Italian Physical Society, and the European Physical Society. I am also a member of the American Academy of Arts and Sciences, the National Academy of Sciences (US), and a Fellow of Academia Sinica.

THE DISCOVERY OF THE J PARTICLE:

A personal recollection

Nobel Lecture, 11 December, 1976
by

SAMUEL C. C. TING
Massachusetts Institute of Technology, Cambridge, Massachusetts, USA
and
CERN, European Organization for Nuclear Research, Geneva, Switzerland

1. PHOTONS AND HEAVY PHOTONS

The study of the interaction of light with matter is one of the earliest known subjects in physics. An example of this can be found in the *Mo Tsu* [1] (the book of Master Mo, Chou Dynasty, China, 4th century B.C.). In the 20th century, many fundamentally important discoveries in physics were made in connection with the study of light rays. The first Nobel Prize in Physics was awarded to W. C. Röntgen in 1901 for his discovery of X-rays.

In modern times, since the work of Dirac, we realized the possibility of the creation of electron-positron pairs by energetic light quanta. The work of W. E. Lamb and R. C. Retherford provided a critical step in the understanding of interactions between photons and electrons. The elegant formulation of quantum electrodynamics by S. Tomonaga, J. Schwinger and R. Feynman, F. J. Dyson, V. F. Weisskopf and others has led to a procedure for calculating observable effects of the proper electromagnetic field of an electron.

In the last decade, with the construction of giant electron accelerators, with the development of sophisticated detectors for distinguishing electrons from other particles, and finally with the building of electron-positron colliding beam storage rings, much has been learnt about the nature of very high energy light quanta in their interactions with elementary particles. The study of interactions between light and light-like particles (the so-called vector mesons, or heavy photons) eventually led to the discovery of a new family of elementary particles—the first of which is the J particle.

My first knowledge of the concept of light quanta and the role they play in atomic physics came from the classical book "The Atomic Spectra" by Herzberg [2], which I picked up in the summer of 1957 when I was working in New York as a summer student. Just before my graduation from college, I received as a Christmas gift from my father the English translation of the book "Quantum Electrodynamics" by Akhiezer and Berestetskii [2]. During my school years at Michigan I managed to go through this book in some detail and worked out some of the formulas in the book myself. Then, during my years as a junior faculty member at Columbia University, I read with great interest a paper by Drell [2], who pointed out the implications of various tests of quantum electrodynamics at short distances using high-energy electron accelerators. I did a theoretical calculation with Brodsky [3] on how to isolate a certain class of Feynman graphs from the muon production of three muons.

There are basically two ways of testing the theory of interactions between photons, electrons, and muons. The low-energy method, like the Lamb shift or $(g-2)$ experiment, tests the theory to high accuracy at a long distance (or small momentum transfer). For example, the most recent experiment done at CERN by Picasso and collaborators [4] to measure the g-factor anomaly of the muon with a muon storage ring, obtained the result:

$(g-2)/2 = 0.001165922 + 0.000000009$ (an accuracy of 10 parts per million).

This result can be compared with calculations of quantum electrodynamics, including corrections from strong and weak interactions. The theoretical number is

$(g-2)/2 = 0.001165921 \pm 0.000000010,$

a most fantastic achievement of both experiment and theory.

The other way of testing quantum electrodynamics involves the study of reactions at large momentum transfers. Using the uncertainty principle $\Delta x \cdot \Delta p \approx h$, this type of experiment, though much less accurate, probes the validity of QED to a large momentum transfer or to a small distance. One such experiment, the process of e^+e^- production by multi-GeV photons in the Coulomb field of the nucleus, has both electromagnetic and strong interaction contributions to the e^+e^- yield. By properly choosing the kinematical conditions we can isolate the contributions from quantum electrodynamics alone and reduce the yield from strong interactions to a few percent level. The momentum transfer to the electron propagator is about 1 GeV; it is related to the effective mass of the e^+e^- pair. The yield of QED pairs is of the order a^3 $(a = 1/137)$. Because the yield is third order in a, to obtain a reasonable amount of events the experiment must be able to handle a high intensity of incident flux. A large acceptance detector is necessary not only to collect the events but also to average the steep angular dependence of the yields.

The effective mass of a pair of particles emitted from the same point is obtained by measuring the momentum of each of the particles p_1 and p_2, and the angles θ_1 and θ_2 between their paths and the incident beam direction, and by identifying the two particles simultaneously so that their masses m_1 and m_2 can be determined. The effective mass m of the pair is defined by:

$$m^2 = m_1^2 + m_2^2 + 2[E_1 E_2 - p_1 p_2 \cos(\theta_1 + \theta_2)],$$

where E_i = total energy of the particle.

A pair spectrometer has two arms, which measure simultaneously the momenta p_1 and p_2 of the particles and the angles θ_1 and θ_2. Owing to the immense size of the equipment required, the physical position of each arm is often preselected. This restricts θ_1 and θ_2 to a relatively narrow band of possible values. Different effective masses may be explored by varying the accepted momentum of the particles p_1 and p_2.

When the two particles are uncorrelated, the distribution of m is normally a smooth function. A 'narrow' resonance will exhibit a sharp peak above this smooth distribution, while a 'wide' resonance will produce a broader bump.

The identification of particles from the spectrometer is done by

i) measuring the charge and momentum of the particle from its trajectory in a magnetic field;

ii) determining for a given trajectory, or a given momentum, the mass of the particle by measuring its velocity and using the relation $p = m \cdot v$.

The measurement of velocity can be done with Čerenkov counters using the Čerenkov effect. For electrons, their additional property of having only electromagnetic interactions can be used. When an electron enters a dense piece of lead, it loses all its energy by a cascading process which releases photons. The amount of light emitted from a lead-lucite sandwich shower counter (or a lead-glass counter) is thus proportional to the energy of the electron.

In October, 1965, I was invited by W. Jentschke, then Director of the Deutsches-Elektronen Synchrotron (DESY) in Hamburg, Germany, to perform my first experiment on e^+e^- production [5]. The detector we used is shown in Figs. 1a and 1b. It has the following properties that are essential to this type of experiment: i) it can use an incident photon flux of $\sim 10^{11}$/s, with a duty cycle of $2-3\%$; ii) the acceptance is very large and is not limited by edges of the magnets or by shielding, being defined by scintillation counters alone; iii) all counters are located such that their surfaces are not directly exposed to the target; iv) to reject the hadron pairs, the Čerenkov counters are separated by magnets so that knock-on electrons from the pions interacting with gas radiators in the first pair of counters LC, RC are swept away by the magnet MA and do not enter the second pair of counters HL, HR. The low-energy knock-on electrons from HL, HR are rejected by shower counters.

The large number of Čerenkov counters and shower counters enables us to perform redundant checks on hadron rejection. Since each Čerenkov counter is 100% efficient on electrons and not efficient on hadrons, the observation that:

the yield of e^+e^- from 3 Čerenkov counters =

the yield of e^+e^- from 4 Čerenkov counters,

ensures that we are measuring pure e^+e^- pairs. The combined rejection is $>>10^8$.

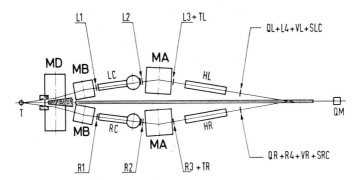

Fig. 1a. Plan view of the spectrometer. MD, MA, MB are dipole magnets; L1, ..., L4, and R1, ..., R4, are triggering counters; LC, RC, and HL, HR are large-aperture threshold Čerenkov counters; SLC, SRC are shower counters; and TL, QL, VL, and TR, QR, VR are hodoscopes. QM is a quantameter.

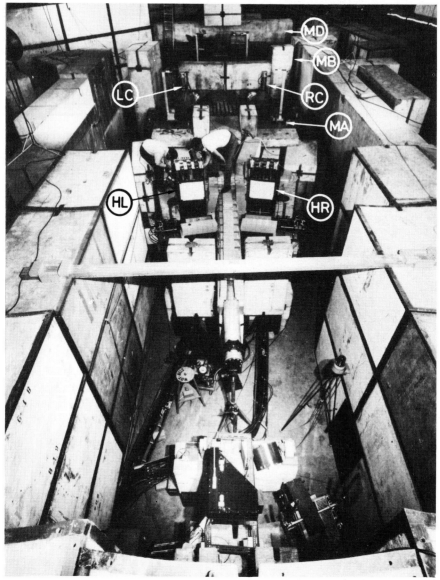

Fig. 1b. Over-all view of my first experiment at DESY. The position of LC, RC, HL, HR. MA, and MD are all marked. The physicist on the left is Dr. A. J. S. Smith; on the right is Dr. C. L. Jordan.

After we had finished this experiment, which showed that quantum electrodynamics correctly describes the pair production process to a distance of $\approx 10^{-14}$ cm, we tuned the spectrometer magnets so that the maximum pair mass acceptance is centred near $m \approx 750$ MeV. We observed a large increase in the e^+e^- yield and an apparent violation of QED. This deviation is caused by an enhancement of the strong interaction contribution to the e^+e^- yield where the incident photon produces a massive photon-like particle, the ρ meson, which decays into e^+e^- [6—8] with a decay probability of order α^2.

In order to show that this is indeed the case, we made another measurement at a larger e^+e^- opening angle and observed an even larger deviation from QED. This is to be expected since the QED process decreases faster than the strong interaction process when we increase the opening angle of the e^+e^- pair.

The observation of $\rho \rightarrow e^+ + e^-$ decay started a series of experiments by my group on this subject [9—12]. Basically the heavy photons ρ, ω, φ, are resonance states of $\pi^+\pi^-(\rho)$, $\pi^+\pi^-\pi^0(\omega)$, K^+K^- or $\pi^+\pi^-\pi^0(\varphi)$ with a rather short lifetime of typically $\approx 10^{-23}—10^{-24}$ s. The widths of these particles are $\Gamma_\rho \approx$ ≈ 100 MeV, $\Gamma_\omega \sim 10$ MeV, and $\Gamma_\varphi \approx 5$ MeV. They are unique in that they all have quantum numbers $\mathcal{J}$ (spin) $= 1$, C (charge conjugation) $= -1$, P (parity) $= -1$. Thus they are exactly like an ordinary light-ray except for their heavy mass. The mass of ρ is $m_\rho \simeq 760$ MeV, and $m_\omega \simeq 783$ MeV; $m_\varphi \approx 1019.5$ MeV.

The production of heavy photons by photons on nucleon and nuclear targets shows that it is a diffraction process very much like the classical scattering of light from a black disk. The experiments on photoproduction of heavy photons and observation of their e^+e^- decay measure the coupling strength between each heavy photon and the photon. The interference between the e^+e^- final state from heavy photon decays and e^+e^- from QED measures the production amplitude of the heavy photon. The interference between these amplitudes can be viewed classically as a simple two-slit experiment, where in front of one of the slits we placed a thin piece of glass (corresponding to $\gamma \rightarrow \rho \rightarrow \gamma \rightarrow$ $\rightarrow e^+e^-$) thus disturbing the interference pattern. The QED pairs alone would correspond to passing of light without the glass in front of the slit. The interference between $\rho(2\pi) \rightarrow e^+ + e^-$ and $\omega(3\pi) \rightarrow e^+ + e^-$ and the interference between $\rho(2\pi) \rightarrow 2\pi$ and $\omega(3\pi) \rightarrow 2\pi$ are measurements of strength of isospin non-conservation in electromagnetic interactions [13].

In the course of these experiments, since the width of ω is ~ 10 MeV and φ is ~ 5 MeV, we developed a detector with a mass resolution of ~ 5 MeV.

Some of the measurements have low event rates. In one particular experiment where we studied the e^+e^- mass spectra in the mass region above the ρ and ω mesons, the yield of e^+e^- pairs was about one event per day, with the full intensity of the accelerator. This implies that for about half a year the whole laboratory was working on this experiment alone. The rate of one event per day also implies that often there were no events for 2—3 days, and then on other days we had 2—3 events. It was during the course of this experiment that we developed the tradition of checking all voltages manually every 30 minutes, and calibrating the spectrometer by measuring the QED yields every 24 hours. To ensure that the detector was stable, we also established the practice of having physicists on shift, even when the accelerator was closed down for maintenance, and never switched off any power supplies. The net effect of this is that for many years our counting room has had a different grounding system from that of the rest of the laboratory. The Control Room for this series of experiments is shown in Fig. 2.

Some of the quantitative results from the above experiments may be explained if we assume that there are three kinds of fundamental building blocks

Fig. 2. Earlier Control Room at DESY. The three other people in the picture are Miss I. Schulz, Dr. U. Becker and Dr. M. Rohde. All have worked with me during the last 10 years.

in the world, known as quarks, which combine to form various elementary particles. The interactions between photons, heavy photons, and nuclear matter are results of interactions of the various quarks.

Sakurai [14] was the first to propose that the electromagnetic interaction of elementary particles may be viewed as through the heavy photon (vector meson) intermediate states.

2. NEW PARTICLES

After many years of work, we have learnt how to handle a high intensity beam of $\sim 10^{11}$ γ/s with a 2—3% duty cycle, at the same time using a detector that has a large mass acceptance, a good mass resolution of $\Delta M \approx 5$ MeV, and the ability to distinguish $\pi\pi$ from e^+e^- by a factor of $>>10^8$.

We can now ask a simple question: How many heavy photons exist? and what are their properties? It is inconceivable to me that there should be only three of them, and all with a mass around 1 GeV. To answer these questions, I started a series of discussions among members of the group on how to proceed. I finally decided to first perform a large-scale experiment at the 30 GeV proton accelerator at Brookhaven National Laboratory in 1971, to search for more heavy photons by detecting their e^+e^- decay modes up to a mass (m) of 5 GeV. Figure 3 shows the photocopy of one page of the proposal; it gives some of the reasons I presented, in the spring of 1972, for performing an e^+e^- experiment in a proton beam rather than in a photon beam, or at the DESY colliding beam accelerator then being constructed.

The best way to search for vector mesons is through production experiments of the type p + p → V⁰ + X . The reasons are:
                                                    ↳ e⁺e⁻

(a) The V⁰ are produced via strong interactions, thus a high production cross section.

(b) One can use a high intensity, high duty cycle extracted beam.

(c) An e⁺e⁻ enhancement limits the quantum number to 1⁻, thus enabling us to avoid measurements of angular distribution of decay products.

Contrary to popular belief, the e⁺e⁻ storage ring is not the best place to look for vector mesons. In the e⁺e⁻ storage ring. the energy is well-defined. A systematic search for heavier mesons requires a continuous variation and monitoring of the energy of the two colliding beams—a difficult task requiring almost infinite machine time. Storage ring is best suited to perform detailed studies of vector meson parameters once they have been found.

Fig. 3. Page 4 of proposal 598 submitted to Brookhaven National Laboratory early in 1972 and approved in May of the same year, giving some of the reasons for performing this experiment in a slow extracted proton beam.

Historically, to my knowledge, the Zichichi Group was the first one to use hadron-hadron collisions to study e⁺e⁻ yields from proton accelerators [15]. This group was the first to develop the earlier shower development method so as to greatly increase the e/π rejection [16]. In later years the Lederman Group made a study of the $\mu^+\mu^-$ yield from proton nuclei collisions [17]. Some of the early theoretical work was done by Preparata [18], Drell and Yan [19], and others.

Let me now go to the J-particle experiment [20—22].

I. To perform a high-sensitivity experiment, detecting narrow-width particles over a wide mass range, we make the following four observations.

i) Since the e⁺e⁻ come from electromagnetic processes, at large mass m, the yield of e⁺e⁻ is lower than that of hadron pairs ($\pi^+\pi^-$, K⁺K⁻, $\bar{p}p$, K⁺$\bar{p}$, etc.) by a factor $<<10^{-6}$.

ii) Thus, to obtain sufficient e⁺e⁻ rates, a detector must be able to stand a high flux of protons, typically of $10^{11}-10^{12}$ protons/s, and

iii) it must be able to reject hadron pairs by a factor of $>>10^8$.

iv) For a detector with finite acceptance, there is always the question of where is the best place to install it to look for new particles. *A priori* we do not know what to do. But we do know that in reactions where ordinary hadrons are produced, the yield is maximum when they are produced at rest in the centre-of-mass system [23]. If we further restrict ourselves to

85

the 90° e⁺e⁻ decay of new particles, then we quickly arrive at the conclusion that the decayed e⁺ or e⁻ emerge at an angle of 14.6° in the laboratory system for an incident proton energy of 28.5 GeV, independent of the mass of the decaying particle.

II. Figure 4 shows the layout of the slow-extracted intense proton beam from the Alternating Gradient Synchrotron (AGS) at Brookhaven, during the period 1973—1974. Our experiment (No. 598) was located in a specially designed beam line (the A-line). To design a clean beam with small spot sizes, I remembered having a conversation with Dr. A. N. Diddens of CERN who had used a slow-extracted beam at the CERN Proton Synchrotron. He advised me to focus the beam with magnets alone without using collimators.

The incident beam of intensity up to 2×10^{12} protons per pulse was focused to a spot size of 3×6 mm². The position of the beam was monitored by a closed-circuit TV. The stability and the intensity of the beam were monitored by a secondary emission counter and six arrays of scintillation counter telescopes, located at an angle of 75° with respect to the beam, and buried behind 12 feet of concrete shielding. Daily calibrations were made of the secondary emission counter with the Al and C foils.

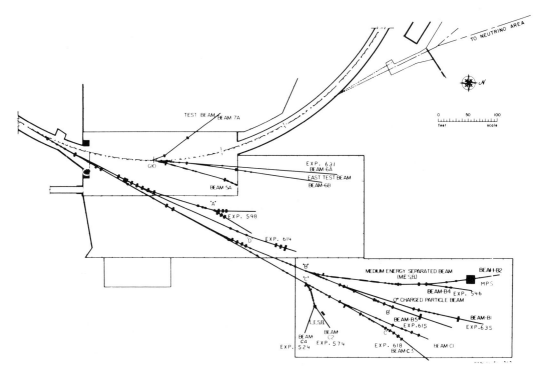

Fig. 4. The AGS East experimental area. The MIT experiment is No. 598 at the end of Station A. Experiment 614 is that of Prof. M. Schwartz (see Ref. 22).

86

III. From our early experience at DESY, we felt the best way to build an electron-pair detector that could handle high intensities, and at the same time have a large mass acceptance and a good mass resolution, is to design a large double-arm spectrometer and to locate most of the detectors behind the magnets so that they would not "view" the target directly. To simplify analysis and to obtain better mass resolution, we used the "p, θ independent" concept in which the magnets bend the particles vertically to measure their momentum, while the production angles ·are measured in the horizontal plane. Figures 5a and 5b show the plan and side views of the spectrometer and detectors.

The main features of the spectrometer are the following:

1) *The target:* The target consists of nine pieces of 1.78 mm thick beryllium, each separated by 7.5 cm so that particles produced in one piece and accepted by the spectrometer do not pass through the next piece. This arrangement also helps us to reject pairs of accidentals by requiring two tracks to come from the same origin.

2) *The magnet system:* The bending powers of the dipole magnets M_0, M_1, M_2 are such that none of the counters sees the target directly. The field of the magnets in their final location was measured with a three-dimensional Hall probe at a total of 10^5 points.

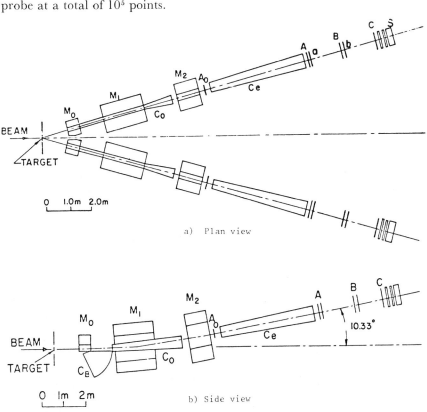

Fig. 5. Schematic diagram of the experimental set-up for the double-arm spectrometer used in our discovery of the J particle. M_0, M_1, and M_2 are dipole magnets; A_0, A, B, and C are 8000-wire proportional chambers; a and b are each 8×8 hodoscopes; S designates three banks of lead-glass and shower counters; C_B, C_0, and C_e are gas Čerenkov counters.

3) *The chambers:* A_0, A, B, and C are multiwire proportional chambers. They consist of more than 8000 very fine, $20 \mu m$ thick, gold-plated wires, 2 mm apart, each with its own amplifier and encoding system. The wire arrangement is shown in Fig. 6. The 11 planes all have different wire orientation. In each of the last three chambers the wires are rotated 60° with respect to each other, so that for a given hit, the numbers of wires add up to a constant—a useful feature for sorting out multitracks and rejecting soft neutrons and γ-rays which do not fire all planes. We developed special gas mixtures to operate the chambers at low voltage and high radiation environment. To help improve the timing resolution, two planes of thin (1.6 mm thick) hodoscopes (8×8) are situated behind each of the chambers A and B. These chambers are able to operate at a rate of ~ 20 MHz and are also able to sort out as many as eight particles simultaneously in each arm.

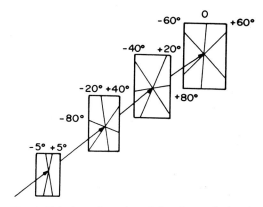

Fig. 6. Relative orientation of the planes of wires in the proportional chambers.

It is essential that all 8000 wires should function properly because to repair a single wire would involve removing close to a thousand tons of concrete.

These chambers and the magnets yield a mass resolution of ± 5 MeV and a mass acceptance of 2 GeV at each magnet current setting. The good mass resolution makes it possible to identify a very narrow resonance. The large mass acceptance is very important when searching over a large mass region for narrow resonances.

4) *Čerenkov counters and shower counters:* The Čerenkov counters marked C_0 and C_e together with the lead-glass and shower counters marked S, enable one to have a rejection against hadron pairs by a factor of $\gg 1 \times 10^8$.

The Čerenkov counter in the magnet (C_0, see Fig. 7a) has a large spherical mirror with a diameter of 1 m. This is followed by another Čerenkov counter behind the second magnet with an elliptical mirror of dimensions 1.5×1.0 m². The Čerenkov counters are filled with hydrogen gas so that the knock-on electrons are reduced to the minimum. As in our earlier DESY experiments, the separation of the two counters by strong magnetic fields ensures that the

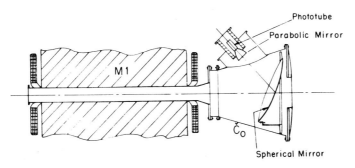

Fig. 7a. Plan view of the C_0 counter shown in its location in the experiment.

small number of knock-on electrons produced in the first counter is swept away and does not enter into the second counter.

To reduce multiple scattering and photon conversion, the material in the beam is reduced to a minimum. The front and rear windows of C_0 are 126 μm and 250 μm thick, respectively. To avoid large-angle Čerenkov light reflection, the mirrors of C_0 and C_e are made of 3 mm thick black lucite, aluminized on the forward (concave) surface only. The mirrors in the experiment were made at the Precision Optical Workshop at CERN. We measured the curvature of the mirrors with a laser gun, and out of the many mirrors that were made a total of 24 were used in this experiment (4 in C_0, 4 in C_e, 16 in C_B).

The counters are painted black inside so that only the Čerenkov light from electrons along the beam trajectory will be focused onto the photomultiplier cathode. Special high-gain, high-efficiency phototubes of the type RCA C31000M are used, so that when we fill the counter with He gas as radiator (where we expect, on the average, $2-3$ photoelectrons) we are able to locate the single photoelectron peak (see Fig. 7b).

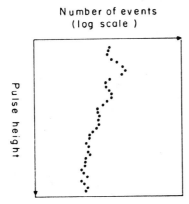

Fig. 7b. Pulse-height spectrum from the phototube (RCA C31000M) of the C_0 Čerenkov counter with He as radiator. Clearly visible are the one, two, and three photoelectron peaks.

The counter C_0 is very close to the target, which is a high-radiation-level area. To reduce random accidentals and dead-time, the excitation voltage on the photomultiplier has to be kept as low as possible. Yet we must still ensure that the counter is efficient. We have to avoid mistakingly setting the voltage so low that the counter is only efficient on an e^+e^- pair from $\pi^0 \to \gamma +$ $+e^++e^-$, which may enter the counter. When C_0 is filled with hydrogen gas, a single electron will yield about eight photoelectrons, a pair will yield about sixteen. The knowledge of the location of one photoelectron peak enables us to distinguish between these two cases. The counters are all calibrated in a test beam to make sure they are 100% efficient in the whole phase space.

At the end of each arm there are two orthogonal banks of lead-glass counters of three radiation lengths each, the first containing twelve elements, the second thirteen, followed by one horizontal bank of seven lead-lucite shower counters, each ten radiation lengths thick, to further reject hadrons from electrons. The subdividing of the lead-glass and lead-lucite counters into ~ 100 cells also enables us to identify the electron trajectory from spurious tracks.

Figure 8 shows an over-all view of the detector with the roof removed. Figure 9 shows the end section of one arm of the detector, showing part of the Čerenkov counter C_e, the proportional chambers, and counters.

Fig. 8. Over-all view of the detector.

Fig. 9. End view of one arm, showing part of the Čerenkov counter C_e, the chambers A, B, C, with part of the 8000 amplifiers X, cables Y, and hodoscopes Z. The lead-glass counter is at the end of chamber U.

5) *A pure electron beam for calibration:* To obtain a high rejection against hadron pairs and to ensure that the detectors are 100% efficient for electrons, we need to calibrate the detectors with a clean electron beam. In an electron accelerator such as DESY we can easily produce a clean electron beam with an energetic photon beam hitting a high-Z target thus creating $0°$ e^+e^- pairs. In a proton accelerator the best way to create a clean electron beam is to use the reaction $\pi^0 \rightarrow \gamma + e^+ + e^-$, tagging the e^+ in coincidence with the e^-. To accomplish this, the very directional Čerenkov counter C_B is placed close to the target and below a specially constructed magnet M_0 (Fig. 10a). This counter also is painted black inside; it is sensitive to electrons above 10 MeV/c and rejects pions below 2.7 GeV/c. The coincidence between C_B and C_0, C_e, the shower counter, and the hodoscopes, indicates the detection of an e^+e^- pair from the process $\pi^0 \rightarrow \gamma + e^+ + e^-$. A typical plot of the relative timing of this coincidence is shown in Fig. 10b. We can trigger on C_B and provide a pure electron beam to calibrate C_0, C_e, the lead-glass and shower counters.

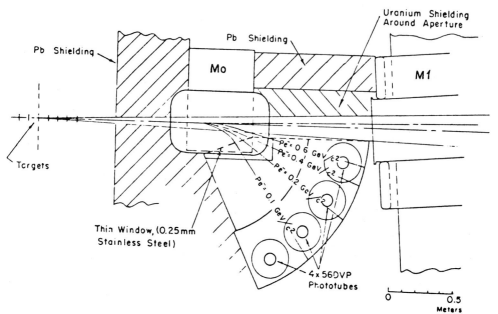

a. Side view of magnet M_0 which bends the various low-energy trajectories (P_e) of $e^{\pm}$ into C_B.

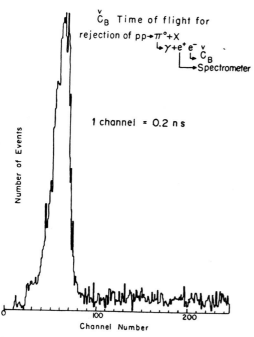

b. The relative timing between an electron pulse from C_B and a positron trigger from the main spectrometer arm or vice versa.

Fig. 10. Measurement of e^+e^- from $\pi^0 \rightarrow \gamma + e^+ + e^-$ decay.

This is another way of setting the voltage of the C_0 counters, since the coincidence between C_e and C_B will ensure that the counter is efficient for a single electron and not a zero degree pair.

6) *Shielding:* As shown in Fig. 8 the detector is large, and with 10^{12} protons incident on a 10% collision length target there are $\sim 10^{12}$ particles generated around the experimental area. To shield the detector and the physicists, we constructed scaled-down wooden models of the concrete blocks, and soon realized that we would need more shielding than was available at Brookhaven. This problem was solved by obtaining all the shielding blocks from the Cambridge Electron Accelerator, which had just closed down. The total shielding used is approximately a) 10,000 tons of concrete, b) 100 tons of lead, c) 5 tons of uranium, d) 5 tons of soap—placed on top of C_0, between M_1 and M_2, and around the front of C_e to stop soft neutrons. Even with this amount of shielding, the radiation level in the target area, one hour after the shutting down of the proton beam, is still 5 röntgen/hour, a most dangerous level.

During the construction of our spectrometers, and indeed during the entire experiment, I encountered much criticism. The problem was that in order to gain a good mass resolution it was necessary to build a spectrometer that was very expensive. One eminent physicist made the remark that this type of spectrometer is only good for looking for narrow resonances—and there are no narrow resonances. Nevertheless, since I usually do not have much confidence in theoretical arguments, we decided to proceed with our original design.

In April 1974, we finished the set-up of the experiment and started bringing an intense proton beam into the area. We soon found that the radiation level in our counting room was 0.2 röntgen/hour. This implied that our physicists would receive the maximum allowable yearly dose in 24 hours! We searched very hard, for a period of two to three weeks, looking for the reason, and became extremely worried whether we could proceed with the experiment at all.

One day, Dr. U. Becker, who has been working with me since 1966, was walking around with a Geiger counter when he suddenly noticed that most of the radiation was coming from one particular place in the mountains of shielding. Upon close investigation we found out that even though we had 10,000 tons of concrete shielding blocks, the most important region—the top of the beam stopper—was not shielded at all! After this correction, radiation levels went down to a safe level and we were able to proceed with the experiment.

From April to August, we did the routine tune-ups and found the detectors performing as designed. We were able to use 10^{12} protons per second. The small pair spectrometer also functioned properly and enabled us to calibrate the detector with a pure electron beam.

IV. Owing to its complexity, the detector required six physicists to operate it. Before taking data, approximately 100 hours were spent ensuring that all the detectors were close to 100% efficient. I list some examples:

i) The efficiency of the Čerenkov counters was measured over the whole phase space, and voltages set so that they were efficient everywhere. A typical result for C_e is shown in Fig. 11a.

ii) The voltages and the response of all the lead-glass and shower counters were calibrated to ensure that the response did not change with time.

iii) The efficiency of the hodoscopes at the far end, furthest away from the photomultiplier tube, was checked.

iv) The timing of the hodoscopes was also checked to ensure that signals from each counter generated by particles produced at the target arrived simultaneously. During the experiment, the time-of-flight of each of the hodoscopes and the Čerenkov counters, the pulse heights of the Čerenkov counters and of the lead-glass and shower counters, the single rates of all the counters together with the wire chamber signals, were recorded and continuously displayed on a storage/display scope.

v) To ensure that the proportional wire chambers were efficient over their whole area, a small test counter was placed behind the chambers at various positions over the chambers' area, and voltage excitation curves were made at those positions. A typical set of curves for all the planes is shown in Fig. 11b.

vi) To check the timing between the two arms, two tests were performed. Firstly, the test counter was physically moved from one arm to the other

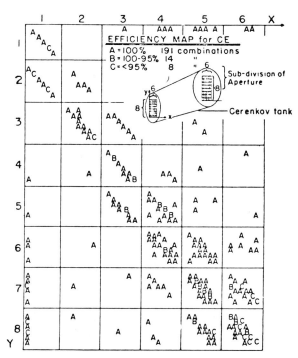

Fig. 11a. Mapping of the efficiency of the C_e counter over its whole phase space. The letters on the plot refer to efficiencies measured for trajectories between the corresponding points marked on the grid at each end of the counter.

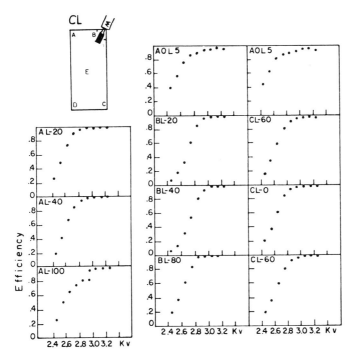

Fig. 11b. Efficiency of all the wire planes as a function of the applied voltage. The measurements were done by placing a small test counter W in various positions, marked A, B, C, D, E, in every chamber.

so that the relative timing could be compared. Secondly, the e^+e^- yield was measured at low mass, $m_{ee} < 2$ GeV/c², where there is an abundance of genuine e^+e^- pairs.

In the early summer of 1974 we took some data in the high mass region of 4—5 GeV. However, analysis of the data showed very few electron-positron pairs.

By the end of August we tuned the magnets to accept an effective mass of 2.5—4.0 GeV. Immediately we saw clean, real, electron pairs.

But most surprising of all is that most of the e^+e^- pairs peaked narrowly at 3.1 GeV (Fig. 12a). A more detailed analysis shows that the width is less than 5 MeV! (Fig. 12b).

Throughout the years, I have established certain practices in the group with regard to experimental checks on our data and on the data analysis. I list a few examples:

i) To make sure the peak we observed was a real effect and not due to instrumentation bias or read-out error of the computer, we took another set of data at a lower magnet current. This has the effect of moving the particles into different parts of the detector. The fact that the peak remained fixed at 3.1 GeV (Fig. 12a) showed right away that a real particle had been discovered.

ii) We used two completely different sets of programs to ensure that the analysis was correct. This means that two independent groups of physi-

95

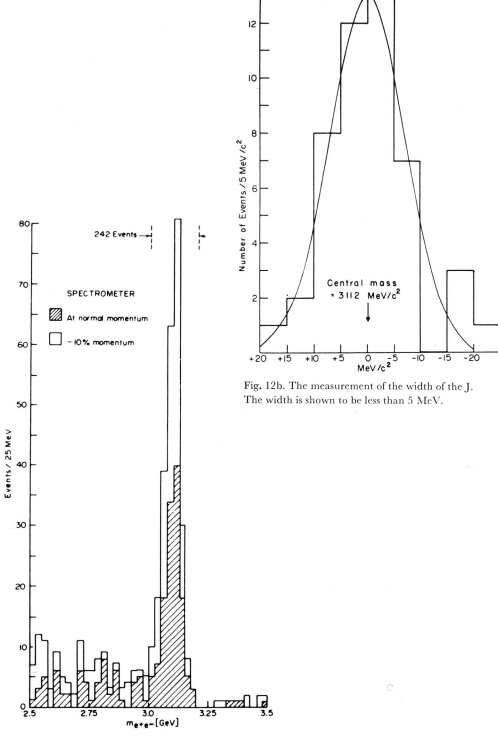

Fig. 12b. The measurement of the width of the J. The width is shown to be less than 5 MeV.

Fig. 12a. Mass spectrum for events in the mass range $2.5 < m_{ee} < 3.5$ GeV/c. The shaded events correspond to those taken at the normal magnet setting, while the unshaded ones correspond to the spectrometer magnet setting at -10% lower than normal value.

cists analysed the data, starting from the reduction of raw data tapes, to form their own data summary tapes, and then performed two sets of Monte Carlo acceptance calculations, two sets of event reconstruction, two sets of data corrections, and finally, two sets of results which must agree with each other. Although this procedure uses twice as much computer time, it provides greater confidence in our results after the two independent approaches have reached the same conclusions.

iii) To understand the nature of various second-order background corrections, we made the following special measurements:

    a) To check the background from pile-up in the lead-glass and shower counters, different runs were made with different voltage settings on the counters. No effect was observed in the yield.

    b) To check the background from scattering from the sides of the magnets, cuts were made in the data to reduce the effective aperture. No significant reduction in the yield was found.

    c) To check the read-out system of the chambers and the triggering system of the hodoscopes, runs were made with a few planes of chambers deleted and with sections of the hodoscopes omitted from the trigger. No unexpected effect was observed on the yield.

    d) Since the true event rate is proportional to incident beam intensity and the accidental backgrounds from the two arms are proportional to the square of the incident intensity, a sensitive way to check the size of the background is to run the experiment again with different intensities. This was done and the background contribution in the peak was found to be unnoticeable.

iv) To understand the nature of production properties of the new peak, we increased the target thickness by a factor of two. The yield increased by a factor of two, not by four.

These and many other checks convinced us that we had observed a real massive particle.

We discussed the name of the new particle for some time. Someone pointed out to me that the really exciting stable particles are designated by Roman characters—like the postulated W^0, the intermediate vector boson, the Z^0, etc.—whereas the "classical" particles have Greek designations like ρ, ω, etc. This, combined with the fact that our work in the last decade had been concentrated on the electromagnetic current $j_\mu(x)$, gave us the idea to call this particle the J particle.

V. I was considering announcing our results during the retirement ceremony for V. F. Weisskopf, who had helped us a great deal during the course of many of our experiments. This ceremony was to be held on 17 and 18 October 1974. I postponed the announcement for two reasons. First, there were speculations on high mass e^+e^- pair production from proton-proton collisions as coming from a two-step process: $p+N \rightarrow \pi+...$, where the pion undergoes a second collision $\pi+N \rightarrow e^++e^-+...$. This could be checked by a measurement based on target thickness. The yield from a two-step process would increase quadratically with target thickness, whereas for a one-step process the yield increases linearly. This was quickly done, as described in point (iv) above.

Most important, we realized that there were earlier Brookhaven measurements [24] of direct production of muons and pions in nucleon-nucleon collisions which gave the μ/π ratio as 10^{-4}, a mysterious ratio that seemed not to change from 2000 GeV at the ISR down to 30 GeV. This value was an order of magnitude larger than theoretically expected in terms of the three known vector mesons, ρ, ω, φ, which at that time were the only possible "intermediaries" between the strong and electromagnetic interactions. We then added the J meson to the three and found that the linear combination of the four vector mesons could not explain the μ^-/π^- ratio either. This I took as an indication that something exciting might be just around the corner, so I decided that we should make a direct measurement of this number. Since we could not measure the μ/π ratio with our spectrometer, we decided to look into the possibility of investigating the e^-/π^- ratio.

We began various test runs to understand the problems involved in doing the e/π experiment. The most important tests were runs of different e^- momenta as a function of incident proton intensities to check the single-arm backgrounds and the data-recording capability of the computer.

On Thursday, 7 November, we made a major change in the spectrometer (see Fig. 13) to start the new experiment to search for more particles. We began by measuring the mysterious e/π ourselves. We changed the electronic logic and the target, and reduced the incident proton beam intensity by almost two orders of magnitude. To identify the e^- background due to the decay of π^0 mesons, we inserted thin aluminium converters in front of the spectrometer to increase the $\gamma \rightarrow e^+ + e^-$ conversion. This, together with the C_B counter which measures the $\pi \rightarrow \gamma + e^+ + e^-$ directly, enabled us to control the major e^- background contribution.

We followed the e/π measurements with another change in the spectrometer by installing new high-pressure Čerenkov counters and systematically measuring hadron pairs (K^+K^-, $\pi^+\pi^-$, $\bar{p}p$, etc.) to find out how many other particles exist that do not decay into e^+e^- but into hadrons. But, after a long search, none was found.

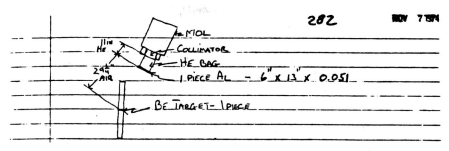

Fig. 13a. Aluminium foil arrangement in front of magnet M_0 in our new experiment to determine the e/π ratio. The converter was used to determine the electron background yield.

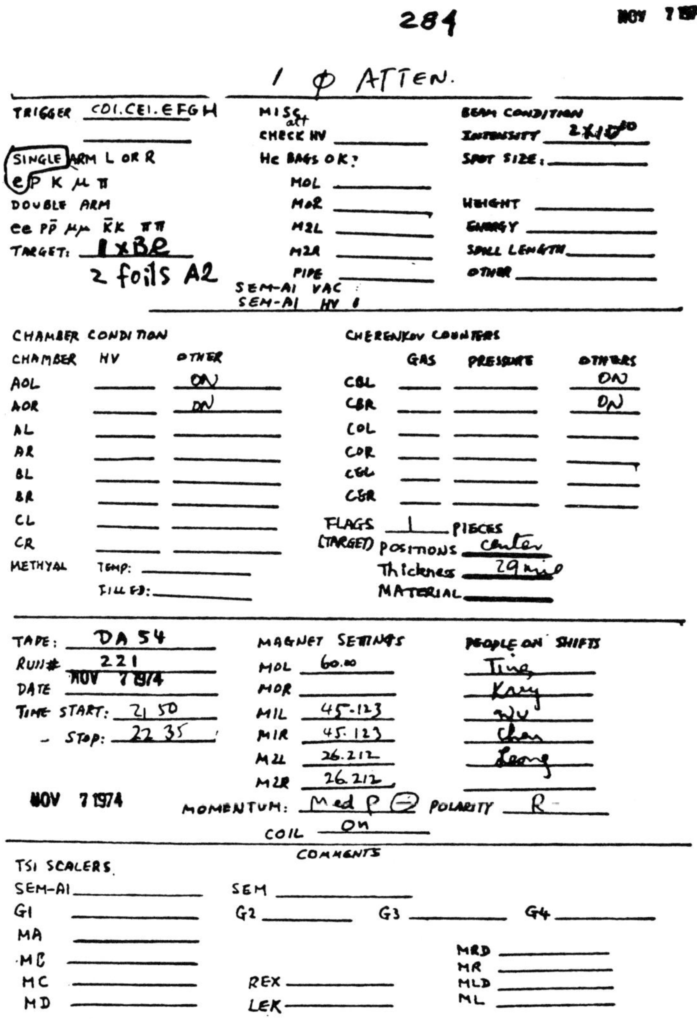
284 NOV 7 1974

1 φ ATTEN.

TRIGGER COI.CEI.EFGH
SINGLE ARM L OR R
e P K μ π
DOUBLE ARM
ee pp̄ μμ KK ππ
TARGET: 1×Be
2 foils Al

MISC. att
CHECK HV
He BAGS OK?
MOL
MOR
M2L
M2R
PIPE
SEM-Al VAC
SEM-Al HV

BEAM CONDITION
INTENSITY 2×10^10
SPOT SIZE:
HEIGHT
ENERGY
SPILL LENGTH
OTHER

CHAMBER CONDITION
CHAMBER HV OTHER
AOL ON
AOR ON
AL
AR
BL
BR
CL
CR
METHYAL TEMP:
FILLED:

CHERENKOV COUNTERS
GAS PRESSURE OTHERS
C0L ON
C0R ON
COL
COR
CEL
CER
FLAGS 1 PIECES
(TARGET) POSITIONS center
Thickness 29 mil
MATERIAL

TAPE: DA 54
RUN# 221
DATE NOV 7 1974
TIME START: 21 50
STOP: 22 35

MAGNET SETTINGS
MOL 60.00
MOR
M1L 45.123
M1R 45.123
M2L 26.212
M2R 26.212
MOMENTUM: Med P ⊖ POLARITY R
COIL On

PEOPLE ON SHIFTS
Ting
Kasy
Wu
Chen
Leong

NOV 7 1974

COMMENTS

TSI SCALERS
SEM-Al
G1
MA
MB
MC
MD
SEM
G2
G3
G4
REX
LEK
MRD
MR
MLD
ML

Fig. 13b. Data sheet for a typical run under the new experimental conditions. Blank spaces imply either data entered in the computer or conditions identical to the prior run. In this run the electrons pass through the right detector arm with a momentum of about 6 GeV. Two pieces of aluminium foil in front of the magnet M_0 serve as converters. [From the group's data book, pp. 282 and 284, 7 November 1974.]

In the meantime, since the end of October, M. Chen and U. Becker and others in the group had been insisting that we publish our results quickly. I was very much puzzled by the $\mu/\pi = 10^{-4}$ ratio and wanted to know how many particles existed. Under pressure, I finally decided to publish our results of J alone.

On 6 November I paid a visit to G. Trigg, Editor of Physical Review Letters, to find out if the rules for publication without refereeing had been changed. Following that visit, I wrote a simple draft in the style of our quantum electrodynamics paper of 1967 (Ref. 5). The paper emphasized only the discovery of J. and the checks we made on the data without mention of our future plans.

On 11 November we telephoned G. Bellettini, the Director of Frascati Laboratory, informing him of our results. At Frascati they started a search on 13 November, and called us back on 15 November to tell us excitedly that they had also seen the J signal and obtained a $\Gamma_{\mu\mu}^{2}/\Gamma_{\text{total}} = 0.8\pm0.2$ keV. Their first spectrum is shown in Fig. 14a. The Frascati Group were able to publish their results in the same issue of Physical Review Letters [25] as ours. Very shortly after, they made a more detailed study of J (Fig. 14b) and also established that its total width is only ~60 keV. (It lives ~1000 times longer than the ρ meson.) They have since made a systematic search for more particles at lower mass—but have found none [26].

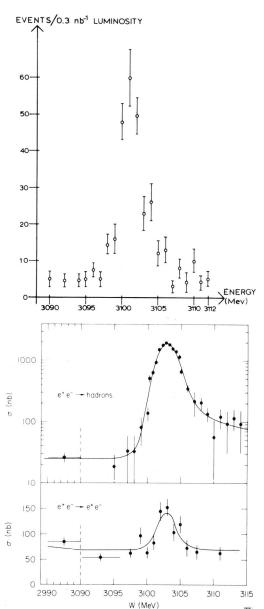

Fig. 14a. Result from one of the Frascati groups on J-particle production. The number of events per 0.3 nb⁻¹ luminosity is plotted versus the total c.m. energy of the machine. (From Ref. 25.)

Fig. 14b. Excitation curves for the reactions $e^{+}+e^{-} \rightarrow$ hadrons and $e^{+}+e^{-} \rightarrow e^{+}+e^{-}$.
The solid line represents the best fit to their data. (From Ref. 26.)

100

VI. Now, immediately after the discovery of J, because of its heavy mass and unusually long lifetime, there were many speculations as to the nature of this particle. Lee, Peoples, O'Halloran and collaborators [27] were able to photo-produce the J particle coherently from nuclear targets with an ~100 GeV photon beam. They showed that the photoproduction of the J is very similar to ρ production and thus were the first to establish that J is a strongly interacting particle.

Pilcher, Smith and collaborators [28] have ingeniously used a large accep-tance spectrometer to perform an accurate and systematic study of J production at energies >100 GeV. By using π beams as well as proton beams, and by measuring a wide range of mass and the momentum transfer dependence of $\mu\mu$ production, they were the first to state that the single muon yield which produced the mysterious $\mu/\pi = 10^{-4}$, which had puzzled me for a long time, comes mostly from the production of muon pairs. The J yield from the π meson seems to be much higher than from the proton.

In Fig. 15 are listed some of the relative yields of J production from various proton accelerators. It seems that I had chosen the most difficult place to discover the J.

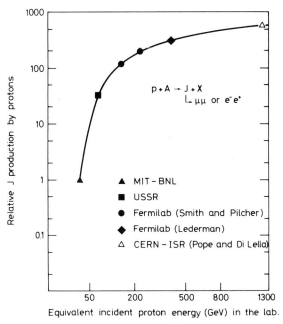

Fig. 15. Relative J production, at 90° in the centre of mass, as a function of the energy of the incident proton beam. For experiments using nuclear targets, a linear A-dependence has been used to obtain the yield on a nucleon. Refs: MIT-BNL: J. J. Aubert et al., Phys. Rev. Letters *33*, 1404 (1974); CERN-ISR: F. W. Büsser et al., Phys. Letters *56B*, 482 (1975); USSR: Yu. M. Antipov et al., Phys. Letters *60B*, 309 (1976); Lederman Group: H. D. Snyder et al., Phys. Rev. Letters *36*, 1415 (1976); Smith-Pilcher Group: K. J. Anderson et al., paper submitted to the 18th Internat. Conf. on High-Energy Physics, Tbilisi, USSR (1976).

101

3. SOME SUBSEQUENT DEVELOPMENTS

The discovery of the J has triggered off many new discoveries. Some of the most important experimental work was done at SLAC [29] and at DESY [30].

The latest results [31] from the 4π superconducting magnet detector, called "Pluto", measuring the $e^+ + e^- \rightarrow$ hadrons near the mass of ψ' (the sister state of J) first discovered at SLAC, are shown in Fig. 16a. The yield of ψ' (and of J) goes up by $>10^2$. It can be seen that an electron-positron storage ring is an ideal machine for studying these new particles. The same group has recently carried out a careful search for new particles at a higher mass region. Their accurate results, shown in Fig. 16b, confirm the indication by SLAC that there may be many more states in this high mass region.

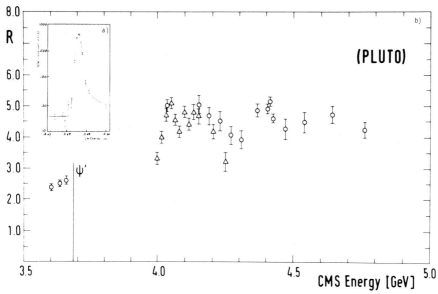

Fig. 16. a) Excitation curve for ψ'. b) Ratio $R = (e^+ + e^- \rightarrow$ hadrons) over $(e^+ + e^- \rightarrow \mu^+ + \mu^-)$, measured by the DESY Pluto group. (Ref. 31.)

One of the most important discoveries after that of the J is the observation by the double-arm spectrometer (DASP) Group at DESY [32] of the chain reaction

$$e^+ + e^- \rightarrow \psi'$$
$$\big\downarrow \rightarrow P_c \rightarrow \gamma_1$$
$$\big\downarrow \rightarrow \gamma_2 + J$$
$$\big\downarrow \rightarrow \mu + \mu.$$

By tuning the storage ring so that the electron-positron energy reaches 3.7 GeV to produce the ψ', using the double-arm spectrometer to select the $J \rightarrow \mu^+ + \mu^-$ events and detecting both the γ_1 and γ_2 as well, they found that the two photons γ_1 and γ_2 are strongly correlated into two groups. The first group has $E_{\gamma_1} = 169 \pm 7$ MeV and $E_{\gamma_2} = 398 \pm 7$ MeV (or vice versa, since they did not

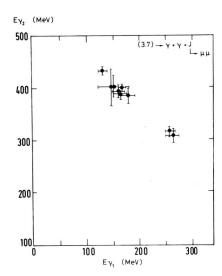

Fig. 17. Scatter plot of the two-photon energies for candidates for the decay $\psi' \rightarrow (J \rightarrow \mu^+ + \mu^-) + \gamma + \gamma$. (Ref. 32.)

determine which γ came first), and the second group has $E_{\gamma_1} = 263 \pm 8$ MeV and $E_{\gamma_2} = 315 \pm 8$ MeV. This correlation, called scatter plot, is shown in Fig. 17. The emission of monochromatic γ-rays indicates the existence of intermediate states with even-spin quantum number.

The narrow width of the J and the existence of the P_c and many other states, strongly suggests that the J may be a bound state of two new quarks. The existence of charmed quarks was first proposed by Bjorken and Glashow [33], and Glashow, Iliopoulos and Maiani [34], originally as a cure for certain difficulties in the weak interaction of hadrons. Indeed, the energy levels of the observed states are very similar to the positronium state discovered by Deutsch in 1951 [35].

Recently there are indications from experiments at BNL [36], from DESY [37, 38], from the Fermi Laboratory [39] and from SLAC [40] of the existence of further narrow states, indications which very much follow the general prediction of Glashow.

4. CONCLUSION

In conclusion, we can ask ourselves some further questions:

1) We know that the photon transforms itself into ρ, ω, and φ with a mass of about 1 GeV. It can transform into J and its various associated states with a mass of about $3-5$ GeV. What happens when we go to higher and higher energies? It seems very unlikely that there should not be many more new series of photon-like particles.

2) The existence of J implies that we need at least four quarks to explain the phenomena observed so far. How many more quarks will we need if we find a new series of particles in higher energy regions?

3) If we need a large family of quarks, are they the real fundamental blocks of nature? Why has none of them been found?

103

REFERENCES

1. See for example: J. Needham, Science and civilization in China (Cambridge University Press, New York, 1962), Vol. 4.

2. G. Herzberg, Atomic spectra and atomic structure (Dover Reprint, New York, 1944). A. I. Akhiezer and V. B. Berestetskii, Quantum electrodynamics (translated by Oak Ridge Technical Information Service, ORNL, Tennessee, USA, 1957). S. D. Drell, Ann. Phys. *4*, 75 (1958).

3. S. J. Brodsky and S. C. C. Ting, Phys. Rev. *145*, 1018 (1966).

4. J. Bailey, K. Borer, F. Combley, H. Drumm, C. Eck, F. J. M. Farley, J. H. Field, W. Flegel, P. M. Hattersley, F. Krienen, F. Lange, G. Petrucci, E. Picasso, H. I. Pizer, O. Runolfsson, R. W. Williams and S. Wojcicki, Phys. Letters *55B*, 420 (1975). E. Picasso, private communication.

5. J. G. Asbury, W. K. Bertram, U. Becker, P. Joos, M. Rohde, A. J. S. Smith, S. Friedlander, C. Jordan and S. C. C. Ting, Phys. Rev. Letters *18*, 65 (1967). H. Alvensleben, U. Becker, W. K. Bertram, M. Binkley, K. Cohen, C. L. Jordan, T. M. Knasel, R. Marshall, D. J. Quinn, M. Rohde, G. H. Sanders and S. C. C. Ting, Phys. Rev. Letters *21*, 1501 (1968).

6. J. G. Asbury, U. Becker, W. K. Bertram, P. Joos, M. Rohde, A. J. S. Smith, C. L. Jordan and S. C. C. Ting, Phys. Rev. Letters *19*, 869 (1967).

7. For theoretical papers on leptonic decay of vector mesons, see:
   M. Gell-Mann, D. Sharp and W. G. Wagner, Phys. Rev. Letters *8*, 261 (1962).
   S. L. Glashow, Phys. Rev. Letters *7*, 469 (1961).
   M. Gell-Mann and F. Zachariasen, Phys. Rev. *124*, 953 (1961).
   Y. Nambu and J. J. Sakurai, Phys. Rev. Letters *8*, 79 (1962).
   S. M. Berman and S. D. Drell, Phys. Rev. B *133*, 791 (1964).
   N. M. Kroll, T. D. Lee and B. Zumino, Phys. Rev. *157*, 1376 (1967).
   H. Joos, Phys. Letters *24B*, 103 (1967).

8. See also: J. K. de Pagter, J. I. Friedman, G. Glass, R. C. Chase, M. Gettner, E. von Goeler, R. Weinstein and A. M. Boyarski, Phys. Rev. Letters *16*, 35 (1966). A. Wehman, E. Engels, L. N. Hand, C. M. Hoffman, P. G. Innocenti, R. Wilson, W. A. Blanpied, D. J. Drickey and D. G. Stairs, Phys. Rev. Letters *18*, 929 (1967). B. D. Hyams, W. Koch, D. Pellett, D. Potter, L. von Lindern, E. Lorenz, G. Lütjens, U. Stierlin and P. Weilhammer, Phys. Letters *24B*, 634 (1967). M. N. Khachaturyan, M. A. Azimov, A. M. Baldin, A. S. Belousov, I. V. Chuvilo, R. Firkowski, J. Hladky, M. S. Khvastunov, J. Manca, A. T. Matyushin, V. T. Matyushin, G. A. Ososkov, L. N. Shtarkov and L. I. Zhuravleva, Phys. Letters *24B*, 349 (1967).

9. H. Alvensleben, U. Becker, W. K. Bertram, M. Chen, K. J. Cohen, T. M. Knasel, R. Marshall, D. J. Quinn, M. Rohde, G. H. Sanders, H. Schubel and S. C. C. Ting, Phys. Rev. Letters *24*, 786 (1970).

10. H. Alvensleben, U. Becker, M. Chen, K. J. Cohen, R. T. Edwards, T. M. Knasel, R. Marshall, D. J. Quinn, M. Rohde, G. H. Sanders, H. Schubel and S. C. C. Ting, Phys. Rev. Letters *25*, 1377 (1970).

11. H. Alvensleben, U. Becker, W. K. Bertram, M. Chen, K. J. Cohen, R. T. Edwards, T. M. Knasel, R. Marshall, D. J. Quinn, M. Rohde, G. H. Sanders, H. Schubel and S. C. C. Ting, Phys. Rev. Letters *25*, 1373 (1970).

12. H. Alvensleben, U. Becker, W. Busza, M. Chen, K. J. Cohen, R. T. Edwards, P. M. Mantsch, R. Marshall, T. Nash, M. Rohde, H. F. W. Sadrozinski, G. H. Sanders, H. Schubel, S. C. C. Ting and S. L. Wu, Phys. Rev. Letters *27*, 888 (1971).

13. For an excellent review of earlier work on ρ-ω interference, see G. Goldhaber, *in* Experimental meson spectroscopy (eds. C. Baltay and A. H. Rosenfeld) (Columbia Univ. Press, New York, 1970), p. 59. See also E. Gabathuler, same Proceedings, p. 645.

14. J. J. Sakurai, Ann. Phys. *11*, 1 (1960) and Nuovo Cimento *16*, 388 (1960). For an excellent review of earlier work, see H. Joos, Review talk at the Internat. Conf. on Elementary Particles, Heidelberg, 1967 (North-Holland Publ. Co., Amsterdam, 1968), p. 349.

15. M. Conversi, T. Massam, Th. Muller, M. A. Schneegans and A. Zichichi, Proc.12th Internat. Conf. on High-Energy Physics, Dubna, 1964 (Atomizdat, Moscow, 1966), p. 895, and T. Massam, Th. Muller and A. Zichichi, Nuovo Cimento *40*, 589 (1965).

16. T. Massam, Th. Muller and A. Zichichi, CERN 63-25 (1963). See also, T. Massam, Th. Muller, M. Schneegans and A. Zichichi, Nuovo Cimento *39*, 464 (1965).

17. J. H. Christenson, G. S. Hicks, L. M. Lederman, P. J. Limon, B. G. Pope and E. Zavattini, Phys. Rev. Letters *25*, 1523 (1970).

18. One of the first theoretical works on dileptonic production from pp collisions is that of: G. Altarelli, R. A. Brandt and G. Preparata, Phys. Rev. Letters *26*, 42 (1971).

19. S. D. Drell and T. M. Yan, Phys. Rev. Letters *25*, 316 (1970).

20. J. J. Aubert, U. Becker, P. J. Biggs, J. Burger, M. Chen, G. Everhart, P. Goldhagen, Y. Y. Lee, J. Leong, T. McCorriston, T. G. Rhoades, M. Rohde, S. C. C. Ting and S. L. Wu, Phys. Rev. Letters *33*, 1404 (1974).

21. J. J. Aubert, U. Becker, P. J. Biggs, J. Burger, M. Chen, G. Everhart, J. W. Glenn III, P. Goldhagen, Y. Y. Lee, J. Leong, P. Mantsch, T. McCorriston, T. G. Rhoades, M. Rohde, S. C. C. Ting and S. L. Wu, Nuclear Phys. *B89*, 1 (1975).

22. See, S. C. C. Ting, Discovery story *in* Adventures in Experimental Physics *5*, 115 (1976).

23. T. T. Wu, private communication. V. Blobel, H. Fesefeldt, H. Franz, B. Hellwig, W. Idschok, J. W. Lamsa, D. Mönkemeyer, H. F. Neumann, D. Roedel, W. Schrankel, B. Schwarz, F. Selonke and P. Söding, Phys. Letters *48B*, 73 (1974).

24. L. B. Leipuner, R. C. Larsen, L. W. Smith, R. K. Adair, H. Kasha, C. M. Ankenbrandt, R. J. Stefanski and P. J. Wanderer, Phys. Rev. Letters *34*, 103 (1975).

25. C. Bacci, R. Baldini Celio, M. Bernardini, G. Capon, R. Del Fabbro, M. Grilli, E. Iarocci, L. Jones, M. Locci, C. Mencuccini, G. P. Murtas, G. Penso, G. Salvini, M. Spano, M. Spinetti, B. Stella, V. Valente, B. Bartoli, D. Bisello, B. Esposito, F. Felicetti, P. Monacelli, M. Nigro, L. Paoluzi, I. Peruzzi, G. Piano Mortari, M. Piccolo, F. Ronga, F. Sebastiani, L. Trasatti, F. Vanoli, G. Barbarino, G. Barbiellini, C. Bemporad, R. Biancastelli, M. Calvetti, M. Castellano, F. Cevenini, V. Costantini, P. Lariccia, S. Patricelli, P. Parascandalo, E. Sassi, C. Spencer, L. Tortora, U. Troya and S. Vitale, Phys. Rev. Letters *33*, 1408 (1974).

26. C. Bemporad, Proc. Internat. Symposium on Lepton and Photon Interactions at High Energies, Stanford, 1975 (SLAC, Calif., USA, 1975), p. 113.

27. B. Knapp, W. Lee, P. Leung, S. D. Smith, A. Wijangco, K. Knauer, D. Yount, D. Nease, J. Bronstein, R. Coleman, L. Cormell, G. Gladding, M. Gormley, R. Messner, T. O'Halloran, J. Sarracino, A. Wattenberg, D. Wheeler, M. Binkley, J. R. Orr, J. Peoples and L. Read, Phys. Rev. Letters *34*, 1040 and 1044 (1975). The group has recently finished a series of experiments on J production with a neutron beam on nuclear targets, and has learned valuable information on the transmission properties of J. M. Binkley, I. Gaines, J. Peoples, B. Knapp, W. Lee, P. Leung, S. D. Smith, A. Wijangco, J. Knauer, J. Bronstein, R. Coleman, G. Gladding, M. Goodman, M. Gormley, R. Messner, T. O'Halloran, J. Sarracino and A. Wattenberg, Phys. Rev. Letters *37*, 571 and 574 (1976).

28. K. J. Anderson, G. G. Henry, K. T. McDonald, J. E. Pilcher, E. I. Rosenberg, J. G. Branson, G. H. Sanders, A. J. S. Smith and J. J. Thaler, Phys, Rev. Letters *36*, 237 (1976), and *37*, 799 and 803 (1976).

29. See, for example, review papers by: R. F. Schwitters, Proc. Internat. Symposium on Lepton and Photon Interactions at High Energies, Stanford, 1975 (SLAC, Calif., USA, 1975), p. 5. G. S. Abrams, same Proceedings, p. 25. G. J. Feldman, same Proceedings, p. 39. A. D. Liberman, same Proceedings, p. 55.

30. For a review of DESY work, see: Review paper by B. H. Wiik, Proc. Internat. Symposium on Lepton and Photon Interactions at High Energies, Stanford, 1975 (SLAC, Calif., USA, 1975), p. 69.

31. J. Burmester, L. Criegee, H. C. Dehne, K. Derikum, R. Devenish, J. D. Fox, G. Franke, G. Flügge, Ch. Gerke, G. Horlitz, Th. Kahl, G. Knies, M. Rössler, G. Wolff, R. Schmitz, T. N. Rangaswamy, U. Timm, H. Wahl, P. Waloschek, G. G. Winter, W. Zimmermann, V. Blobel, H. Jensing, B. Koppitz, E. Lohrmann, A. Bäcker, J. Bürger, C. Grupin, M. Rost, H. Meyer and K. Wacker, DESY preprint 76/53 (1976). Also, E. Lohrmann, private communication.

32. W. Braunschweig, H.-U. Martyn, H. G. Sander, D. Schmitz, W. Sturm, W. Wallraff, K. Berkelman, D. Cords, R. Felst, E. Gadermann, G. Grindhammer, H. Hultschig, P. Joos, W. Koch, U. Kötz, H. Krehbiel, D. Kreinick, J. Ludwig, K.-H. Mess, K. C. Moffeit, A. Petersen, G. Poelz, J. Ringel, K. Sauerberg, P. Schmüser, G. Vogel, B. H. Wiik, G. Wolf, G. Buschhorn, R. Kotthaus, U. E. Kruse, H. Lierl, H. Oberlack, R. Pretzl, M. Schliwa, S. Orito, T. Suda, Y. Totsuka and S. Yamada, Phys. Letters *57B*, 407 (1975).

33. B. J. Bjorken and S. L. Glashow, Phys. Letters *11*, 255 (1964). See also earlier paper by S. L. Glashow and M. Gell-Mann, Ann. Phys. *15*, 437 (1961).

34. S. L. Glashow, J. Iliopoulos and L. Maiani, Phys. Rev. D *2*, 1285 (1970).

35. M. Deutsch. Phys. Rev. *82*, 455 (1951).

36. E. Cazzoli, A. M. Cnops, P. L. Connolly, R. I. Louttit, M. J. Murgtagh, R. B. Palmer, N. P. Samios, T. T. Tso and H. H. Williams, Phys. Rev. Letters *34*, 1125 (1975).

37. W. Braunschweig, H.-U. Martyn, H. G. Sander, D. Schmitz, W. Sturm, W. Wallraff, D. Cords, R. Felst, R. Fries, E. Gadermann, B. Gittelman, H. Hultschig, P. Joos, W. Koch, U. Kötz, H. Krehbiel, D. Kreinick, W. A. McNeely, K. C. Moffeit, P. Petersen, O. Römer, R. Rüsch, B. H. Wiik, G. Wolf, G. Grindhammer, J. Ludwig, K. H. Mess, G. Poelz, J. Ringel, K. Sauerberg, P. Schmüser, W. De Boer, G. Buschhorn, B. Gunderson, R. Kotthaus, H. Lierl, H. Oberlack, M. Schliwa, S. Orito, T. Suda, Y. Totsuka and S. Yamada, Phys. Letters *63B*, 471 (1976).

38. J. Burmester, L. Criegee, H. C. Dehne, K. Derikum, R. Devenish, J. D. Fox, G. Franke, G. Flügge, Ch. Gerke, G. Horlitz, Th. Kahl, G. Knies, M. Rössler, G. Wolff, R. Schmitz, T. N. Rangaswamy, U. Timm, H. Wahl, P. Waloschek, G. G. Winter, W. Zimmermann, V. Blobel, H. Jensing, B. Koppitz, E. Lohrmann, A. Bäcker, J. Bürger, C. Grupin, M. Rost, H. Meyer and K. Wacker, DESY preprint 76/50 (1976), and private communication from B. Wiik.

39. B. Knapp, W. Lee, P. Leung, S. D. Smith, A. Wijangco, J. Knauer, D. Yount, J. Bronstein, R. Coleman, G. Gladding, M. Goodman, M. Gormley, R. Messner, T. O'Halloran, J. Sarracino, A. Wattenberg, M. Binkley, I. Gaines and J. Peoples, Phys. Rev. Letters 37, 882 (1976).

40. G. Goldhaber, F. M. Pierre, G. S. Abrams, M. S. Alam, A. M. Boyarski, M. Breidenbach, W. C. Carithers, W. Chinowsky, S. C. Cooper, R. G. DeVoe, J. M. Dorfan, G. J. Feldman, C. E. Friedberg, D. Fryberger, G. Hanson, J. Jaros, A. D. Johnson, J. A. Kadyk, R. R. Larsen, D. Lüke, V. Lüth, H. L. Lynch, R. J. Madaras, C. C. Morehouse, H. K. Nguyen, J. M. Paterson, M. L. Perl, I. Peruzzi, M. Piccolo, T. P. Pun, P. Rapidis, B. Richter, B. Sadoulet, R. H. Schindler, R. F. Schwitters, J. Siegrist, W. Tanenbaum, G. H. Trilling, F. Vannucci, J. S. Whitaker and J. E. Wiss, Phys. Rev. Letters 37, 255 (1976). I. Peruzzi, M. Piccolo, G. J. Feldman, H. K. Nguyen, J. E. Wiss, G. S. Abrams, M. S. Alam, A. M. Boyarski, M. Breidenbach, W. C. Carithers, W. Chinowsky, R. G. DeVoe, J. M. Dorfan, G. E. Fischer, C. E. Friedberg, D. Fryberger, G. Goldhaber, G. Hanson, J. A. Jaros, A. D. Johnson, J. A. Kadyk, R. R. Larsen, D. Lüke, V. Lüth, H. L. Lynch, R. J. Madaras, C. C. Morehouse, J. M. Paterson, M. L. Perl, F. M. Pierre, T. P. Pun, P. Rapidis, B. Richter, R. H. Schindler, R. F. Schwitters, J. Siegrist, W. Tanenbaum, G. H. Trilling, F. Vannucci and J. S. Whitaker, Phys. Rev. Letters 37, 569 (1976).

William N. Lipscomb

WILLIAM N. LIPSCOMB

Although born in Cleveland, Ohio, USA, on December 9, 1919, I moved to Kentucky in 1920, and lived in Lexington through my university years. After my bachelors degree at the University of Kentucky, I entered graduate school at the California Institute of Technology in 1941, at first in physics. Under the influence of Linus Pauling, I returned to chemistry in early 1942. From then until the end of 1945 I was involved in research and development related to the war. After completion of the Ph.D., I joined the faculty of the University of Minnesota in 1946, and moved to Harvard University in 1959. Harvard's recognitions include the Abbott and James Lawrence Professorship in 1971, and the George Ledlie Prize in 1971.

The early research in borane chemistry is best summarized in my book "Boron Hydrides" (W. A. Benjamin, Inc., 1963), although most of this and later work is in several scientific journals. Since about 1960, my research interests have also been concerned with the relationship between three-dimensional structures of enzymes and how they catalyze reactions or how they are regulated by allosteric transformations.

Besides memberships in various scientific societies, I have received the Bausch and Lomb honorary science award in 1937; and, from the American Chemical Society, the Award for Distinguished Service in the Advancement of Inorganic Chemistry, and the Peter Debye Award in Physical Chemistry. Local sections of this Society have given the Harrison Howe Award and Remsen Award. The University of Kentucky presented to me the Sullivan Medallion in 1941, the Distinguished Alumni Centennial Award in 1965, and an honorary Doctor of Science degree in 1963. A Doctor Honoris Causa was awarded by the University of Munich in 1976. I am a member of the National Academy of Sciences U.S.A. and of the American Academy of Arts and Sciences, and a foreign member of the Royal Netherlands Academy of Sciences and Letters.

My other activities include tennis and classical chamber music as a performing clarinetist.

THE BORANES AND THEIR RELATIVES

Nobel Lecture, December 11, 1976
by
WILLIAM N. LIPSCOMB
Harvard University, Cambridge, Massachusetts, USA

This year, 1976, the Nobel Prize in Chemistry has been awarded for research in pure inorganic chemistry, in particular the boranes. May I say that I am most pleased and profoundly grateful. My own orientation to this field has been, as it has in all of my studies, the relationships of the chemical behavior of molecules to their three-dimensional geometrical and electronic structures. The early work on the molecular structures of boranes by X-ray diffraction led to a reasonable basis for a theory of chemical bonding different from that which is typical in carbon chemistry, and yielded an understanding of the pleasing polyhedral-like nature of these compounds. Assimilated by the preparative chemists, the principles helped to establish a large body of a hitherto unknown chemistry, which made a reality of the expectation that boron, next to carbon in the periodic table, should indeed have a complex chemistry.

In these nearly thirty years both the theoretical and experimental methods have been applied by us and others to areas of inorganic, physical, organic and biochemistry. For examples, these areas include low temperature X-ray diffraction techniques, and the theoretical studies of multicentered chemical bonds including both delocalized and localized molecular orbitals. An early example is extended Hückel theory, originally developed for studies of the boranes, and even now one of the most widely applicable approximate methods for theoretical studies of bonding in complex molecules. More soundly based theories are presently in use by my research students for studying how enzymes catalyze reactions, details of which are based on the three-dimensional structures by X-ray diffraction methods. Besides illuminating particular problems, these developments may contribute toward the redefinition of areas of chemistry, and thereby broaden the chemist's view. Our research in the boranes and their related molecular species crosses areas of inorganic, experimental physical, theoretical and organic chemistry, and includes applications in biochemistry. More simply stated, the area is the study of the relationships of molecular structure to function.

BORANES, AND EARLY STRUCTURE STUDIES

By now, large numbers of chemical compounds related to polyborane chemistry exist: boron hydrides, carboranes, metalloboranes, metallocarboranes, mixed compounds with organic moieties, and others. These discoveries of preparative chemists are relatively recent. Long ago, Alfred Stock established borane chemistry. He developed the experimental techniques which were required

110

for the preparation of the volatile and potentially explosive compounds, B_2H_6, B_4H_{10}, B_5H_9, B_5H_{11} and B_6H_{10}, and the relatively stable white crystalline $B_{10}H_{14}$. This work, beautifully summarized in his Baker Lectures,[1] was celebrated at the Third International Meeting on Boron Chemistry this past July in Munich, 100 years after his birth. Sidgwick[2] wrote, "All statements about the hydrides of boron earlier than 1912, when Stock began to work on them, are untrue."

Aside from the classification as either an N+4 or an N+6 series, no simple basis for these unusual formulas was foreseen before their structures were established. A B_6 octahedron (Fig. 1) was known in certain crystalline borides, and the B_{12} iscosahedron (Fig. 2) was found in boron carbide, but no one realized that a systematic description of the boron arrangements in these hydrides might be based on fragments of these polyhedra. Most electron diffraction work before 1940 supported more open structures, which Pauling[3] described in terms of resonating one-electron bonds. In 1940—1941 Stitt[4] produced infrared and thermodynamic evidence for the bridge structure of B_2H_6 (Fig. 3). More general realization of the correctness of this structure followed the theoretical studies,[5-8] and especially the infrared work of Price.[9] The three-center bridge BHB bond was clearly formulated by Longuet-Higgins.[8]

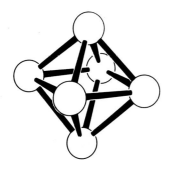

Fig. 1. The B_6 octahedron, which occurs in certain metal borides, in which each boron atom is bonded externally to a boron atom of another octahedron. In $B_6H_6^{-2}$ or $C_2B_4H_6$, a terminal hydrogen atom is bonded externally to each B or C atom.

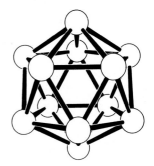

Fig. 2. The B_{12} icosahedron, which occurs in boron carbide $B_{12}C_3$, in elementary boron, and in $B_{12}H_{12}^{-2}$. The three isomers of $C_2B_{10}H_{12}$ also have this icosahedral arrangement in which there is one externally bonded hydrogen on each B or C atom.

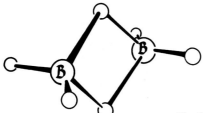

Fig. 3. The geometrical structure of B_2H_6.

The first of the higher hydrides to be structurally characterized was $B_{10}H_{14}$ (Fig. 4). Kasper, Lucht and Harker[10] showed that the boron arrangement was a fragment of a B_{12} icosahedron in which there are four bridge BHB bonds in the open face. Next was B_5H_9,[11, 12] (Fig. 5), a fragment of the B_6 octahedron, and then B_4H_{10}[13, 14] (Fig. 6), a B_4 unit from these polyhedra. Both of these structures were established by X-ray diffraction in our laboratory, and by electron diffraction at the California Institute of Technology. Our X-ray diffraction results on B_5H_{11}[15] (Fig. 7) and tetrahedral B_4Cl_4[16] then set the stage for the beginning of the theory of bonding. The B_6H_{10} structure,[17, 18] (Fig. 8) completing the compounds found by Stock, was to be one of our later X-ray diffraction studies, which were to include many other boranes and related molecules.

It was actually in 1946 that I decided to enter this area of inorganic chemistry. At that time, no reliable methods were generally available for accumulation of large amounts of X-ray diffraction data at low temperatures. Our methods[19] paralleled those in Fankuchen's laboratory[20] at the then Polytechnic Institute of Brooklyn, but were quite independent. Because of the special difficulties of working with the volatile boranes, I chose among other topics, a series of X-ray diffraction studies of single crystals grown at low temperatures from low melting liquids for which putative residual entropy problems

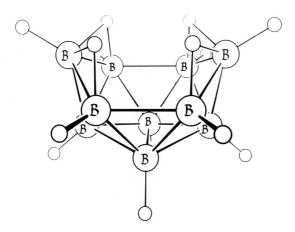

Fig. 4. $B_{10}H_{14}$.

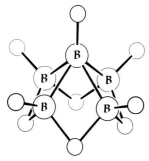

Fig. 5. B_5H_9.

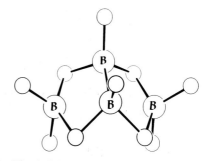

Fig. 6. B_4H_{10}.

112

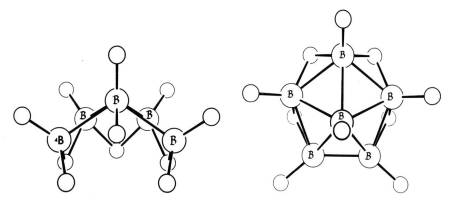

Fig. 7. B_5H_{11}.

Fig. 8. B_6H_{10}.

existed: N_2O_2, CH_3NH_2, CH_3OH, N_2H_4, $COCl_2$ and H_2O_2. The subsequent low temperature studies of single crystals of these volatile and unstable boranes were not without hazards. Vacuum line techniques were learned as we needed them. Fortunately, no serious injuries were incurred as a result of several explosions resulting from cracks in these vacuum systems. I was relieved, on one occasion, when I had taken Russell Grimes to a hospital in Cambridge after one of these explosions to hear the doctor tell me, "Louis Fieser sends me much more interesting cases than you do." I still have in my office the air gun which I, or my young son, used on a number of occasions to destroy a cracked vacuum system from a safe distance. We also had chemical surprises, for example, when we found a presumed B_8 hydride to be B_9H_{15}.[21] Our only chemical analysis of this compound was the count of the numbers of boron and hydrogen atoms in the electron density map, which was calculated in those days from rough visual estimates of intensities of diffraction maxima on films.

THREE-CENTER BONDS AMONG BORON ATOMS

At the fortunate time in 1953 of W. H. Eberhardt's sabbatical, he, Crawford and I examined[22] the open boron hydrides B_2H_6, B_4H_{10}, B_5H_9, B_5H_{11} and $B_{10}H_{14}$ from the viewpoint of three-center bonds; and we studied B_5H_9, the unknown polyhedral molecule B_4H_4, the then hypothetical ions $B_6H_6^{-2}$ (Fig. 1) and $B_{12}H_{12}^{-2}$ (Fig. 2) from the viewpoint of molecular orbitals. Longuet-Higgins[23] also, independently, formed an early molecular orbital description almost like ours. One of the simple consequences of these studies was that electron deficient molecules, defined as having more valence orbitals than electrons, are not really electron deficient. I mean by this non-sequitur that the three-center two-electron bonds make possible a simple description of these molecules and ions as filled orbital species. Filled molecular orbitals were later extended to closed polyhedral compounds B_nH_n for all values of n from 5 to 24, all of which have a formal charge of -2, even though hypothetical B_4H_4 is neutral. In fact, all of the experimentally known ions, for $6 \leqslant n \leqslant 12$, do have -2 charge.

113

In addition to $B_6H_6^{-2}$ (Fig. 1) and $B_{12}H_{12}^{-2}$ (Fig. 2), those polyhedra for $5 \leqslant n \leqslant 10$ are shown in Fig. 9. The isoelectronic series $C_2B_{n-2}H_n$ is known for $5 \leqslant n \leqslant 12$.

Equations for the atom, orbital and electron balance were formulated in our paper of 1954, allowing prediction of many new chemical species. One simple form of these rules is exemplified for a neutral hydride formula B_pH_{p+q} in which each boron atom has at least one terminal hydrogen atom. Define the number of BHB bridges as s, the number of three-center BBB bonds as t, the number of two-center BB bonds as y and the number of extra terminal hydrogens on each BH unit as x. Then

$$s+x = q$$

$$s+t = p$$

$$p = t+y+q/2$$

The first equation is the hydrogen balance. The second comes from the fact that each of the p boron atoms supplies four orbitals and only three electrons, and the extra orbital is utilized in one of the two types of three-center bond. Finally, if each BH unit is recognized as contributing a pair of electrons, these p pairs are used in BBB or BB bonds, or in half of the pairs required for the extra hydrogens, s and x. These rules, and the accompanying valence structures, are especially helpful in describing those polyboron compounds which are open, but they are also useful for closed polyhedral molecules and ions.

Fig. 9. Structures for the boron and carbon arrangements in some of the polyhedral molecules $C_2B_{n-2}H_n$, which are known for $5 \leqslant n \leqslant 12$. The isoelectronic anions are known for $6 \leqslant n \leqslant 12$.

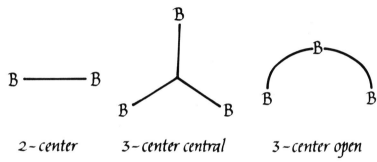

2-center   3-center central   3-center open

Fig. 10. The three types of bonds within the boron framework of a borane structure, or an equivalent carborane structure, are a BB bond, and the two types of three-center bonds. As shown below, the open three-center bond is known only for BCB bonds, not BBB bonds.

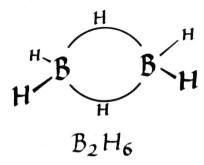

B_2H_6

Fig. 11. Bonds in B_2H_6, according to three-center bond theory.

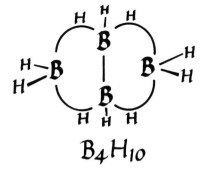

B_4H_{10}

Fig. 12. Bonds in B_4H_{10}.

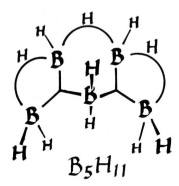

B_5H_{11}

Fig. 13. Bonds in B_5H_{11}.

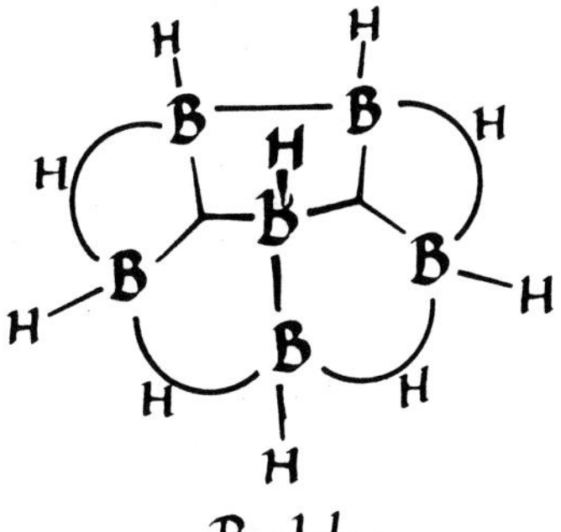

B_6H_{10}

Fig. 14. Bonds in B_6H_{10}.

    There are two kinds of three-center bonds among three boron atoms (Fig. 10). The central three-center bond involves positive overlap among hybrid orbitals from each of three boron atoms, while the open three-center bond involves, on the central atom, a π orbital which overlaps in a bonding manner with an orbital from each of the adjacent boron atoms. The less compact B_2H_6, B_4H_{10}, B_5H_{11} and B_6H_{10} structures (Figs. 11—14) are well described

115

with the use of these three-center bonds, omitting open three-center BBB bonds for the moment. However, B_5H_9 (Fig. 15) requires a resonance hybrid of four valence structures, related by the four-fold symmetry; and $B_{10}H_{14}$ (Fig. 16) requires a resonance hybrid of 24 valence structures.

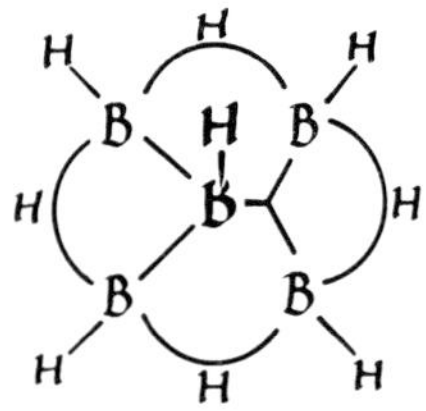

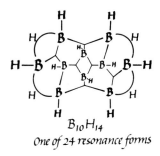

B_5H_9

One of 4 resonance forms

Fig. 15. One of four resonance structures for B_5H_9. The other three are obtained by reorientation of the framework bonds by 90° about the molecular four-fold axis.

$B_{10}H_{14}$

One of 24 resonance forms

Fig. 16. One of the 24 resonance structures for $B_{10}H_{14}$, omitting open three-center bonds.

Three-center bond theory was further developed in the following 22 years.[24] I realized that the valence rules implied the existence of a large body of boron chemistry, and then ventured predictions, some of which were actually verified experimentally. Dickerson[25] and I formalized my intuitive approach into a theory of connectivity of various bonding patterns within the three-center description. Also, geometrical constraints were introduced in order to avoid overcrowding of hydrogen atoms and to preserve known bonding angles about boron atoms among the boranes.[26] More recently, Epstein[27] and I reformulated the topology using central three-center BBB bonds, to the exclusion of open three-center BBB bonds. The recent work on localized molecular orbitals which has led to the restriction of open three-center bonds, so far, to BCB bonds is exemplified in a later part of this manuscript.

MOLECULAR ORBITAL STUDIES OF BORANES

Molecular orbitals are more appropriate for describing the valence structures of the polyhedral molecules and ions, and the more compact polyhedral fragments. Two simple examples will suffice. In B_5H_9 there are three pairs of electrons in the boron framework, which has four-fold symmetry. The bonding is beautifully described without resonance, by a simple σ and π set of molecular orbitals[22, 24, 28] (Fig. 17). These orbitals are similar to the bonding orbitals, for example, between planar four-fold cyclobutadiene (C_4H_4) and a CH^+ placed along the four-fold axis to give the carbonium ion $C_5H_5^+$.

116

A similar σ, π situation occurs[28] if a BH unit is removed from icosahedral $B_{12}H_{12}^{-2}$ leaving $B_{11}H_{11}^{-2}$ having five atomic orbitals containing four electrons (Fig. 18). This set of five orbitals gives σ, π molecular orbitals which can bond to a similar set of σ, π orbitals from another atom or group of atoms supplying two more electrons. I suggested, conceptually, adding H_3^+ to predict $B_{11}H_{14}^-$, for example. Although recognizing the similarity of this set of orbitals to those in C_5H_5, which was known to form ferrocene $Fe(C_5H_5)_2$, I did not then go quite so far as to suggest bonding of this $B_{11}H_{11}^{-2}$ fragment to a transition metal. Later, Hawthorne did so, using these ideas as a starting point, and thereby created the large family of metalloboranes and metallocarboranes[29] (Fig. 19).

In the early 1960's, when large scale computing facilities became available to us, Roald Hoffmann and Lawrence Lohr independently programmed the

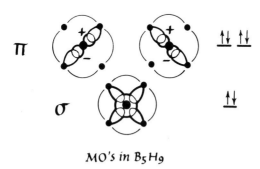

π

σ

MO's in B_5H_9

Fig. 17. Symmetry molecular orbitals in the boron framework of B_5H_9. The σ molecular orbital is a five-centered one, and each of the π components is actually an open three-center bond.

Fig. 18. Five atomic orbitals, containing four electrons remain when a neutral BH unit is removed from the apex of $B_{12}H_{12}^{-2}$, or $C_2B_{10}H_{12}$. These five atomic orbitals form a σ(bonding), π (bonding) and δ (antibonding) set of five molecular orbitals, like those in the π electron system of $C_5H_5^-$.

Five AO's to apex in $B_{12}H_{12}^{-2}$

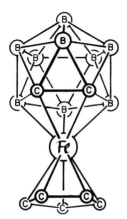

Fig. 19. The structure of $(B_9C_2H_{11})Fe(C_5H_5)$, a metallocarborane derivative.

117

extended Hückel method in my research group. Its first application was to boron chemistry,[30] where, particularly in the carboranes (compounds of boron, carbon and hydrogen), the charge distributions predicted sites of electrophilic and nucleophilic substitution. One of the rather simple rules which emerged was that nucleophilic attack occurs in a polyhedral carborane at a boron atom closest to carbon, while electrophilic attack was preferred at a boron furthest removed from carbon. Experimental studies of boranes and carboranes in which one or more hydrogens had been replaced by a halogen or by an amine group confirmed these predictions. The extended Hückel method became for a time the most widely used program for the study of molecular theory and reactions in complex organic and inorganic molecules. For example, the Woodward-Hoffmann rules, and related orbital concepts, were tested by their inventors[31] with the use of this theory.

I thought then that progress in structure determination, for new polyborane species and for substituted boranes and carboranes, would be greatly accelerated if the ^{11}B nuclear magnetic resonance spectra, rather than X-ray diffraction, could be used. One approach was empirical,[32] while the other was purely theoretical. This latter approach required the development of a theory for fairly reliable calculation of chemical shifts of ^{11}B from first principles of quantum mechanics.[33] This theory, the coupled Hartree-Fock method for a molecule in a magnetic or electric field, yielded molecular constants good to a few to several percent[34] for many diatomic molecules. A striking result was the prediction of the paramagnetic nature of diatomic BH.[35] However, the application of this method to the complex boranes still lies in the future, even after 13 years of effort. While we understand some of the contributions to chemical shift, diamagnetic and large temperature-independent paramagnetic effects, the use of this method for structure determination of complex polyboranes is still somewhat limited.

These programs yielded accurate self-consistent field molecular orbitals, which were explored in other areas of chemistry, as well as in the boranes and carboranes. One example is the first accurate calculation of the barrier to internal rotation in ethane.[36] At this point, my research students and I set out to explore the gap between extended Hückel theory and self-consistent field theory. We achieved by stages[37, 38] a molecular orbital theory[39] still being extended, which was applicable to large polyboranes and other molecules, and which had essentially the accuracy of self-consistent field methods. Molecular orbital methods which do not go beyond symmetry orbitals tend to make each molecule a separate case. Hence we began only a few years ago to explore the connections between these symmetry orbitals and the three-center bonds of the previous section.

LOCALIZED MOLECULAR ORBITALS

Ordinarily, molecular orbitals are classified according to their symmetry types. However, it is possible to make linear combinations of molecular orbitals of different symmetries in such a way that the total electron density of the molecule remains invariant. The most popular methods are those of Edmiston and Ruedenberg[40] who maximize

$$\sum_i \iint \Phi_i(1)\, \Phi;(1) \frac{1}{r_{12}}\, \Phi_i(2)\, \Phi_i(2)\, dV_1 dV_2$$

and of Boys[41] who minimizes

$$\sum_i \iint \Phi_i(1)\, \Phi_i(1)\, r^2_{12}\, \Phi_i(2)\, \Phi_i(2)\, dV_1 dV_2$$

These procedures, respectively, maximize the repulsions of those electron pairs within each molecular orbital, and minimize the orbital self-extension of each electron pair. Thus, in slightly different manner, the symmetry orbitals are converted into linear combinations which are a good approximation to the localized electron-pair bond. These objective procedures, without adjustable parameters, have been compared in some detail.[42] They provide support of three-center bond descriptions within a theoretical chemical framework. Also, they test the level at which two-center and three-center bonds require some further delocalization. These studies have also provided preferred descriptions of valence structures, often eliminating or reducing the need for resonance hybrids.

Open three-center and central three-center BBB bonds are almost equivalent descriptions. Including both types there are 111 resonance structures for $B_{10}H_{14}$, of which 24 are based only on central three-center bonds. In B_5H_{11} (Fig. 20) two slightly unsymmetrical central three-center BBB bonds are

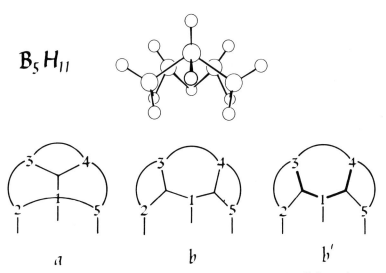

Fig. 20. Three valence structures for B_5H_{11} include (a) the disfavored open three-center bond, (b) the symmetrical central three-center bonds, and (b') the localized slightly unsymmetrical three-center bonds. For clarity, one terminal B-H bond has been omitted at each boron site in (a), (b) and (b').

found[43] by both localization procedures (Fig. 20b′), whereas the open three-center description is not favored. In a series of studies of localized molecular orbitals in all of the boron hydrides, carboranes, and ions of known geometry, we have never found an open three-center BBB bond. However, open three-center BCB bonds do exist. For example, the open three-center BCB bond[44] occurs twice in 1,2—$C_2B_4H_6$ (Fig. 21), when the Edmiston-Ruedenberg procedure is used. A comparison of these results with those of the Boys procedure is given below. In the simplest molecular orbital description of an open three-center bond, the electron pair is distributed as e/2, e, e/2 among these three atoms. It is probable that the extra nuclear charge of carbon stabilizes this distribution, to give open three-center bonds rather than nearly equivalent central three-center bonds, when carbon is the middle atom.

Another new general result is that almost every single bond within a triangulated borane or carborane framework shows some donation to the nearest adjacent atoms (Fig. 22). This tendency for multi-centered bonding usually involves 10 per cent or less of the electron pair. In B_4H_{10}, about 0.2 e is donated[43] from the single BB bond to each of atoms B_1 and B_4, which themselves are relatively electron deficient because of the open three-center bonds of the hydrogen bridges (Fig. 23). This donation then causes these

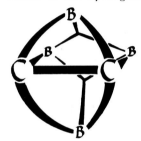

Fig. 21. Localized molecular orbitals are shown in the framework of 1,2-$C_2B_4H_6$. The open three-center bonds go through carbon. An external hydrogen has been omitted at each B or C atom.

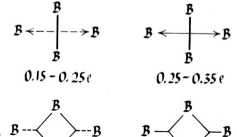

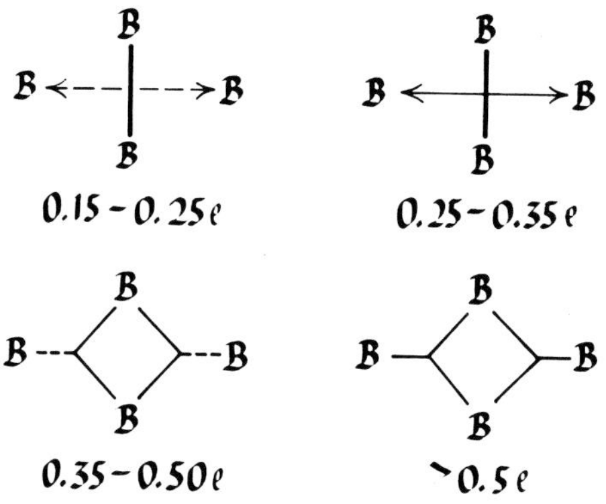

Fig. 22. Notation is shown for amounts of single bond donation to adjacent boron atoms. Unsymmetrical donation may also occur.

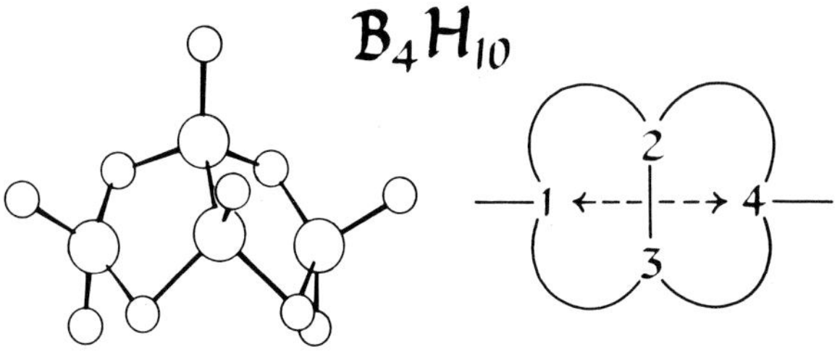

Fig. 23. Single bond donation in B_4H_{10} is about 0.19e from the B_2B_3 bond to each of the outer doubly bridged BH_2 groups of the molecule.

120

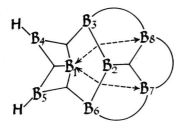

$$B_8 \ H_{13}^{-}$$

Fig. 24. Single bond donation is shown in $B_8H_{13}^{-}$.

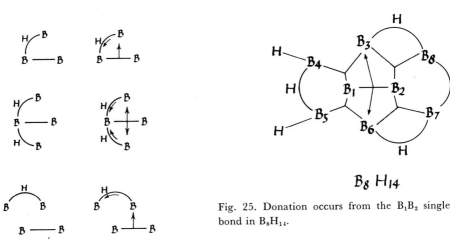

$$B_8 \ H_{14}$$

Fig. 25. Donation occurs from the B_1B_2 single bond in B_8H_{11}.

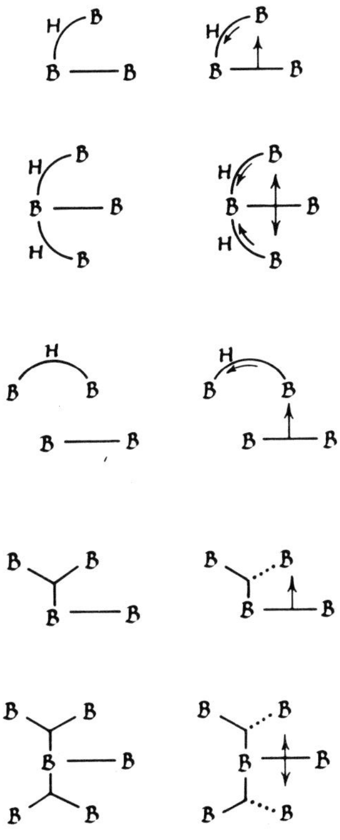

Fig. 26. Some common patterns of single bond donation cause hydrogen atom displacement and electron withdrawal from the atom to which donation occurs.

hydrogen bridges to become unsymmetrical, displaced toward B_2 and B_3, in accord with the results obtained from our X-ray diffraction study. More generally, this donation causes electron withdrawal along other bonds in the molecule, whether or not hydrogen bridges are available for accommodating this electron displacement. Two additional examples are illustrated in $B_8H_{13}^{-}$ and in the predicted structure of B_8H_{14}, respectively[15] (Fig. 24 and 25). I have abstracted from these examples some typical modes of single bond donation, and accompanying electron withdrawal or hydrogen displacement, in Fig. 26. These and similar valence diagrams may be useful in understanding intramolecular distortions and reaction mechanisms.

121

A new type of bonding, which is conceptually transferable among these molecules, is described as fractional three-center bonds.[46] Its simplest interpretation is the replacement of a pair of resonance structures by a single valence structure (Fig. 27). The fractional use of orbitals, indicated by dotted lines, increases the apparent number of bonds to a given boron above the usual four, in an element in the first row of the periodic table. However, the Pauli exclusion principle is not violated because less than a full atomic orbital is required at a fractional bond. Indeed, the localized molecular orbitals are themselves derived from wavefunctions for which the exclusion principle is rigorously introduced. The use of fractional bonds to reduce the number of resonance hybrids, often to a single preferred structure, is not limited to boranes and their relatives. Our rather extensive studies of bonding among atoms other than boron have indicated that these simplified localized molecular orbitals may be an informative and useful alternative to the more conventional valence bond and molecular orbital descriptions in other parts of the periodic table. A very simple example, carboxylate anion,[47] is shown in Fig. 28.

Fractional bonds to atom B_2 in $4,5—C_2B_4H_8$ are preferred[48] over a resonance hybrid of a single and a central three-center bond, and also are preferred over the open three-center bond (Fig. 29). Also, the bonding of the two carbon atoms in this carborane by both a single bond and a central three-center bond has not been found in boranes, and, in particular, does not occur in B_6H_{10} which

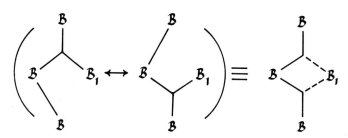

Fig. 27. Equivalence is shown of the two fractional three-center bonds to a resonance hybrid of a single bond and a three-center bond.

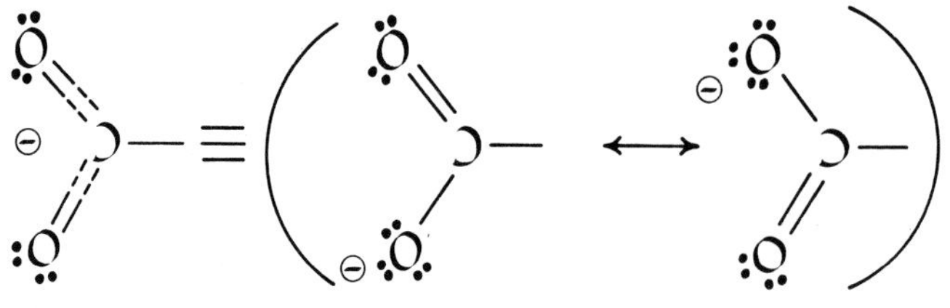

Fig. 28. The four localized molecular orbitals in carboxylate anion have a charge distribution which shows displacement toward oxygen. On the left, the equivalent resonance hybrid is given.

122

$4,5-C_2B_4H_8$

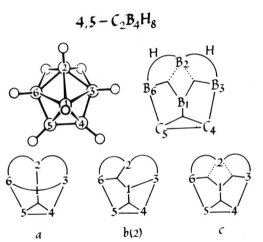

Fig. 29. Localized orbitals in $4,5-C_2B_4H_8$ show fractional donation to atom B_2 as dotted lines.

$B_{10}H_{14}$

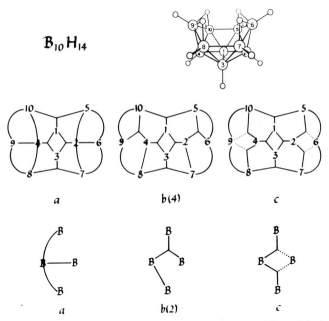

Fig. 30. The pattern of fractional bonds, dotted toward B_6 and B_9, in $B_{10}H_{11}$ can be expected when there is resonance of the type shown in the central diagram, or when one is tempted to draw open three-center BBB bonds as shown on the left. The fractional bond description is preferred.

is isoelectronic with $4,5-C_2B_4H_8$. Fractional bonds give a particularly simple valence description[15] of bonding in $B_{10}H_{14}$ (Fig. 30), where the single valence structure (Fig. 30c) replaces a resonance hybrid of 24 central three-center bond structures. A very similar simplification[15] occurs in $B_{10}H_{14}^{-2}$, where the two pairs of fractional bonds are dotted toward atoms B_2 and B_4, rather than toward B_6 and B_9.

Similar pairs of fractional bonds are found by Boys' localization procedure in the polyhedral carboranes $1,2-C_2B_4H_6$ (Fig. 31) and $1,7-C_2B_{10}H_{12}$ (Fig. 32). Perhaps this procedure tends to exaggerate the separation of charge centroids of bonds when they lie at or near a single center. For this reason, we tend to prefer[42] the almost equivalent open three-center bonds, as found by the Edmiston-Ruedenberg procedure in $1,2-C_2B_4H_6$. When it becomes economically feasible to test this alternative in $1,7-C_2B_{10}H_{12}$, I would guess that localized open three-center bonds will be found, centered at carbon atoms, in this molecule, like those in $1,2-C_2B_4H_6$.

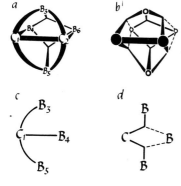

Fig. 31. In $1,2-C_2B_4H_6$ the Edmiston-Ruedenberg localization yields open three-center bonds at carbon, while the Boys localization gives fractional three-center bonds. The latter procedure gives greater emphasis to separation of orbital centroids when they are on the same atom.

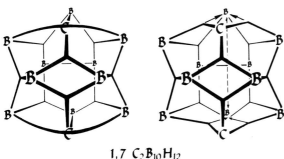

$1,7 \ C_2B_{10}H_{12}$

Fig. 32. A situation parallel to that of Fig. 31 may occur in $1,7-C_2B_{10}H_{12}$, where the Boys localization (right side) shows fractional bonds. The open three-center bond description may be found by the Edmiston-Ruedenberg procedure, if and when the calculations can be made.

Fractional three-center bonds are not always unique, particularly in aromatic hydrocarbons, or in those boranes which have a valence pattern similar to that in the aromatics. An example of this orientational ambiguity occurs in the boron framework bonds in B_5H_9 (Fig. 33). Actually, the two valence structures represent extremes over a 45° range of orientation angle, about the four-fold axis. There is a continuum of valence structures between these extremes. Moreover, this ambiguity continues throughout the whole 360°, in accord with the four-fold symmetry which the electron density must have in this molecule. All of these valence structures are equally preferred, and each has a total electron density which is consistent with the four-fold molecular symmetry.

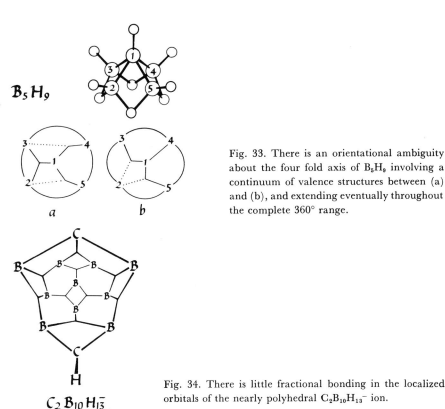

$B_5 H_9$

a   *b*

Fig. 33. There is an orientational ambiguity about the four fold axis of B_5H_9 involving a continuum of valence structures between (a) and (b), and extending eventually throughout the complete 360° range.

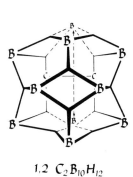

$C_2 B_{10} H_{\overline{13}}$

Fig. 34. There is little fractional bonding in the localized orbitals of the nearly polyhedral $C_2B_{10}H_{13}^-$ ion.

$1,2\ C_2 B_{10} H_{12}$

Fig. 35. The localized orbitals obtained for $1,2\text{-}C_2B_{10}H_{12}$ by Boys' procedure are the same as those found in $1,7\text{-}C_2B_{10}H_{12}$ in spite of the difference in positions of carbon atoms relative to boron atoms.

In more complex molecules one can find various degrees of simplicity in the bonding patterns of localized molecular orbitals. In $C_2B_{10}H_{13}^-$, which has a somewhat open near-icosahedral C_2B_{10} arrangement, the bonding is especially simple,[49] not requiring resonance or appreciable fractional bonding (Fig. 34). In $1,2\text{—}C_2B_{10}H_{12}$, another simple idea occurs: the bonding, as found by Boys' procedure, is to a good approximation just like that in $1,7\text{—}C_2B_{10}H_{12}$ in spite of the very different positions of the two carbon atoms relative to each other and to their boron neighbors (Fig. 35). Thus there is some tendency for bonding invariance in closely related geometrical structures. In iso-$B_{18}H_{22}$,

125

we find[50] both single bond donation, from B_4B_8 and $B_{14}H_{18}$, and fractional bonds, to B_6 and B_{16} (Fig. 36). Here, the single bond donations are greater toward B_9, which is relatively electron deficient, than toward B_3 and B_{13}. In $B_{20}H_{16}$ there is a remarkable amount of single-bond donation, particularly toward the electron deficient B_9—B_{16} atoms, inclusive (Fig. 37), and the valence structure of each half is clearly like that in $B_{10}H_{14}^{-2}$ (Fig. 38) rather than like that in $B_{10}H_{14}$ (Fig. 30).

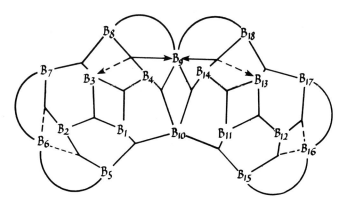

Fig. 36. Single bond donation and fractional bonds occur in iso-$B_{18}H_{22}$, a molecule having a two-fold axis only, and no terminal hydrogen atoms on atoms B_9 and B_{10}.

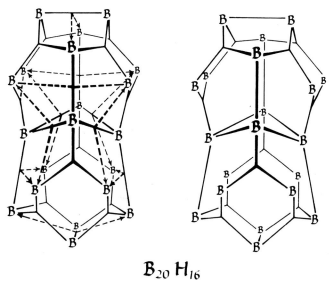

$B_{20}H_{16}$

Fig. 37. Donation and non-donation localized orbitals are shown for $B_{20}H_{16}$, in which the four borons nearest the equatorial belt have no terminal hydrogens. Boron atoms B_9B_{16}, inclusive, are particulary electron deficient, and receive substantial donation from single bonds. Each of these eight boron atoms has only two framework bonds in the figure at the right.

126

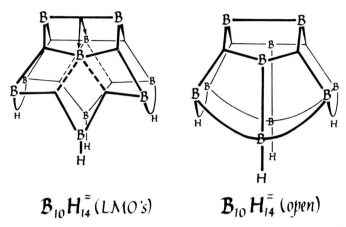

$$B_{10}H_{14}^= (LMO's) \qquad B_{10}H_{14}^= (open)$$

Fig. 38. A relationship similar to that in $B_{20}H_{16}$ occurs in $B_{10}H_{14}^{-2}$. The preferred localized orbital structure is shown on the left side, while the open three-center bond structure without donation is an oversimplified valence structure.

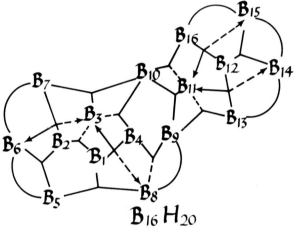

$$B_{16}H_{20}$$

Fig. 39. A rather complex pattern of localized orbitals is shown for $B_{16}H_{20}$. Bond donations can be withdrawn by the reader in order to discover the preferred valence bond structures of the simpler theory. This single valence structure replaces a resonance hybrid of 216 valence structures based upon central three-center bonds and single bonds. Atoms B_9 and B_{10} do not have terminal hydrogens.

The rather complex localized molecular orbitals in $B_{16}H_{20}$ (Fig. 39) are dominated by the three-center bond approximation; in addition they are modified by single bond donation accompanied by electron withdrawal from atoms to which donation occurs.[50] With recognition that atoms B_9 and B_{10} have no terminal hydrogens attached to them, I offer the reader a challenge to find the close relative valence structures which do not have fractional bonding or single bond donation in this molecule.

Finally, the bonding in reaction intermediates is a new area of study, primarily by purely theoretical methods. In BH_5 (Fig. 40) there is only a very weak donor bond from H_2 to the vacant orbital of BH_3.[51-55] This weakness is probably due to the absence of a pathway for back donation. On the other hand, in the dimerization of two BH_3 molecules to form B_2H_6, donation of electron density from one terminal H to B of the other BH_3 group is balanced by a symmetrically related donation toward the first BH_3 group[56] (Fig. 41). Our other recent progress in theoretical studies of bonding in reaction intermediates, such as B_3H_7 and B_4H_8, shows that the more stable transient species may have a vacant orbital[57] on one boron atom, because of the strain involved when that vacant orbital is filled by converting a terminal BH bond to a

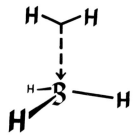

Fig. 40. Fractional donation of a single bond between two hydrogen atoms to the vacant orbital of a slightly pyramidal, nearly planar, BH_3 group. The resulting BH_5 molecule is a very short-lived reaction intermediate.

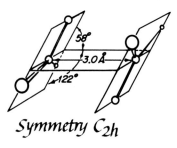

Symmetry C_{2h}

Fig. 41. Approximate geometry of the transition state when two BH_3 molecules form B_2H_6. This geometry is favored over that in an unsymmetrical approach of two BH_3 molecules.

bridge BHB bond. Actually less is known of the detailed reaction mechanisms for reactions of boranes and their related compounds than is known for organic reactions of comparable complexity. Surely, this is a fruitful area for future research.

I shall stop here, omitting descriptions of bonding in large polyhedral borane anions and other related compounds. Also, polyhedral rearrangements, hydrogen atom tautomerism, and particularly the use of bonding theory in bringing some degree of order to chemical transformations of the boranes have been omitted. Attention has thus been concentrated on those aspects of chemical bonding which have been especially illuminated by the molecular and crystal structures that we and others have studied over these many years.

My original intention in the late 1940's was to spend a few years understanding the boranes, and then to discover a systematic valence description of the vast numbers of "electron deficient" intermetallic compounds. I have made little progress toward this latter objective. Instead, the field of boron chemistry has grown enormously, and a systematic understanding of some of its complexities has now begun.

It remains to give credits where they really belong, to my research associates: graduate students, undergraduates, postdoctoral fellows and my other colleagues who have coauthored nearly all of these studies. For the figures of this manuscript, and of the lecture, I thank Jean Evans. I am most grateful to the Office of Naval Research who supported this research during the period from 1948 to 1976, a remarkably long time. I am most aware of the great influence of Linus Pauling on my whole scientific career. Finally, this manucript is dedicated to the memory of my sister, Helen Porter Lipscomb, composer, teacher and performer.

REFERENCES

1. Stock, A. 1933. *Hydrides of Boron and Silicon*. The George Fisher Baker Non-Resident Lectureship in Chemistry at Cornell University. Cornell University Press, Ithaca, New York.
2. Sidgwick, N. V. 1950. *The Chemical Elements and their Compounds*. The Clarendon Press, Oxford, p. 338.
3. Pauling, L. 1940. *The Nature of the Chemical Bond*. The George Fisher Baker Non-Resident Lectureship in Chemistry at Cornell University. Cornell University Press, Ithaca, New York.
4. Stitt, F. 1940. "The Gaseous Heat Capacity and Restricted Internal Rotation of Diborane." J. Chem. Phys. *8*, 981—986. Stitt, F. 1941. "Infra-Red and Raman Spectra of Polyatomic Molecules. XV. Diborane." J. Chem. Phys. *9*, 780—785.
5. Longuet-Higgins, H. C. and R. P. Bell. 1943. "The Structure of the Boron Hydrides." J. Chem. Soc., 250—255.
6. Pitzer, K. S. 1945. "Electron Deficient Molecules. I. The Principles of Hydroboron Structures." J. Am. Chem. Soc. *67*, 1126—1132.
7. Mulliken, R. S. 1947. "The Structure of Diborane and Related Molecules." Chem. Rev. *41*, 207—217.
8. Longuet-Higgins. 1949. "Substances Hydrogenées avec Défaut d'Electrons." J. Chim Phys. *46*, 268—275.
9. Price, W. C. 1947. "The Structure of Diborane." J. Chem. Phys. *15*, 614. Price, W. 1948. "The Absorption Spectrum of Diborane." J. Chem. Phys. *16*, 894—902.
10. Kasper, J. S., C. M. Lucht and D. Harker. 1950. "The Crystal Structure of Decaborane, $B_{10}H_{11}$." Acta Cryst. *3*, 436—455.
11. Dulmage, W. J. and W. N. Lipscomb. 1951. "The Molecular Structure of Pentaborane." J. Am. Chem. Soc. *73*, 3539. Dulmage, W. J. and W. N. Lipscomb. 1952. "The Crystal and Molecular Structure of Pentaborane." Acta Cryst. *5*, 260—264.
12. Hedberg, K., M. E. Jones and V. Schomaker. 1951. "On the Structure of Stable Pentaborane." J. Am. Chem. Soc. *73*, 3538—3539. Hedberg, K., M. E. Jones and V. Schomaker. 1952. "The Structure of Stable Pentaborane." Proc. Nat. Acad. Sci. *38*, 679—686.
13. Nordman, C. E. and W. N. Lipscomb. 1953. "The Molecular Structure of B_4H_{10}." J. Am. Chem. Soc. *75*, 4116—4117. Nordman, C. E. and W. N. Lipscomb. 1953. "The Crystal and Molecular Structure of Tetraborane." J. Chem. Phys. *21*, 1856—1864.
14. Jones, M. E., K. Hedberg and V. Schomaker. 1953. "On the Structure of Tetraborane." J. Am. Chem. Soc. *75*, 4116.
15. Lavine, L. and W. N. Lipscomb. 1954. "The Crystal and Molecular Structure of B_5H_{11}." J. Chem. Phys. *22*, 614—620.
16. Atoji, M. and W. N. Lipscomb. 1953. "The Molecular Structure of B_4Cl_4." J. Chem. Phys. *21*, 172.

Atoji, M. and W. N. Lipscomb. 1953. "The Crystal and Molecular Structure of B_4Cl_4." Acta Cryst. *6*, 547—550.

17. Eriks, K., W. N. Lipscomb and R. Schaeffer. 1954. "The Boron Arrangement in a B_6 Hydride." J. Chem. Phys. *22*, 754—755.

18. Hirshfeld, F. L., K. Eriks, R. E. Dickerson, E. L. Lippert, Jr. and W. N. Lipscomb. 1958. "Molecular and Crystal Structure of B_6H_{10}." J. Chem. Phys. *28*, 56—61.

19. Abrahams, S. C., R. L. Collin, W. N. Lipscomb and T. B. Reed. 1950. "Further Techniques in Single-Crystal X-ray Diffraction Studies at Low Temperatures." Rev. Sci. Instr. *21*, 396—397.

20. Kaufman, H. S. and I. Fankuchen. 1949. "A Low Temperature Single Crystal X-ray Diffraction Technique." Rev. Sci. Instr. *20*, 733—734.

21. Dickerson, R. E., P. J. Wheatley, P. A. Howell and W. N. Lipscomb. 1957. "Crystal and Molecular Structure of B_9H_{15}." J. Chem. Phys. *27*, 200—209.

22. Eberhardt, W. H., B. Crawford, Jr. and W. N. Lipscomb. 1954. "The Valence Structure of the Boron Hydrides." J. Chem. Phys. *22*, 989.

23. Longuet-Higgins, H. C. and M. de V. Roberts. 1954. "The Electronic Structure of the Borides MB_6." Proc. Roy. Soc. (London) *A224*, 336—347.
    Longuet-Higgins, H. C. and M. de V. Roberts. 1955. "The Electronic Structure of an Icosahedron of Boron Atoms." Proc. Roy. Soc. (London) *A230*, 110—119.

24. Lipscomb, W. N., *Boron Hydrides*. (W. A. Benjamin, Inc. 1963).

25. Dickerson, R. E. and W. N. Lipscomb. 1957. "Semitopological Approach to Boron-Hydride Structures." J. Chem. Phys. *27*, 212—217.

26. Lipscomb, W. N. 1964. "Geometrical Theory of Boron Hydrides." Inorg. Chem. *3*, 1683—1685.

27. Epstein, I. R. and W. N. Lipscomb. 1971. "Boron Hydride Valence Structures: A Topological Approach." Inorg. Chem. *10*, 1921—1928.

28. Moore, E. B., Jr., L. L. Lohr, Jr. and W. N. Lipscomb. 1961. "Molecular Orbitals in Some Boron Compounds." J. Chem. Phys. *35*, 1329—1334.

29. Hawthorne, M. F. 1968. "The Chemistry of the Polyhedral Species Derived from Transition Metals and Carboranes." Accounts of Chem. Res. *1*, 281—288.

30. Hoffmann, R. and W. N. Lipscomb. 1962. "Boron Hydrides: LCAO-MO and Resonance Studies." J. Chem. Phys. *37*, 2872—2883.
    Hoffmann, R, and W. N. Lipscomb. 1962. "Theory of Polyhedral Molecules. I. Physical Factorizations of the Secular Equation." J. Chem. Phys. *36*, 2179—2189.
    Hoffmann, R. and W. N. Lipscomb. 1962. "Theory of Polyhedral Molecules. III. Population Analyses and Reactivities for the Carboranes." J. Chem. Phys. *36*, 3489—3493.

31. Woodward, R. B. and R. Hoffmann. 1970. *The Conservation of Orbital Symmetry*. Verlag Chemie GmbH, Academic Press.

32. Eaton, G. R. and W. N. Lipscomb. 1969. *NMR Studies of Boron Hydrides and Related Compounds*. W. A. Benjamin, Inc.

33. Stevens, R. M., R. M. Pitzer and W. N. Lipscomb. 1963. "Perturbed Hartree-Fock Calculations. I. Magnetic Susceptibility and Shielding in the LiH Molecule." J. Chem. Phys. *38*, 550—560.

34. Lipscomb, W. N. 1972. "Molecular Properties." MTP International Review of Science, Theoretical Chemistry. Physical Chemistry Series One. Volume 1. Editors: A. D. Buckingham and W. Byers Brown. Butterworths, London, England. pp. 167—196.

35. Hegstrom, R. A. and W. N. Lipscomb. 1968. "Paramagnetism in Closed-Shell Molecules." Rev. Mod. Phys. *40*, 354—358.

36. Pitzer, R. M. and W. N. Lipscomb. 1963. "Calculation of the Barrier to Internal Rotation in Ethane." J. Chem. Phys. *39*, 1995—2004.

37. Newton, M. D., F. P. Boer and W. N. Lipscomb. 1966. "Molecular Orbital Theory for Large Molecules. Approximation of the SCF LCAO Hamiltonian Matrix." J. Am. Chem. Soc. *88*, 2353—2360.

130

38. Boer, F. P., M. D. Newton and W. N. Lipscomb. 1966. "Molecular Orbitals for Boron Hydrides Parameterized from SCF Model Calculations." J. Am. Chem. Soc. *88*, 2361—2366.

39. Halgren, T. A. and W. N. Lipscomb. 1972. "Approximations to Self-Consistent Field Molecular Wavefunctions." Proc. Nat. Acad. Sci. USA *69*, 652—656.
    Halgren, T. A. and W. N. Lipscomb. 1973. "Self-Consistent Field Wavefunctions for Complex Molecules. The Approximations of Partial Retention of Diatomic Differential Overlap. J. Chem. Phys. *58*, 1569—1591.

40. Edmiston, C. and K. Ruedenberg. 1963. "Localized Atomic and Molecular Orbitals." Rev. Mod. Phys. *35*, 457—465.

41. Boys, S. F. 1966. *Quantum Theory of Atoms, Molecules and the Solid State*. (P. O. Löwdin, Ed.). Academic Press, New York. pp. 253—262.

42. Kleier, D. A., T. A. Halgren, J. H. Hall, Jr. and W. N. Lipscomb. 1974. "Localized Molecular Orbitals for Polyatomic Molecules. I. A Comparison of the Edmiston-Ruedenberg and Boys Localization Methods." J. Chem. Phys. *61*, 3905—3919.

43. Switkes, E., W. N. Lipscomb and M. D. Newton. 1970. "Localized Bonds in Self-Consistent-Field Wave Functions for Polyatomic Molecules. II. Boron Hydrides." J. Am. Chem. Soc. *92*, 3847—3853.

44. Epstein, I. R., D. S. Marynick and W. N. Lipscomb. 1973. "Localized Orbitals for 1,2- and 1,6-Dicarbahexaborane(6). The Open Three-Center Bond, and Implications for Carborane Topology." J. Am. Chem. Soc. *95*, 1760—1766.

45. Hall, J. H., Jr., D. A. Dixon, D. A. Kleier, T. A. Halgren, L. D. Brown and W. N. Lipscomb. 1975. "Localized Molecular Orbitals for Polyatomic Molecules. II. Structural Relationships and Charge Distributions for Open Boron Hydrides and Ions." J. Am. Chem. Soc. *97*, 4202—4212.

46. Marynick, D. S. and W. N. Lipscomb. 1972. "Self-Consistent Field Wave Function and Localized Orbitals for 2,4-Dicarbaheptaborane(7). The Fractional Three-Center Bond." J. Am. Chem. Soc. *94*, 8692—8699.

47. Dixon, D. A. and W. N. Lipscomb. 1976. "Electronic Structure and Bonding of the Amino Acids Containing First Row Atoms." J. Biol. Chem. *251*, 5992—6000.

48. Marynick, D. S. and W. N. Lipscomb. 1972. "A Self-Consistent Field and Localized Orbital Study of 4,5-Dicarbahexaborane(8)." J. Am. Chem. Soc. *94*, 8699—8706.

49. Tolpin, E. I. and W. N. Lipscomb. 1973. "Crystal and Molecular Structure of Tetramethylammonium C,C'-Diphenylundecahydrodicarbanido-dodecaborate(1-)." Inorg. Chem. *12*, 2257—2262.

50. Dixon, D. A., D. A. Kleier, T. A. Halgren and W. N. Lipscomb. 1976. "Localized Molecular Orbitals for Polyatomic Molecules. IV. Large Boron Hydrides." J. Am. Chem. Soc. *98*, 2086—2096.

51. Kreevoy, M. M. and J. E. C. Hutchins. 1972. "H_2BH_3 as an Intermediate in Tetrahydridoborate Hydrolysis." J. Am. Chem. Soc. *94*, 6371—6376.

52. Pepperberg, I. M., T. A. Halgren and W. N. Lipscomb. 1976. "A Molecular Orbital Study of the Role of BH_5 in the Hydrolysis of BH_4^-." J. Am. Chem. Soc. *98*, 3442—3451.

53. Hoheisel, C. and W. Kutzelnigg. 1975. "Ab Initio Calculation Including Electron Correlation of the Structure and Binding Energy of BH_5 and $B_2H_7^-$." J. Am. Chem. Soc. *97*, 6970—6975.

54. Collins, J. B., P. v. R. Schleyer, J. S. Binkley, J. A. Pople and L. Radom. 1976. J. Am. Chem. Soc., *98*, 3436—3441 (1976).

55. Hariharan, P. C., W. A. Latham and J. A. Pople. 1972. "Molecular Orbital Theory of Simple Carbonium Ions." Chem. Phys. Lett. *14*, 385—388.

56. Dixon, D. A., I. M. Pepperberg and W. N. Lipscomb. 1974. "Localized Molecular Orbitals and Chemical Reactions. II. A Study of Three-Center Bond Formation in the Borane-Diborane Reaction." J. Am. Chem. Soc. *96*, 1325—1333.

57. Dupont, J. A. and R. Schaeffer. 1960. "Interconversion of Boranes. I. A. Kinetic Study of the Conversion of Tetraborane-10 to Pentaborane-11." J. Inorg. Nucl. Chem. *15*, 310—315.

Baruch S. Blumberg

BARUCH S. BLUMBERG

I was born in 1925, in New York City, the second of three children of Meyer and Ida Blumberg. My grandparents came to the United States from Europe at the end of the 19th century. They were members of an immigrant group who had enormous confidence in the possibilities of their adopted country. I received my elementary education at the Yeshiva of Flatbush, a Hebrew parochial school, and, at an early age, in addition to a rigorous secular education, learned the Hebrew Testament in the original language. We spent many hours on the rabbinic commentaries on the Bible and were immersed in the existential reasoning of the Talmud at an age when we could hardly have realized its impact.

After attending Far Rockaway High School I joined the U.S. Navy in 1943 and finished college under military auspices. I was commissioned as a Deck Officer, served on landing ships, and was the commanding officer of one of these when I left active duty in 1946. My interest in the sea remained. In later years I made several trips as a merchant seaman, held a ticket as a Ships Surgeon, and, while in medical school, occasionally served as a semi-professional hand on sailing ships. Sea experience placed a great emphasis on detailed problem solving, on extensive planning before action, and on the arrangement of alternate methods to effect an end. These techniques have application in certain kinds of research, particularly in the execution of field studies.

My undergraduate degree in Physics was taken at Union College in upstate New York and in 1946 I began graduate work in mathematics at Columbia University. My father, who was a lawyer, suggested that I go to medical school, and I entered The College of Physicians and Surgeons of Columbia University in 1947. I enjoyed my four years at the College immensely. Robert Loeb was the chairman of the Department of Medicine and exerted a marked influence on the entire college. There was a strong emphasis on basic science and research in the first two years (we hardly saw a patient till our third year), and we learned practical applications only in our last years.

Between my third and fourth years, Harold Brown, our professor of parasitology, arranged for me to spend several months at Moengo, an isolated mining town, accessible only by river, in the swamp and high bush country of northern Surinam. While there we delivered babies, performed clinical services, and undertook several public health surveys, including the first malaria survey done in that region. Different people had been imported into the country to serve as laborers in the sugar plantations, and they, along with the indigenous American Indians, provided a richly heterogeneous population.

Hindus from India, Javanese, Africans (including the Djukas, descendents of rebelled slaves who resided in autonomous kingdoms in the interior), Chinese, and a smattering of Jews descended from 17th century migrants to the country from Brazil, lived side by side. Their responses to the many infectious agents in the environment were very different. We were particularly impressed with the enormous variation in the response to infection with *Wuchereria bancroftia* (the filariad which causes elephantiasis), and my first published research paper was on this topic. This experience was recalled in later years when I became interested in the study of inherited variation in susceptibility to disease. Nature operates in a bold and dramatic manner in the tropics. Biological effects are profound and tragic. The manifestations of important variables may often be readily seen and measured, and the rewards to health in terms of prevention or treatment of disease can be great. As a consequence, much of our field work has been done in tropical countries.

I was an intern and assistant resident on the First (Columbia) Division at Bellevue Hospital in lower New York from 1951 to 1953. It is difficult to explain the fascination of Bellevue. In the days before widespread health insurance, many of the city's poor were hospitalized at Bellevue, including many formerly middle class people impoverished by the expenses of chronic illness. The wards were crowded, often with beds in the halls. Scenes on the wards were sometimes reminiscent of Hogarth's woodcuts of the public institutions of 18th century London. Despite this, morale was high. We took great pride that the hospital was never closed; any sick person whose illness warranted hospitalization was admitted, even though all the regular bed spaces were filled. A high scientific and academic standard was maintained. Our director, Dickinson W. Richards, and his colleague, Andre F. Cournand, received the Nobel Prize for their work on cardio-pulmonary physiology. Anyone who has been immersed in the world of a busy city hospital, a world of wretched lives, of hope destroyed by devastating illness, cannot easily forget that an objective of bio-medical research is, in the end, the prevention and cure of disease.

I spent the following two years as a Clinical Fellow in Medicine at Columbia Presbyterian Medical Center working in the Arthritis Division under Dr. Charles A. Ragan. I also did experimental work on the physical biochemistry of hyaluronic acid with Dr. Karl Meyer. From 1955 to 1957, I was a graduate student at the Department of Biochemistry at Oxford University, England, and a member of Balliol College. I did my Ph.D. thesis with Alexander G. Ogston on the physical and biochemical characteristics of hyaluronic acid. Professor Ogston's remarkable combination of theory and experiment guided the scientific activity in his laboratory. He has served as a model to me on how to train students; I hope I have measured up to his standard. Sir Hans Krebs was the chairman of the Department of Biochemistry. I have profited by conversations with him, particularly when (in 1972) I was a visiting fellow at Trinity College and we had opportunities to discuss our mutual interests in the history of science.

Oxford science at that time was influenced by the 19th and 20th century

British and European naturalists, scientists and explorers who went to the world of nature—often to distant parts of it—to make the observations which generated their hypotheses. Anthony C. Allison was then working in the Department of Biochemistry and introduced me to the concept of polymorphism, a term introduced by the lepidopterist E. B. Ford of the Department of Zoology. In 1957 I took my first West African trip (to Nigeria) and was introduced to the special excitement of that part of the world. I found the Nigerians warmhearted and friendly with a spontaneous approach to life. We collected blood specimens from several populations (including the nomadic pastoral Fulani and their domestic animals) and studied inherited polymorphisms of the serum proteins of milk and of hemoglobin. This approach was continued in many subsequent field trips, and it eventually led to the discovery of several new polymorphisms and, in due course, the hepatitis B virus.

I worked at the National Institutes of Health from 1957 until 1964. This was during a period of rapid growth for the NIH, and I continued to develop my research on polymorphisms and their relation to disease. This led to the formation of the Section on Geographic Medicine and Genetics, which was eventually assigned to an epidemiology branch directed by Thomas Dublin, from whom I learned the methods of epidemiology. The NIH was a very exciting place, with stimulating colleagues including J. Edward Rall, Jacob Robbins, J. Carl Robinson, Kenneth Warren, Seymour Geisser, and many others. The most important connection I made, however, was with W. Thomas London (who later came to The Institute for Cancer Research), who has become a colleague, collaborator, and good friend with whom I have worked closely for fifteen years. Tom was an essential contributor to the work on Australia antigen and hepatitis B, and without him it could not have been done.

I came to The Institute for Cancer Research in 1964 to start a program in clinical research. The Institute was, and is, a remarkable research organization. Our director, Timothy R. Talbot, Jr., has a deep respect for basic research and a commitment to the independence of the investigators. Above all, people are considered an end in themselves, and the misuse of staff to serve some abstract goal is not tolerated. Jack Schultz was a leading intellectual force in the Institute, and his foresighted, humane view of science, his honesty and his good sense influenced the activities of all of us. Another important characteristic is the dedication and intelligence of our administrative and maintenance staffs, which contributes to the strong sense of community which pervades our Institute.

Over the course of the next few years we built up a group of investigators from various disciplines and from many countries (Finland, France, Italy, Poland, Venezuela, England, India, Korea, China, Thailand, Singapore) who, taken together, did the work on Australia antigen. Alton I. Sutnick (now Dean of the Medical College of Pennsylvania) was responsible for much of the clinical work at Jeanes Hospital. Some of the early workers included Irving Millman, Betty Jane Gerstley, Liisa Prehn, Alberto Vierucci, Scott Mazzur, Barbara Werner, Cyril Levene, Veronica Coyne, Anna O'Connell,

135

Edward Lustbader, and others. There were many field trips during this period to the Philippines, India, Japan, Canada, Scandinavia, Australia, and Africa. It has been an exciting and pleasant experience surrounded by stimulating and friendly colleagues.

At present, we are conducting field work in Senegal and Mali, West Africa, in collaboration with Professor Payet of Paris, formerly the Dean of the Medical School of Dakar, with Professor Sankalé, his successor in Dakar, and a group of other French and Sengalese colleagues, including Drs. Larouzé and Saimot.

I am Professor of Medicine at the University of Pennsylvania and attend ward rounds with house staff and medical students. I am also a Professor of Anthropology and have taught Medical Anthropology for eight years. I have learned a great deal from my students.

My non-scientific interests are primarily in the out-of-doors. I have been a middle distance runner (very non-competitive) for many years and also play squash. We canoe on the many nearby lakes and rivers of Pennsylvania and New Jersey. I enjoy mountain walking and have hiked in many parts of the world on field trips. With several friends we own a farm in western Maryland which supplies beef for the local market. Shoveling manure for a day is an excellent counterbalance to intellectual work.

My wife, Jean, is an artist who has recently become interested in print making. We have four children of whom I am very proud: Anne, George, Jane, and Noah. They are all individualists, which makes for a turbulent and noisy household, still we miss the two oldest who are now away at college. We live in the center of old Philadelphia, a few blocks from Independence Hall. The city has appreciated its recognition by the Nobel Award in our Bicentennial Year.

AUSTRALIA ANTIGEN AND THE BIOLOGY OF HEPATITIS B.

Nobel Lecture, December 13, 1976
by
BARUCH S. BLUMBERG
The Institute for Cancer Research, The Fox Chase Cancer Center,
Philadelphia, Pennsylvania, U.S.A.

The discovery of the infectious agent associated with hepatitis B and the elucidation of new mechanisms for its dissemination are the consequences of a series of studies involving many investigators in our laboratory in Philadelphia. The particular directions the work has followed have been a product of the interests and personalities of the investigators, physicians, technicians, students and others who have come to our laboratory. It has resulted in a complex body of data which crosses the boundaries of several disciplines. I have been fortunate in having as co-workers dedicated, and highly motivated scientists. We have had a warm, friendly and congenial atmosphere and I am grateful to my colleagues for bringing these qualities to their work.

POLYMORPHISM AND INHERITED VARIATION

E. B. Ford, the Oxford zoologist, lepidoptorist and geneticist, defined polymorphims as "the occurrence together in the same habitat of two or more (inherited) discontinuous forms of a species, in such proportions, that the rarest of them cannot be maintained merely by recurrent mutation" (1). Examples of polymorphism are the red blood cell groups in which the different phenotypes of a system may occur in high frequencies in many populations. This, according to Ford's view, would be unlikely to occur as a consequence of recurrent mutation operating alone to replace a phenotype lost by selection. Another example is the sickle cell homoglobin system. In this, Hb^S genes may be lost from the population each time a homozygote (who has sickle cell disease) fails to contribute to the next generation because of death before the reproductive age. The heterozygotes (Hb^S/Hb^A) are, however, thought to be differentially maintained in the population because individuals with this phenotype are less likely to succumb to falciparum malaria and consequently survive to contribute genes to the next generation. The theory implies that there are different selective values to the several forms of polymorphisms. This notion has been questioned recently since it has been difficult to demonstrate selective differences for most polymorphisms. Independent of the biological causes for the generation and maintenance of polymorphisms, the concept unifies a large number of interesting biological data. No two people are alike and polymorphisms probably account for a great deal of variation in humans. There are other interesting implications of polymorphisms. In some instances the presence of a small amount of a material may be associated with one effect and the presence of larger amounts of the same material with a very different effect. One gene for hemoglobin S protects against malaria, while two genes result in the (often) fatal sickle cell disease. Polymorphisms may produce antigenic differences. Antigenic variants of ABO and other red blood cell groups may result in transfusion reactions. Differences in Rh red blood cell groups may cause life threatening antigenic reactions between a mother and her child late in pregnancy and at the time of birth. Polymorphic antigens may have an effect when one human's tissues interacts with another's in blood transfusion, transplantation, pregnancy, intercourse, and possibly, as we shall see, when human antigens are carried by infectious agents.

Oliver Smithies (who had been a graduate student of A. G. Ogston, my mentor at Oxford) developed the ingenious starch gel electrophoresis method which allowed the seperation of serum proteins on the basis of complex characteristics of their size and shape. With this, he distinguished several electrophectically different polymorphic serum proteins (haptoglobins, trans-ferrins, etc.). In 1957 and for several years after, in collaboration with Anthony C. Allison who was then in the Department of Biochemistry in Oxford, we studied these variants in Basque, European, Nigerian, and Alaskan, (2, 3) populations and found striking variations in gene frequencies. At the same time, I acquired experince and some skill in mounting field studies. Using this and similar techniques in the following years I studied inherited variants in other populations and regions. These included red blood cell and serum groups in Spanish Basque, Alaskan and Canadian Indians, and Eskimos; β-amino isobutyric acid excretion in Eskimos, Indians, and Micronesians; protein and red blood cell antigens in Greece, and various variants in North and South American Indians and in U.S. blacks and whites (4—7). We identified several "new" polymorphisms in animals. With Michael Tombs, another of Ogstons' pupils, we discovered a polymorphism of alpha lactalbumin in the "Zebu" cattle of the pastoral Fulani of northern Nigeria (8). Later, Jacob Robbins and I found a polymorphism of the thyroxine binding pre-albumin of *Macaca mulatta* (9). From these studies, and those of other in-vestigators, the richness and variety of biochemical and antigenic variation in serum became strikingly apparent.

In the summer of 1960 Allison came to my laboratory at the National Institutes of Health. We decided to test the hypothesis that patients who received large numbers of transfusions might develop antibodies against one or more of the polymorphic serum proteins (either known or unknown) which they themselves had not inherited, but which the blood donors had. We used the technique of double diffusion in agar gel (as developed by Professor Ouchterlony of Goteborg) to see whether precipitating antibodies had formed in the transfused patients which might react with constituents present in the sera of normal persons.

After testing sera from 13 multiply transfused patients (defined as a person who had received 25 units of blood or more), we found a serum which contained a precipitating antibody (10). It was a very exciting experience to see these precipitin bands and realize that our prediction had been fulfilled. The antibody developed in the blood of a patient (Mr. C. de B.), who had received many transfusions for the treatment of an obscure anemia. He was extremely cooperative and interested in our research and on several occasions came to Maryland from his home in Wisconsin for medical studies and to donate blood.

During the course of the next few months we found that the antibody in Mr. C. de B.'s blood reacted with inherited antigenic specificities on the low density lipoproteins. We termed this the Ag system; and it has subsequently been the subject of genetic, clinical and forensic studies (11).

We continued to search for other precipitating systems in the sera of transfused patients on the principle that this approach had resulted in one significant discovery and that a further search would lead to other interesting findings. During my last year at Bethseda, Dr. Harvey Alter, a hematologist, came to work with us. We also had been joined by Mr. Sam Visnich, a former Navy jet fighter and commercial airline pilot, who, during a slack period in aviation, came to work in our laboratory as a technician.

In 1963 we had been studying the sera of a group of hemophilia patients from Mt. Sinai Hospital in New York City which had been sent to us by Dr. Richard Rosenfield, the director of the blood bank. Antibodies against the Ag proteins were not common in this group of sera, but one day we saw a precipitin band which was unlike any of the Ag precipitins. It had a different configuration, it did not stain readily with Sudan black (suggesting a low lipid content compared to the Ag precipitin) but did stain red with Azocarmine, indicating that protein was a major component. There was a major difference in the distribution of the sera with which the transfused hemophilia patient reacted. Most of the anti-Ag antisera reacted with a large number (usually about 50—90%) of the panel sera, but the serum from the hemophilia patient reacted with only one of 24 sera in the panel, and that specimen was from an Australian aborigine (12, 13). We referred to the reactant as Australia antigen, abbreviated Au. The original Australian sera had been sent to us by Dr. Robert Kirk. We subsequently went to Western Australia to collect and test a large number of additional sera.

We now set out to find out why a precipitin band had developed between the sera of a hemophilia patient from New York and an aborigine from Australia. At the outset we had no set views on where this path might lead, although our investigation was guided by our prior experience with the Ag polymorphism. In preparing this "history" of the discovery of Au, I constructed an outline based on a hypothetico-deductive structure, showing the actual events which led to the discovery of the association of Au with hepatitis. From this it is clear that I could not have planned the investigation at its beginning to find the cause of hepatitis B. This experience does not encourage an approach to basic research which is based exclusively on specific-goal-directed programs for the solution of biological problems.

The next step was to collect information on the distribution of Au and anti-Au in different human populations and disease groups. We had established a collection of serum and plasma samples, later to develop into the Blood Collection of the Division of Clinical Research of The Institute for Cancer

Research which now numbers more than 200,000 specimens. The antigen was very stable; blood which had been frozen and stored for 10 years or more still gave strong reactions for Au. There were some instances in which blood had been collected from the same individual for 6 or more successive years. If the sera were positive on one occasion, they were in general positive on subsequent testings; if negative initially, they were consistently negative. Presence or absence of Au appeared, at least in the early experiments, to be an inherent characteristic of an individual.

We were able to use our stored sera for epidemiological surveys and in a short time accumulated a considerable amount of information on the world-wide distribution of Au. It was very rare in apparently normal populations from the United States; only 1 of 1000 sera tested was positive. However, it was quite common in some tropical and Asian populations (for example, 6% in Filipinos from Cebu, 1% in Japanese, 5—15 % in certain Pacific Ocean populations). We will come back to a consideration of the hypothesis which was generated from this set of epidemiologic observations after consideration of an interesting disease association discovered at about the same time.

Sam Visnich had been asked to select from our collection the sera of patients who had received transfusions, in order to search for more anti-Au antisera. He decided, however, to use them both as potential sources of antibody and also in the panels against which anti-Au sera were tested. Included among the transfused sera were specimens from patients with leukemia who had received transfusions. A high frequency of Au, rather than anti-Au, was found in this group. We subsequently tested patients with other diseases and found Au only in transfused patients.

On the basis of these observations we made several hypotheses. Although they sound like alternative ones, they in fact are not, and over the course of subsequent years, in a sense, all of them have been supported and are still being tested.

One hypothesis stated that, although Au may be rare in normal populations, individuals who have Au are more likely to develop leukemia than are individuals who do not have the antigen. That is, there is a common susceptibility factor which makes it more likely for certain people both to have Au and to develop leukemia. We also suggested that Au might be related to the infectious agent (virus) which is said to be the cause of leukemia.

A corollary of the susceptibility hypothesis is that individuals who have a high likelihood of developing leukemia would be more likely to have Au. Young Down's syndrome (Mongolism) patients are more likely to develop leukemia than are other children; estimations of the increased risk vary from 20 to 2000 times that of children without Down's syndrome. I had in 1964 moved to The Institute for Cancer Research in Philadelphia to start its Division of Clinical Research. While there we tested the sera of Down's syndrome patients resident in a large institution and found that Au was very common in this group ($\sim 30\%$ were Au positive); the prediction generated by our hypothesis was fulfilled by these observations, a very encouraging finding (14). The presence of the antigen in people living closer to Philadelphia also made it possible to more readily study persons with Au. Until this time all the individuals with Au who had been identified either lived in Australia, or some other distant place, or were sick with leukemia.

Down's syndrome patients were admitted to the Clinical Research Unit (located in our sister institution, Jeanes Hospital) for clinical study. We found again that the presence or absence of Au seemed to be a consistent feature of an individual. If Au was present on initial testing, then it was present on subsequent testing; if absent initially, it was not found later. In early 1966 one of our Down's syndrome patients, James Bair, who had originally been negative, was found to have Au on a second test. Since this was an aberrant finding we admitted James to the Unit. There was no obvious change in his clinical status. Because he apparently had developed a "new" protein, and since many proteins are produced in the liver we did a series of "liver chemistry" tests. These showed that between the first testing (negative for Au) and the subsequent testing (positive for Au) James had developed a form of chronic anicteric hepatitis.

On 6/28/66, the day of his admission to the Clinical Research Unit, my colleague, Alton I. Sutnick, wrote the following dramatic note in the patient's chart.

"SGOT slightly elevated! Prothrombin time low! We may have an indication of [the reason for] his conversion to Au+."

His prediction proved correct. The diagnosis of hepatitis was clinically confirmed by liver biopsy on 7/20/66, and we now began to test the hypothesis that Au was associated with hepatitis (15). First, we compared the transaminase (SGPT) levels in males with Down's syndrome who had Au and those who did not. The SGPT levels were slightly but significantly higher in the Au(+) individuals. Secondly, we asked clinicians in Pennsylvania to send us blood samples from patients with acute hepatitis. W. Thomas London, and others in our laboratory soon found that many hepatitis patients had Au in their blood early in their disease, but the antigen usually disappeared from their blood, after a few days or weeks. Another dramatic incident occurred which added to our urgency in determining the nature of the relation of Au to hepatitis. Miss (now Dr.) Barbara Werner was the first technician in our laboratory in Philadelphia. She had been working on the isolation of Au by extensions of the methods developed by Alter and Blumberg during the earlier work in Bethesda. Early in April of 1967 she noticed that she was not in her usual state of good health. She was well aware of our observations that Au was related to hepatitis and, one evening, tested her own serum for the presence of Au. The following morning a faint but distinct line appeared, the first case of viral hepatitis diagnosed by the Au test. She subsequently developed icteric hepatitis and, fortunately, went on to a complete recovery.

By the end of 1966 we had found that Au was associated with acute viral hepatitis. In our published report (14) we said:

"Most of the disease associations could be explained by the association of Au(1) with a virus, as suggested in our previous publications. The discovery of the frequent occurrence of Au(1) in patients with virus hepatitis raises the possibility that the agent present in some cases of this disease may be Australia antigen or be responsible for its presence. The presence of Australia antigen in the thalassemia and hemophilia patients could be due to virus introduced by transfusions."

That is, we made the hypothesis that Au was (or was closely related to) the etiologic agent of "viral" hepatitis and we immediately set about to test it. Our original publication did not elicit wide acceptance; there had been many previous reports of the identification of the causative agent of hepatitis and our claims were naturally greeted with caution. Indeed, an additional paper on Australia antigen and acute viral hepatitis (15) which extended our findings published in 1967 was initially rejected for publication on the grounds that we were proposing another "candidate virus" and there were already many of these.

Confirmation of our findings and the first definitive evidence on the relation of Au to post-transfusion hepatitis came soon. Dr. (now Professor) Kazuo Okochi, then at the University of Tokyo, had followed a line of inquiry very similar to ours. He had started with the investigation of anti-Ag (lipoprotein) antisera, and we had corresponded on this subject. Professor Okochi then found an antiserum in a patient with chronic myelogenous leukemia which was different from the anti-Ag precipitins. He also found that it was associated with liver damage. During my several field trips to Japan I had lectured on Australia antigen. Professor Okochi sent the unusual antiserum to us to compare with anti-Australia antigen; we found that they were identical. He confirmed our finding of the association of Au with hepatitis and then proceeded to do the first definitive transfusion study. He found that Au could be transmitted by transfusion and that it led to the development of hepatitis in some of the people who received it, and that some transfused patients developed anti-Au (16, 17). The Au-hepatitis association was also confirmed in 1968 by Dr. Alberto Vierucci (18) who had worked in our laboratory and Dr. Alfred M. Prince (19).

We had made some preliminary observations in Philadelphia in collaboration with Dr. John Senior of the University of Pennsylvania on the transfusion of donor blood which was found to contain Au. We then developed a protocol for a controlled, long term study to determine whether donor bloods which had Au were more likely to transmit hepatitis than those which did not. In 1969 we heard from Prof. Okochi that he had already embarked on a similar transfusion studies. In June of that year he visited our laboratory in Philadelphia and showed us his data. These, in his (and our) opinion demonstrated with a high probability, that donor blood containing Australia antigen was much more likely to transmit hepatitis than donor blood which did not contain the antigen. (Similar studies were later done by Dr. David Gocke (20) in the United States and the same conclusions were reached.) We immediately stopped the experimental study and established the practice of excluding donor bloods with Australia antigens in the hospitals where we were testing donor units. This was a dramatic example of how technical information may completely change an ethical problem. Before Okochi's data had become available it was a moral necessity to determine the consequences of tranfusing

142

blood containing Australia antigen; and it had to be done in a controlled and convincing manner since major changes in blood transfusion practice were consequent on the findings. As soon as the conclusion of Okochi's well controlled studies were known to us, it became untenable to administer donor blood containing Australia antigen. *Autre temps, autre moeurs.*

It was, however, possible to do a study to evaluate the efficacy of Au screening on post-transfusion hepatitis using historical controls, which appears to be valid. Senior and his colleagues had completed an analysis of post-transfusion hepatitis in Philadelphia General Hospital before the advent of screening and found an 18 % frequency of post-transfusion hepatitis. In the fall of 1969 we started testing all donor blood and excluding Au positive donors. Senior and others undertook a similar study one year after the screening program was in progress. They found that the frequency of post-transfusion hepatitis had been reduced to 6 %, a striking improvement (21).

The practical application of an initially esoteric finding had come about only two years after the publication of our paper on the association between Au and hepatitis (14). In retrospect, one of the major factors contributing to the rapid application of the findings was the simplicity of the immunodiffusion test. Another was our program of distributing reagents containing antigen and antibody to all investigators who requested them. We did this until this function was assumed by the National Institutes of Health.

Following the confirmation of the association of hepatitis with Australia antigen, a large number of studies were published, and, in a relatively short time, the routine use of the test in blood banks became essentially universal in the United States and many other countries. It has been estimated that the annual saving resulting from the prevention of post-transfusion hepatitis amounts to about half a billion dollars in the United States.

VIROLOGY

Virological methods (i.e. tissue culture, animal inoculation, etc.) had been used for many years prior to our work to search for hepatitis virus but had not been very productive. Our initial discoveries were based primarily on epidemiologic, clinical, and serological observations. Here, I will try to review the early virology work from our laboratory (Robinson has reviewed much of the recent work (22)).

Bayer *et al.* (23), using the isolation techniques initially introduced by Alter and Blumberg (24), examined isolated Au with the electron microscope. They found particles about 20 nm in diameter which were aggregated by anti-Au antiserum. There were also sausage like particles of the same diameter, but much elongated (Figure 1, 2). Subsequently Dane, Cameron and Briggs identified a larger particle about 42 nm in diameter with an electron dense core of about 27 nm (25). It is probable that this represents the whole virus particle. Both the 20 nm and 42 nm particles contain Australia antigen on their surfaces and this is now termed hepatitis B surface antigen (HBsAg). The surface antigen can be removed from Dane particles by the action of detergents to reveal the core which has its own antigen, hepatitis B core antigen

143

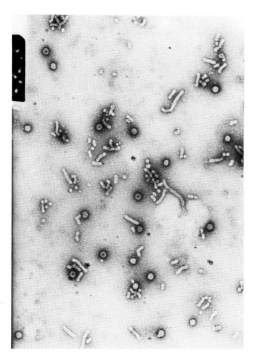

Fig. 1. Electron micrograph showing the several kinds of particles associated with hepatitis B virus (see Figure 2). Magnification = 90,000X. Electron micrograph prepared by E. Halpern and L. K. Weng.

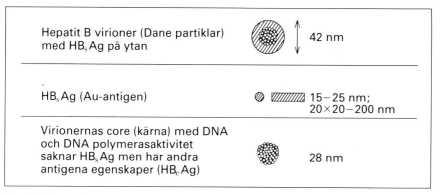

Hepatit B virioner (Dane partiklar) med HB$_s$Ag på ytan		42 nm
HB$_s$Ag (Au-antigen)		15–25 nm; 20×20–200 nm
Virionernas core (kärna) med DNA och DNA polymerasaktivitet saknar HB$_s$Ag men har andra antigena egenskaper (HB$_c$Ag)		28 nm

Fig. 2. Diagram showing appearance of particles associated with hepatitis B virus, the large or Dane particle (top), small surface antigen particle and the sausage shaped particle (middle), and the core of the Dane particle (bottom). (Adapted from E. Lycke, Läkartidningen *73*, 1976.)

(HBcAg). Antibodies to both these antigens (anti-HBs, anti-HBc) can be detected in human blood. The surface antigen can be detected in the peripheral blood by the methods we initially introduced and by more sensitive methods which have since been developed. Anti-HBs is often found in the peripheral blood after infection and may persist for many years. It may also be detected in people who have not had clinical hepatitis. Anti-HBc is usually associated with the carrier state, (i.e. persistent HBsAg in the blood) but may occur without it. HBcAg itself has not been identified in the peripheral blood.

144

Anti-HBc is also found commonly during the active phase of acute hepatitis, before the development of anti-HBs but in general does not persist as long as anti-HBs.

DNA has been isolated from the cores of Dane particles and is associated with a specific DNA polymerase. Robinson has shown that the DNA is in the form of double stranded rings (22). Jesse Summers, Anna O'Connell and Irving Millman of our Institute have confirmed these findings and provided a model for the molecule which appears to have double and single stranded regions (Fig. 3) (26).

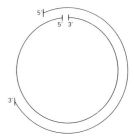

Fig. 3. Structure of the DNA extracted from Dane particles proposed by Summers et al. (26). The position of the gaps in the single strands, and the location of the 5′ and 3′ ends are shown.

Using immunofluorescent and electron microscope studies, hepatitis B core particles have been identified in the nuclei of liver cells of infected patients. HBsAg is found in the cytoplasm. It is thought that assembly of the large particles occurs in the cytoplasm and that large and small particles (surface antigen only) emerge from the cells and eventually find their way to the peripheral blood.

VACCINE AGAINST HEPATITIS B

In 1968 we were informed by the Federal government, who provided most of the funds for our work, that they would like to see applications of the basic research they had funded for many years. It occurred to us that the existence of the carrier state provided an unusual method for the production of a vaccine. We presumed that the very large amounts of HBsAg present in the blood could be separated from any infectious particles and used as an antigen for eliciting the production of antibodies. The antibodies in turn would protect against infection with the virus. Irving Millman and I applied separation techniques for isolating and purifying the surface antigen and proposed using this material as a vaccine. To our knowledge, this was a unique approach to the production of a vaccine; that is, obtaining the immunizing antigen directly from the blood of human carriers of the virus. In October, 1969, acting on behalf of the ICR we filed an application for a patent for the production of a vaccine. This patent was subsequently (January, 1972) granted in the United States and other countries (27).

There are observations in nature which indicate that antibody against the surface antigen is protective. In their early studies, Okochi and Murakami observed that transfused patients with antibody were much less likely to develop hepatitis than those without it (17). In a long term study, London (36) has shown that patients on a renal dialysis unit, and the staff who served them, were much less likely to develop hepatitis if they had anitbody then if they did not (Fig. 4). Edward Lustbader has used this data to develop a statistical method for rapidly evaluating the vaccine (28).

There have now been several animal and human studies of the vaccine and the results are promising (29—32, 54, 55). It should be possible to determine the value of the vaccine within the next few years.

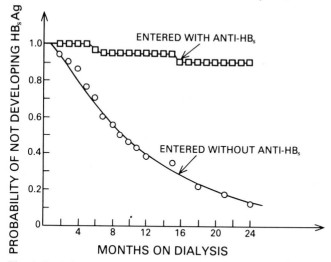

Fig. 4. Probability of not developing HBsAg for patients admitted to a renal dialysis unit with and without anti-HBs. The patients with anti-HBs are relatively well protected while those without antibody are very likely to develop infection (adapted from Lustbader et al. (28)).

VARIATION IN RESPONSE TO INFECTION WITH HEPATITIS B

A physician is primarily interested in how a virus interacts with humans to cause disease. But this is only part of the world of the virus. Our introduction to studies on hepatitis B was not through patients with the disease, but rather through asymptomatic carriers and infected individuals who developed antibody. Therefore, many of our investigations have been of infected but apparently healthy people. There are a variety of responses to infection:

1) Development of acute hepatitis proceeding to complete recovery. Transient appearance of HBsAg and anti-HBc. Subsequent appearance of anti-HBs which may be persistent.

2) Development of acute hepatitis proceeding to chronic hepatitis. HBsAg and associated anti-HBc are usually persistent.

3) Chronic hepatitis with symptoms and findings of chronic liver disease not preceded by an episode of acute hepatitis. HBsAg and anti-HBc are persistent.

4) Carrier state. Persistent HBsAg and anti-HBc. Carrier is asymptomatic but may have slight biochemical abnormalities of the liver.

5) Development of persistent anti-HBs without detectable HBsAg or symptoms.

6) Persistent HBsAg in patients with an underlying disease often associated with immune abnormalities, i.e., Down's syndrome, lepromatous leprosy,

chronic renal disease, leukemia, primary hepatic carcinoma. Usually associated with anicteric hepatitis.

7) Formation of complexes of antigen and antibody. These may be associated with certain "immune" diseases such as periarteritis nodosa.

FAMILY STUDIES

In our first major paper on Australia antigen (13) we described family clustering of Au in a Samaritan family from Israel which had been studied by the anthropologist Batsheva Bonné. From it we inferred the hypothesis that the persistent presence of Au was inherited as a simple autosomal recessive trait. The genetic hypothesis has proven to be very useful not in the sense that it is necessarily "true" (exceptions to the simple hypothesis were noted by us and others very soon (33)), but because it has generated many interesting studies on the family distributions of responses to infection with hepatitis B. We suggested that hepatitis virus may have several modes of transmission. It can be transmitted horizontally from person to person similar to "conventional" infectious agents. This is seen in the transmission of hepatitis B virus (HBV) by transfusion. Other forms of direct and indirect horizontal transmission exist; for example, sputum, the fecal-oral route, and perhaps, by hematophagous insects (see below). It has even been reported to have been spread by computer cards (34), an extraordinary example of adaptation by this ingenious agent! HBV may also be transmitted vertically. If the genetic hypothesis were sustained, then it would imply that the capacity to become persistently infected is controlled (at least in part) as a Mendelian trait. The data are also consistent with the notion that the agent could be transmitted with the genetic material; that the virus could enter the nucleus of its host and in subsequent generations act as a Mendelian trait. The data also suggest a maternal effect. A re-analysis of our family data showed that in many populations more of the offspring were persistent carriers when the mother was a carrier than when the father was a carrier. Many investigators have now shown that women who have acute type B hepatitis just before and/or during delivery or women who are carriers can transmit HBV to their offspring, who then also become carriers. This may be a major method for the development of carriers in some regions, for example, Japan. Interestingly, this mechanism does not appear to operate in all populations. This suggests that some aspects of delivery and parent child interaction, differing in different cultures, as well as biological characteristics may affect transmission.

The family is an essential human social unit. It is also of major importance in the dissemination of disease. A large part of our current work is directed to an understanding of how the social and genetic relations within a family affect the spread of hepatitis virus.

HOST RESPONSES TO HUMAN ANTIGENS AND HEPATITIS B VIRUS. KIDNEY TRANSPLANTATIONS

W. Thomas London, Jean Drew, Edward Lustbader and others in our laboratory have undertaken an extensive study of the patients in a large renal dialysis unit in Philadelphia (36, 37). The renal patients can be characterized on the basis of their response to infection with hepatitis B. Patients who develop antibody to HBsAg are significantly more likely to reject transplanted kidneys that are not completely matched for HLA antigens than patients who become carriers of HBsAg (Fig. 5) (37). Since many of the patients became exposed to hepatitis B while on renal dialysis, their response to infection can be determined prior to transplantation. In this patient population there is a correlation between development of anti-HBs and the subsequent development of anti-HLA antibodies after transplantation. We have also found a correlation between the development of anti-HLA and anti-HBs in transfused hemophilia patients and in pregnant women. Hence, there appears to be a correlation between the response to infection with HBV and the immunologic response to polymorphic human antigens in tissue transplants. Further, from preliminary studies it appears that donor kidneys from males are much more likely to be rejected by patients with anti-HBs than by patients without anti-HBs. These differences were not observed when the kidneys were from female donors. Dr. London is now extending his observations to other transplants, in particular, bone marrow, to determine whether a similar relation exists.

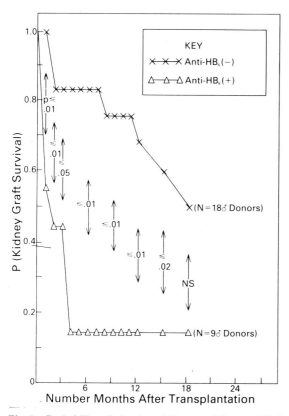

Fig. 5a. Probability of rejecting a kidney graft by renal dialysis patients who received kidneys from male donors. There is a significant difference in rejection rate between patients who were carriers and those who developed anti-HBs (37).

148

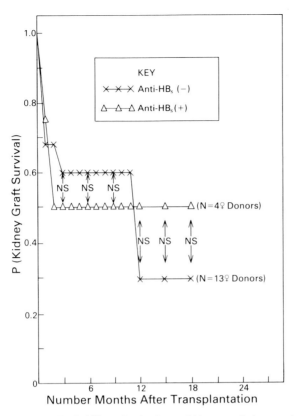

Fig. 5b. Probability of rejecting a kidney graft by renal dialysis patients who received kidneys from female donors. There is no difference in the rejection rates between the two groups of patients (37).

SEX OF OFFSPRING AND FERTILITY OF INFECTED PARENTS

In many areas of the world, including many tropical regions (i.e. the Mediterranean, Africa, southeast Asia, and Oceania) the frequency of HBsAg carriers is very high. In these regions most of the inhabitants will eventually become infected with HBV and respond in one of the several ways already described. Our family studies and the mother-child studies show that there is a maternal effect. Jana Hesser (then a graduate student in Anthropology working in our laboratory) and Ioanna Economidou, Stephanos Hadziyannis, and our other Greek colleagues collected information on the sex of the offspring of parents in a Greek town in southern Macedonia. In this community the probability of infection with HBV is very high and a majority of the parents had evidence of infection, i.e., detectable HBsAg and/or anti-HBs in their blood. It was found that if either parent was a carrier of HBsAg there were significantly more male offspring than in other matings (38). In subsequent studies using the Greek data and additional data from Mali in West Africa, London, Drew, and Veronique Barrois (a post-doctoral trainee from Paris) have found that there is a deficiency of male offspring when parents have anti-HBs (39). This had led London and his colleagues to test the hypo-

149

thesis that anti-HBs has specificities in common with H-Y or other antigens determined by genes on the Y chromosome. If these observations are supported by additional studies, then HBV may have a significant effect on the composition of populations in places where it is common, which includes the most populous regions of the world. The ratio of males and females in a population has a profound effect on population size as well as on the sociology of the population. This connection of HBV with sex selection may also explain why there is a greater likelihood of rejection of male kidneys by renal patients with anti-HBs, and indicate how kidneys can be better selected for transplantation. Transplantation of organs and pregnancy have certain immunologic features in common. Rejection of male kidneys and "rejection" of the male fetus may be mediated by similar biological effects.

PRIMARY HEPATIC CARCINOMA

The project with which we are most concerned at present is the relation of hepatitis B to primary hepatic carcinoma (PHC), and methods for the prevention of the disease. PHC is the most common cancer in men in many parts of Africa and Asia. For many years investigators in Africa including Payet (40), Davies (41), and Steiner (42) have suggested that hepatitis could be the cause of PHC. With the availability of sensitive tests for Australia antigen it became possible to test this hypothesis; it has now been established that there is a striking association of hepatitis B with PHC (43, 45) (Table 1). In our studies in Senegal and Mali, Bernard Larouzé and others found that essentially all the patients had been infected with HBV and that most had

Table 1. Frequency of HBsAg, anti-HBc and anti-HBs in primary hepatic carcinoma (PHC) and controls in Senegal and Mali, West Africa. RIA = radioimmunoassay; "p" is the two tailed probability obtained from Fisher's Exact Test (adopted from Larouzé et al. (45).

| | Test | PATIENTS | | | | CONTROLS | | | | |
		No. Tested	+	--	% +	No. Tested	+	--	% +	p
Senegal	HBsAg									
PHC	RIA	39	31	8	79.4	53	6	47	11.3	4×10^{-11}
	Anti-HBc	39	35	4	89.7	58	16	42	27.6	1×10^{-9}
	Anti-HBs	39	8	31	20.5	58	26	32	44.8	0.02
	Total									
	Exposed	39	37	2	94.8	58	38	20	65.1	8×10^{-4}
Mali	HBsAg									
PHC	RIA	21	10	11	47.6	38	2	36	5.2	4×10^{-4}
	Anti-HBc	20	15	5	75.0	40	10	30	25.0	5×10^{-4}
	Anti-HBs	21	8	13	38.0	40	17	23	42.5	0.95
	Total									
	Exposed	21	19	2	90.4	40	25	15	62.0	0.02

evidence of current infection (presence of HBsAg and/or anti-HBc). Oh-bayashi and his colleagues (44) had reported several families of patients with PHC in which the mothers were carriers. In our study in Senegal (56) we found that a significantly larger number of mothers of PHC patients were carriers of HBsAg compared with controls, and that none of the fathers of the cases had anti-HBs. In control families, on the other hand, 48 % of the fathers developed antibody (Table 2). The hypothesis we have made is that, in some families, children will be infected by their mothers, *in utero*, at the time of birth, and/or shortly afterwards during the period when there is intimate contact between mother and children. In some cases, the infected child will proceed through several stages to the development of PHC. At each stage, only a fraction of the infected individuals will proceed to the next stage, and this will depend on other factors in the host and in the environment. The stages include, retention of the antigen (carrier state), development of chronic hepatitis, development of cirrhossis and finally,

Table 2. Frequency of HBsAg, anti-HBc and anti-HBs in patients with primary hepatic carcinoma (PHC) and controls, and in the parents of patients and controls. The studies were conducted in Dakar, Senegal, West Africa. I.D. = HBsAg by immunodiffusion; RIA = HBsAg by radioimmunoassay. (Adopted from Larouzé et al. (56).)

	Primary Hepatic Carcinoma (PHC)			Controls			p
	N	+	% +	N	+	% +	
HBsAg(+) ID	28	9	32.1 %	28	5	17.9 %	0.35
HBsAg(+) RIA	28	22	78.6 %	28	16	57.1 %	0.15
anti-HBc(+)	28	25	89.2 %	28	18	64.3 %	0.05
anti-HBs(+)	28	7	25.0 %	28	18	64.3 %	6×10^{-3}
HBsAg(+), anti-HBc(+) and/or anti-HBs(+)*	28	27	96.4 %	28	26	92.9 %	0.99
	Mothers of PHC			Mothers of Controls			
HBsAg(+) ID	28	15	53.6 %	28	3	10.7 %	1×10^{-3}
HBsAg(+) RIA	28	20	71.4 %	28	4	14.3 %	3×10^{-5}
anti-HBc(+)	28	20	71.4 %	28	9	32.1 %	6.9×10^{-3}
anti-HBs(+)	28	3	10.8 %	28	15	53.6 %	1×10^{-3}
HBsAg(+), anti-HBc(+) and/or anti-HBs(+)*	28	21	75.0 %	28	19	67.9 %	0.76
	Fathers of PHC			Fathers of Controls			
HBsAg(+) ID	27	2	7.4 %	27	3	11.1 %	0.99
HBsAg(+) RIA	27	5	18.5 %	27	5	18.5 %	1.00
anti-HBc(+)	27	5	18.5 %	27	8	29.6%	0.52
anti-HBs(+)	27	0	0	27	13	48.1 %	3×10^{-5}
HBsAg(+), anti-HBc(+) and/or anti-HBs(+)*	27	5	18.5 %	27	18	66.6 %	7×10^{-6}

* Any evidence of infection with HBV.

development of PHC (Figure 6). We are currently testing this hypothesis in prospective studies in West Africa (45). If it is true, then prevention of PHC could be achieved by preventing infection with HBV, and the vaccine we have introduced, in association with appropriate public health measures, could reduce the amount of infection. This might also involve the use of gamma-globulin in the newborn children of carrier mothers and such studies are now being conducted by Beasley and his colleagues in Taipei. We are now considering the appropriate strategies that might be used to control hepatitis infection and, hopefully, cancer of the liver.

PATHOGENESIS OF PRIMARY HEPATOCELLULAR CARCINOMA

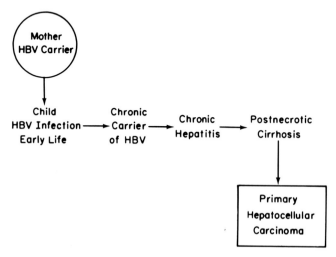

Fig. 6. Scheme for the pathogenesis of primary hepatic carcinoma showing the sequence of stages leading to PHC.

TRANSMISSION BY INSECTS

HBsAg has been detected by several investigators (including Prince, Smith, Muniz and others (46, 47, 48)) in mosquitos collected in the field in areas where HBsAg is common in the human population. In 1971 we collected mosquitoes in Uganda and Ethiopia and found Au antigen in individual mosquitoes (57). In more extensive studies in Senegal we found a field infection rate of about 1 in 100 for *Anopheles gambiae* and also identified the antigen in several other species of mosquitoes (58). It is not known if HBV replicates in mosquitoes, but it has been reported that it can be detected in mosquitoes many weeks after feeding and it has been found in a mosquito egg. Feeding experiments have been conducted with the North American bedbug (*Cimex lectularius*) which show that this insect can also carry the antigen (49). Wills, in our laboratory, has found a very high infection rate ($\sim 60\%$) in the tropical bedbug *Cimex hemipterus* collected from the beds of individuals known to be carriers of hepatitis B (61). Bedbugs could transfer blood (and the virus) from one occupant of a bed to another. If it is in fact a vector of hepatitis, then it

152

could provide a frequent non-venereal (and unromantic) form of connubial spread. It may also provide a means for transmission from mother (or father) to young children who may share the parents' bed in early life; and this would be related to the child rearing practices of a community.

Insect transmission may be important in the program for the control of hepatitis B infection and for the prevention of chronic liver disease and primary hepatic carcinoma. An understanding of the role of insects in the spread of infection, particularly its transmission from mother to children, would help in designing effective strategies for control.

HEPATITIS B AS A POLYMORPHISM

The original discovery of hepatitis B resulted from the study of serum antigen polymorphisms. Its identification as an infectious agent does not diminish the value of this concept. It is useful to view infection with HBV not only as a "conventional" infection but also as a transfusion or transplantation reaction; and our studies on renal transplantation are an example of this.

HBV appears to have only a small amount of nucleic acid, probably only sufficient to code for a few proteins. Much of the coat (and possibly other portions of the virus) could be produced by the genes of the host. Millman and his colleagues found that the surface antigen contains material with antigenic specificities in common with serum proteins including IgG, transferrin, albumin, beta-lipoprotein and others (50). If this is true then the antigenic makeup of the virus would be, at least in part, a consequence of the antigenic characteristics of the host from whence it came; and this, as suggested by our sex studies, may include male antigens. In our discussion of the "Icron" concept (a name we introduced which is an acronym on the Institute for Cancer Research) (51), we pointed out that the responses of the putative host to HBV may be dictated in part by the nature of the "match" between the antigens of the host and virus (i.e., the virus acts as if it were a polymorphic human antigen). London and Werner have described this in a review of these concepts (52, 60). If person A is infected with HBV particles which contain proteins that are antigenically very similar to his own, then he will have little immunologic response and will tend to develop a persistent infection with the virus. On the other hand if the proteins of the agent are antigenically different from his, he will develop an immune response to the virus (i.e., anti-HBs) and will have a transient infection. During the course of infection in person A, new particles will be synthesized which contain antigenic characteristics of A. Person A, in turn can infect person B and the same alternatives present themselves. If the relevant proteins of B are antigenically similar to the antigens of A and the antigens of the HBV produced by A, then B could develop a persistent infection. If they are different, then antibody can form, as described above. (A derivative of this hypothesis is that inflammatory disease of the liver is associated with the immune response to the infectious agent rather than solely with replication of the agent.) A further possibility is that the virus has complex antigens; that some may match the host and some may not and that both persistent infection and development of antibodies may

153

occur. The persistent antigens and the antibody in the same individual would have different specificities, and this occurrence has been described (59).

This view of the agent as an Icron introduces an interesting element into the epidemiology of infectious agents in which not only the host and virus are factors, but also the previous host or hosts of the agent. If, in fact, the agent does replicate in insects, (see above) the antigenic characteristics of previous human hosts may be affected by transmission through another species. This in turn might have an effect on the response of the next host.

BIOETHICS AND THE CARRIER STATE

During the course of our work a number of bioethical questions have arisen (53). Experience has shown that these bioethical considerations cannot be separated from "science," that answers cannot be provided on a "purely scientific" basis, and that our technical knowledge is inseparably intertwined with bioethical concerns.

It has been recognized that hepatitis B may be transmitted by means other than transfusion, i.e. by contact, fecal-oral spread, insects, etc. With the introduction of the screening test many carriers were identified. It is estimated that there are one million such carriers in the United States and more than 100 million in the world. This has led to a situation which may be unique in medicine. Although some carriers may be able to transmit hepatitis by means other than blood transfusion, this is probably not true for many (or most) carriers. There are studies which show that spread of infection from carriers in health care occupations to patients may not be common. At present there is no satisfactory method of identifying the infectious carriers although it appears that carriers with "e" antigen, an unusual antigen originally described by Magnius (62), are much more likely to transmit disease. Despite this, carriers have had professional and social difficulties. Health care personnel who are carriers have been told that they must leave their jobs. In some cases carriers have changed their pattern of social beavior because of the fear they might spread disease to people with whom they come in contact. What appeared to be happening was the development of a class of individuals stigmatized by the knowledge that some member of the "class" could transmit hepatitis.

The bioethical problems that are raised from the studies of hepatitis carriers can be viewed as a conflict between public health interests and individual liberty. When the risk to the public is clear, and the restrictions on personal liberties are small, there is little problem in arriving at appropriate regulations. For example, the transfusion of blood containing hepatitis B antigen is a disadvantage to the patient recipient and it has been stopped. The denial of the right to donate blood is not a great infringement of personal activity and the individuals concerned and society have agreed to accept this moderate restriction. The problems raised by person-to-person transmission are more difficult. The extent of the hazard to the public is not clear, since it is not (now) possible to distinguish carriers who transmit disease from those who do not. On the other hand, if all carriers are treated as infectious, the hazards imposed on the carrier may be enormous, i.e., loss of job and ability to continue in the same profession, restriction of social and family contacts, etc. What is clear is that for a very large number of carriers, the risk of transmitting hepatitis by person-to-person contact must be very small. All members of the carrier class should not be stigmatized because some can transmit hepatitis.

On a broader level, the ethical issue is raised as to the extent to which biological knowledge about individuals should impinge on daily lives. Is it appropriate to regulate the risks inherent in people living together and interacting with each other? An issue has been raised with respect to hepatitis because the test can be easily done and because millions of people are tested as part of blood donor programs. As a consequence of these tets, this particular group of carriers has been identified. There are carriers of other agents, some of them potentially more hazardous (i.e., staphylococcus, typhoid) who are not routinely tested and therefore not placed at a disadvantage.

It is hoped that many of these problems can be resolved by continued research into the nature of the hepatitis carrier state, and that carriers who have already been identified will not be jeopardized during this period when necessary information is not available.

A characteristic of many large scale public health control programs is the emergence of problems that were not anticipated prior to the institution of the program. For example, the control of malaria has in many areas resulted in a markedly decreased infant mortality with a large increase in population. When this has not been accompanied by a concomitant increase in food production, the nourishment and well-being of the population have actually decreased.

With the availability of the serologic and environmental tests for hepatitis B, it is now possible to begin the design of control measures for this disease. If the heptatitis B vaccine is found to be effective, then it may also be of value in preventing the development of the carrier state. We are now attempting to investigate the biology of the hepatitis B agent to learn whether some of the consequences of control can be known before the program begins. An example already discussed is the possible effect of HBV infection on sex ratio. The role of the virus in the life of the insects in which it is found is not known, but may be profound; and there may be other effects on the ecology that are not now obvious.

We hope to continue the study of these broad problems to be as well prepared as possible when and if attempts are made to eliminate or decrease the frequency of the hepatitis B virus.

REFERENCES

1. Ford, E. B. Genetics for medical students, Metheun, London, 1956, p. 202.
2. Allison, A. C., Blumberg, B. S., and ap Rees, W. Haptoglobin types in British, Spanish Basque and Nigerian African populations, Nature, *181:* 824—825, 1958.
3. Blumberg, B. S., Allison, A. C., and Garry, W. The haptoglobins and hemoglobins of Alaskan Eskimos and Indians. Ann. Human Genet. *23:* 349—356, 1959.
4. Alberdi, F., Allison, A. C., Blumberg, B. S., Ikin, E. W., and Mourant, A. E. The blood groups of the Spanish Basques. J. Roy Anthrop. Inst. *87:* 217—221, 1957.
5. Corcoran, P. A., Allen, F. H., Jr., Allison, A. C., Blumberg, B. S. Blood groups of Alaskan Eskimos and Indians. Am. J. Phys. Anthropol. *17:* 187—193, 1959.
6. Allison, A. C., Blumberg, B. S., and Gartler, S. M. Urinary excretion of beta-amino-isobutyric acid in Eskimo and Indian populations of Alaska. Nature *183:* 118—119, 1959.
7. Blumberg, B. S., and Gartler, S. M. High prevalence of high level beta-amino-iso-butyric acid excretors in Micronesians. Nature *184:* 1990—1992, 1959.
8. Blumberg, B. S. and Tombs, M. T. Possible polymorphism of bovine alpha-lactalbumin. Nature *181:* 683—684, 1958.
9. Blumberg, B. S., and Robbins, J. Thryoxine-serum protein complexes. Advan. Thyroid Res. 461—465, 1961.
10. Allison, A. C., and Blumberg, B. S. An isoprecipitation reaction distinguishing human serum protein types. Lancet *1:* 634—637, 1961.
11. Blumberg, B. S., Dray, S., and Robinson, J. C. Antigen polymorphism of a low-density beta-lipoprotein. Allotypy in human serum. Nature *194:* 656—658, 1962.
12. Blumberg, B. S. Polymorphisms of serum proteins and the development of isoprecipitins in transfused patients. Bull. N. Y. Acad. Med. *40:* 377—386, 1964.
13. Blumberg, B. S., Alter, H. J. and Visnich, S. A "new" antigen in leukemia sera. J. Am. Med. Assoc. *191:* 541—546, 1965.
14. Blumberg, B. S., Gerstley, B. J. S., Hungerford, D. A., London, W. T., and Sutnick, A. I. A serum antigen (Australia antigen) in Down's syndrome leukemia and hepatitis. Ann. Int. Med. *66:* 924—931, 1967.
15. London, W. T., Sutnick, A. I. and Blumberg, B. S. Australia antigen and acute viral hepatitis. Ann. Int. Med. *70:* 55—59, 1969.
16. Okochi, K. and Murakami, S. Observations on Australia antigen in Japanese. Vox Sang. *15:* 374—385, 1968.
17. Okochi, K., Murakami, S., Ninomiya, K. and Kaneko, M. Australia antigen, trans-fusion and hepatitis. Vox Sang. *18:* 289—300, 1970.
18. Vierucci, A., Bianchini, A. M., Morgese, G., Bagnoli, F. and Messina, G. L'antigen Australia. 1. Rapporti con l'epatite infettiva e da siero. Una ricerca in pazienti pediatrici. Pediatria Internazione XVIII, No. 4, 1968.
19. Prince, A. M. An antigen detected in the blood during the incubation period of serum hepatitis. Proc. Nat. Acad. Sci. *60:* 814, 1968.
20. Gocke, D. J. and Kavey, N. B. Correlation with disease and infectivity of blood donors. Lancet *1:* 1055—1059, 1969.
21. Senior, J. R., Sutnick, A. I., Goeser, E., London, W. T., Dahlke, M. D. and Blumberg B. S. Reduction of post-transfusion hepatitis by exclusion of Australia antigen from donor blood in an urban public hospital. Am. J. Med. Sci. *267:* 171—177, 1974.
22. Robinson, W. S. and Lutwick, L. I. The virus of hepatitis, type B. N. Engl. J. Med. *295:* 1168—1175, 1976.
23. Bayer, M. E., Blumberg, B. S. and Werner, B. Particles associated with Australia antigen in the sera of patients with leukemia, Down's syndrome and hepatitis. Nature *218:* 1057—1059, 1968.
24. Alter, H. J. and Blumberg, B. S. Studies on a "new" human isoprecipitin system (Australia antigen). Blood 27(3): 297—309, 1966.

25. Dane, D. S., Cameron, C. H. and Briggs, M. Virus-like particles in serum of patients with Australia antigen-associated hepatitis. Lancet *1:* 695—698, 1970.

26. Summers, J., O'Connell, A. and Millman, I. Genome of hepatitis B virus: Restriction enzyme cleavage and structure of DNA extracted from Dane particles. Proc. Nat. Acad. Sci. *72:* 4597—4601, 1975.

27. Blumberg, B. S. and Millman, I. Vaccine against viral hepatitis and process. U.S. Patent Office No. 3,636,191, (1972).

28. Lustbader, E. D., London, W. T. and Blumberg, B. S. Study design for a hepatitis B vaccine trial. Proc. Nat. Acad. Sci. *73:* 955—959, 1976.

29. Purcell, R. H. and Gerin, J. L. Hepatitis B subunit vaccine: A preliminary report of safety and efficacy tests in chimpanzees. Am. J. Med. Sci. *270:* 395—399, 1975.

30. Hilleman, M. R., Buynak, E. B., Roehm, R. R., Tytell, A. A., Bertland, A. V., and Lampson, S. P. Purified and inactivated human hepatitis B vaccine: Progress report. Am. J. Med. Sci. *270:* 401—404, 1975.

31. Maupas, P. Coursaget, P. Goudeau, A., Drucker, J., Bagros, P. Immunisation against hepatitis B in man. Lancet *1:* 1367—1370, 1976.

32. Buynak, E. B., Roehm, R. R., Tytell, A. A., Bertland, A. U., Lampson, G. P., and Hilleman, M. R. Vaccine against human hepatitis B. J. Am. Med. Assoc. *235:* 2832—2834, 1976.

33. Blumberg, B. S. Australia antigen: The history of its discovery with comments on genetic and family aspects. *In* Viral Hepatitis and Blood Transfusion, edited by G. N. Vyas, H. A. Perkins and R. Schmid, Grune & Stratton, New York, 1972, pp. 63—83.

34. Patterson, C. P., Boyer, K. M., Maynard, J. E. and Kelly, P. C. Epidemic hepatitis in a clinical laboratory. J. Am. Med. Assoc. *230:* 854—857, 1974.

35. Blumberg, B. S., London, W. T., Lustbader, E. D., Drew, J. S. and Werner, B. G. Protection vis-a-vis de l'hépatite B par l'anti-HBs chez des malades hémodialysés. *In* Hépatite a Virus B et Hémodialyse, Flammarion Médecine-Sciences, Paris, 1975, pp. 175—183.

36. London, W. T., Drew, J. S., Lustbader, E. D., Werner, B. G. and Blumberg, B. S. Host response to hepatitis B infection among patients in a chronic hemodialysis unit. Kidney Int. (in press) 1977.

37. London, W. T., Drew, J. S., Blumberg, B. S., Grossman, R. A., and Lyons, P. S. Association of graft survival with host response to hepatitis B infection in patients with kidney transplants. N. Engl. J. Med. *296:* 241—244, 1977.

38. Hesser, J. E., Economidou, J. and Blumberg, B. S. Hepatitis B surface antigen (Australia antigen) in parents and sex ratio of offspring in a Greek population. Human Biol. *47:* 415—425, 1975.

39. Drew, J. S., London, W. T., Lustbader, E. D. and Blumberg, B. S. Cross reactivity between hepatitis B surface antigen and an antigen on male cells. Proc. of the 1977 March of Dimes Birth Defects Conference (in press) 1977.

40. Payet, M., Camain, R., Pene, P. Le cancer primitif du foie, étude critique a propos de 240 cas. Rev. Intern. Hepatol. *4:* 1—20, 1956.

41. Davies, J. N. P. Hepatic neoplasm. The Liver, edited by E. A. Gall, F. K. Mostofi. Baltimore, Williams and Wilkins, 1973, pp. 361—369.

42. Steiner, P. D. and Davies, J. N. P. Cirrhosis and primary liver carcinoma in Uganda Africans. Br. J. Cancer *11:* 523—534, 1957.

43. Blumberg, B. S., Larouzé, B., London, W. T., Werner, B., Hesser, J. E., Millman, I., Saimot, G. and Payet, M. The relation of infection with the hepatitis B agent to primary hepatic carcinoma. Am. J. Path. *81:* 669—682, 1975.

44. Ohbayashi, A., Okochi, K. and Mayumi, M. Familial clustering of asymptomatic carriers of Australia antigen and patients with chronic liver disease or primary liver cancer. Gastroenterol. *62:* 618—625, 1972.

45. Larouzé, B., Blumberg, B. S., London, W. T., Lustbader, E. D., Sankale, M., and Payet, M. Forecasting the development of primary hepatic carcinoma by the use of risk factors. Studies in West Africa. J. Nat. Canc. Inst. *58:* 1557—1561, 1977.

46. Prince, A. M., Metselaar, D. Kafuko, G. W., Mukwaya, L. G., Ling, C. M. and Overby, L. R. Hepatitis B antigen in wild-caught mosquitoes in Africa. Lancet *2:* 247—250, 1972.

47. Smith, J. A., Ogunba, E. O., and Francis, T. I. Transmission of Australia Au(1) antigen by Culex mosquitoes. Nature *237:* 231—232, 1970.

48. Muniz, F. J. and Micks, D. W. The persistence of hepatitis B antigen in *Aedes aegypti*. Mosquito News *33:* 509—511, 1973.

49. Newkirk, M. M., Downe, A. E. R., and Simon, J. B. Fate of ingested hepatitis B antigen in blood-sucking insects. Gastroenterol. *69:* 982—987, 1975.

50. Millman, I., Hutanen, H., Merino, F., Bayer, M. E. and Blumberg, B. S. Australia antigen: Physical and chemical properties. Res. Commun. Chem. Path. Pharm. *2:* 667—686, 1971.

51. Blumberg, B. S., Millman, I., Stunick, A. I. and London, W. T. The nature of Australia antigen and its relation to antigen-antibody complex formation. J. Exp. Med. 134: 320—329, 1971.

52. London, W. T., Sutnick, A. I., Millman, I., Coyne, V. Blumberg, B. S. and Vierucci, A. Australia antigen and hepatitis: Recent observations on the serum protein polymorphism, infectious agent hypotheses. C.M.A.J. *106:* 480—485, 1972.

53. Blumberg, B. S. Bioethical questions related to hepatitis B antigen. Am. J. Clin. Path. *65:* 848—853, 1976.

54. Krugman, S., Giles, J. P., and Hammond, J. Viral hepatitis, type B (MS2 strain). Studies on active immunization. J. Am. Med. A. *217:* 41—45, 1971.

55. Maugh, T. H. Hepatitis B: A new vaccine ready for human testing. Science *188:* 137—138, 1975.

56. Larouzé, B., London, W. T., Saimot, G., Werner, B. G., Lustbader, E. D., Payet, M., and Blumberg, B. S. Host responses to hepatitis B infection in patients with primary hepatic carcinoma and their families. A case/control study in Senegal, West Africa. Lancet *2:* 534—538, 1976.

57. Blumberg, B. S., Wills, W., Millman, I., and London, W. T. Australia antigen in mosquitoes. Feeding experiments and field studies. Res. Comm. CP *6:* 719—732, 1973.

58. Wills, W., Saimot, G., Brochard, C., Blumberg, B. S., London, W. T., Dechene, R., and Millman, I. Hepatitis B surface antigen (Australia antigen) in mosquitoes collected in Senegal, West Africa. Am. J. Trop. M. *25:* 186—190, 1976.

59. Raunio, V. K., London, W. T., Sutnick, A. I., Millman, I., and Blumberg, B. S. Specificities of human antibodies to Australia antigen. P. Soc. Exp. M. *134:* 548—557, 1970.

60. Werner, B. and London, W. T. Host responses to hepatitis B infection: Hepatitis B surface antigen and host proteins. Ann Int. Med. *83:* 113—114, 1975.

61. Wills, W., Larouzé, B., London, W. T., Blumberg, B. S., Millman, I., Pourtaghra, M., and Coz, J. Hepatitis B surface antigen in West African mosquitoes and bedbugs, Abstract 25th Annual Joint Meeting of the American Society of Tropical Medicine and Hygiene and the Royal Society of Tropical Medicine and Hygiene, Philadelphia, Pennsylvania, November 3—5, 1976.

62. Magnius, L. O. Characterization of a new antigen-antibody system associated with hepatitis B. Clin. Exp. Im. *20:* 209--216, 1975.

D. Carleton Gajdusek

D. CARLETON GAJDUSEK

My scientific interests started before my school years, when as a boy of five years I wandered through gardens, fields and woods with my mother's entomologist-sister, Tante Irene, as we overturned rocks and sought to find how many different plant and animal species of previously hidden life lay before us. We cut open galls to find the insects responsible for the tumors, and collected strange hardening gummy masses on twigs which hatched indoors to fill the curtains with tiny praying mantises, and discovered wasps with long ovipositors laying their eggs into the larvae of wood-boring beetles. In petri dishes we watched some leaf-eating insects succumb to insecticide poison while others survived, and on exciting excursions visited the laboratories and experimental greenhouses of the Boyce Thompson Institute for Plant Research in my hometown of Yonkers, New York, where my aunt, Irene Dobroscky, worked, studying in the 1920's virus inclusions in the cells of leaf-hoppers.

In my first years at school I had problems with my teachers for carrying to school insect-killing jars, correctly labeled "Poison: potassium cyanide". As a grade schoolboy, I met at the Boyce Thompson Institute laboratories the quiet, amused, watchful and guiding eyes of the mathematician and physical chemist, Dr. William J. Youden, who enjoyed letting me play with his hand cranked desk calculator, with his circular or cylindrical slide rules, and with models of crystal lattice structure, and on his laboratory bench where he taught me to prepare colloidal gold solution time color reactions and to manufacture mercuric thiocyanate snake-generating tablets. Before I was ten years old I knew that I wanted to be a scientist like my aunt and my quiet mathematician tutor. I rejected completely, as did my younger brother, Robert, who is now a poet and critic, the interests of our father and maternal grandfather in business, which had made our life style possible.

My life and outlook were greatly influenced by the polyglot immigrant Eastern European communities, adjacent and unwillingly interlaced, living in the carpet, elevator and copper wire manufacturing and sugar refining city of Yonkers, just upstream on the Hudson River from the New York megalopolis and possessing a schoolbook history of a Seventeenth Century Royal Dutch land grant of Indian land to Johng Heer (hence Yonkers) Adrian van der Donck. The cimbalon in our living room, beside the piano, Romanian and Hungarian gypsies who fiddled the *czardas* and *halgatos* at our family festivities and camped in the empty store adjacent to my father's butcher shop, an uninterrupted flow of loud conversation in many tongues, rarely English, and kitchen odors of many Hapsburg cuisines filling our crowded expanded-family-filled home, gave me an orthodox and optimistic view of America as a land of change and possibility which I never lost. Below our almost rural hilltop home—our family had "risen"—clustered the factories, churches, shops and two to four family houses of immigrant factory workers and tradesmen in the valleys of the almost obliterated Nepperhan and Tuckahoe Indian-named creeks. In this hollow stood Hungarian, Slovak and Polish Catholic and Russian Orthodox churches and a Presbyterian mission to the factory workers. (This exciting conglomeration of Eastern Europeans has been later displaced by Mediterranean and Caribbean and, still later, Black Americans, all similarly "melting".)

My father, Karl Gajdusek, was a Slovak farm boy from a small village near Senica, who had left home as an adolescent youth to immigrate to America before World War I, alone and without speaking English, to become a butcher in the immigrant communities of Yonkers, where he met and married my mother, Ottilia Dobroczki. Her parents had also come, each alone, as youthful immigrants from Debrecen, Hungary to America. On my father's side we were a family of farmers and tradesmen, vocations which never interested my brother or myself, but my father's temperament for laughter and ribald fun, lust for life in work and play, music, song, dance and food, and above all, conversation, affected us strongly. On my mother's side were the more somber academic and aesthetic aspirations of four university educated first generation American siblings and a heroic interest in fantasy and inquiry, in the classics and culture, nature, nurture and process. Because of my mother's unquenchable interest in literature and folklore, my brother and I were reared listening to Homer, Hesiod, Sophocles, Plutarch and Virgil long before we learned to read.

I was born on September 9, 1923 in the family home we still own, while my maternal grandparents and my mother's youngest sister shared the home. My brother arrived nineteen months later. He and I grew up closely together; for every move I made further into mathematics and the sciences, he moved further into poetry, music and the other arts. In 1930 we traveled to Europe to visit our relatives, mostly those of my father's large family, which he had abandoned twenty years earlier. My brother and I were left for months in my father's birthplace with his old father and the huge remaining family (the squire had sired some twenty five children), while our parents toured European capitals.

Back in America, my early school years were those of great happiness: I liked school and the enchanting family excursions up the Hudson valley were frequent. My Tante Irene was working on problems of economic entomology in the Philippines and South East Asia, and exotic artifacts and natural history specimens, particularly the beautiful giant leafhoppers clad in batik-like patterns, arrived to fascinate me. On her return from the Orient she took me on ever broader excursions to collect insects, to watch the emergence of the seventeen-year cicadas and to attend scientific meetings in the American Museum of Natural History. I became an early habitué of New York city's museums, attending courses on Egyptology at the Metropolitan Museum of Art on schoolday afternoons after my fifth grade classes and at weekend and evening lectures on entomology, geology and botany at the Museum of Natural History.

Today, I and my large family of adopted sons from New Guinea and Micronesia still occupy, on our frequent visits to New York city, our family home in which I was born fifty-three years ago. Here, the boys recently discovered, while installing new attic insulation, daguerreotypes and tintypes of the family taken in towns east of the Danube and in turn-of-the-century New York city and also school notebooks which once belonged to my mother, her siblings, my brother, and myself. From this home, too, we buried both of my maternal grandparents, and my father and mother. On the occasion of my pagan mother's death, the unavoidably close proximity of Slovak Catholic and Russian Orthodox churches, both named Holy Trinity, led to the confusion which resulted in burying her with ministrations of the wrong denomination, which she would have enjoyed, when I attemped to assuage, by asking the funeral director to call in the priest, the pious Roman Catholic relatives of my irreverent father, at whose earlier funeral the Slovak priest had declined to officiate.

I started to read seriously before puberty. Books by Scandinavian authors, Henrik Ibsen and Sigrid Undset, were among the earlier works I read myself. I devoured enthusiastically three biographical works which must have had a profound effect on me: René Vallery-Radot's biography of his father-in-law, Louis Pasteur; Eve Curie's biography of her mother, Marie Curie; and Paul de Kruif's "Microbe Hunters." I then stenciled the twelve names of microbiologists whom de Kruif had selected on the steps leading to my attic chemistry laboratory, where they remain today. At about this time, when I was about ten years old, I wrote an essay on why I planned to concentrate on chemistry, physics, and mathematics, rather than classical biology, in preparation for a career in medicine. Dr. Youden had succeeded in making it clear to me that education in mathematics, physics and chemistry was the basis for the biology of the future.

During the summers of my thirteenth to sixteenth years, I was often working at the Boyce Thompson Laboratories. Under Dr. John Arthur's tutelage, I synthesized and characterized a large series of halogenated aryloxyacetic acids, many previously unsynthesized. The series of new compounds I derived from these failed to yield the fly-killing potency anticipated, but when they were tested several years later for their phytocidal capacity one of my new compounds, 2,4-dichlorophenoxyacetic acid, became the weed killer of commerce; and the Institute based its patent rights to royalties on my boyhood laboratory notebooks—the only venture I have had which involved commerce.

My experiences at the Boyce Thompson, especially with Youden, directed me towards physics at the University of Rochester, where I hoped to fulfill my plan, formulated in boyhood from my readings and teachings of my aunt and Youden, of studying mathematics, physics, and chemistry in preparation for a career in medical research.

From 1940 to 1943 I studied at the University of Rochester under Victor Weisskopf in physics; Curt Stern, Don Charles, David Goddard, Jim Goodwin, in biology; Vladimir Seidel in mathematics; and Ralph Helmkamp in chemistry. In the summer of 1941 I was inspired by the marine embryology course of

163

Viktor Hamburger's at Woods Hole Marine Biology Laboratories. In those years of my teens I learned to love mountaineering, hiking, canoeing and camping with a passion as great as that for science.

At nineteen to twenty-two years of age while at Harvard Medical School, I worked with John T. Edsall in the laboratory of protein physical chemistry, and with James L. Gamble in his laboratory of electrolyte balance at Boston Children's Hospital. Thereafter, at ages of twenty-five and twenty-six, I worked at Caltech with Linus Pauling and John Kirkwood, where I was also greatly influenced by Max Delbrück, George Beadle, Walter Zechmeister and James Bonner. It was at Caltech that my peers—fellow postdoctoral students and young investigators (Gunther Stent, Jack Dunitz, Elie Wollman, Benoit Mandelbrot, David Shoemaker, John Cann, Harvey Itano, Aage Bohr, Ole Maaloe, Ted Harold, John Fincham, Reinhart Ruge, Arnold Mazur, Al Rich, and others)—had a profound effect on my intellectual development, goals and appreciation of quality in creative life, and on my career. This was the "Golden Age" at Caltech and the many close friends working in several different disciplines, as well as our mentors, have remained mutually stimulating coworkers in science and, above all, lasting personal friends for the past thirty years. With the group of students about Linus Pauling, John Kirkwood, Max Delbrück and George Beadle, I spent many days and evenings in wide-ranging discussions in the laboratories and at the Atheneum, and in even more protracted exchanges on camping and hiking trips to the deserts and mountains of the West, of Mexico and Canada. Max and Mannie Delbrück were often the hosts for our group at their home, and the prime organizers of many of our expeditions. This period of less than two years at Caltech has given me a group of friends who are interested critics of my work, who together with my major teachers in clinical and laboratory investigation, comprise, perhaps unwittingly, the jury whose judgements I most respect.

I had not counted on my captivation with clinical pediatrics. Children fascinated me, and their medical problems (complicated by the effect of variables of varying immaturity, growth, and maturation upon every clinical entity that beset them) seemed to offer more challenge than adult medicine. I lived and worked within the walls of Boston Children's Hospital through much of medical school. Thereafter, I started my postgraduate specialty training in clinical pediatrics which I carried through to Specialty Board qualification, while also working in the laboratory of Michael Heidelberger at Columbia University College of Physicians and Surgeons, while at Caltech, and while with John Enders on postgraduate work at Harvard. I have never abandoned my clinical interests, particularly in pediatrics and neurology, which were nurtured by a group of inspiring bedside teachers: Mark Altschuler, Louis K. Diamond, William Ladd, Frank Ingraham, Sidney Gellis, and Canon Ely at Harvard; Rustin McIntosh, Hattie Alexander, Dorothy Anderson, and Richard Day at Babies Hospital, Columbia Presbyterian Medical Center in New York; Katie Dodd, Ashley Weech, Joe Warkany, and Sam Rappaport at Cincinnati Children's Hospital, and Ted Woodward of Baltimore.

In 1951 I was drafted to complete my military service from John Enders' laboratory at Harvard to Walter Reed Army Medical Service Graduate School as a young research virologist, to where I was called by Dr. Joseph Smadel. I found that he responded to my over-ambitious projects and outlandish schemes with severity and metered encouragement, teaching me more about the methods of pursuing laboratory and field research, and presenting scientific results, than any further theoretical superstructure, which he assumed I already possessed.

From him and from Marcel Baltazard of the Institut Pasteur of Teheran, where I worked in 1952 and 1953 on rabies, plague, arbovirus infections, scurvy and other epidemic disease in Iran, Afghanistan and Turkey, I learned of the excitement and challenge offered by urgent opportunistic investigations of epidemiological problems in exotic and isolated populations. My quest for medical problems in primitive population isolates took me to valleys of the Hindu Kush, the jungles of South America, the coast and inland ranges of New Britain, and the swamps and high valleys of Papua New Guinea and Malaysia, but always with a base for quiet contemplation and exciting laboratory studies with John Enders in Boston, Joe Smadel in Washington, and Frank Burnet in Melbourne. To these teachers I am indebted for guidance and inspiration and for years of encouragement and friendship.

To Joe Smadel I also owe the debt of further sponsorship and encouragement, and recognition of my scientific potential for productive research which led him to create for me several years later a then-unique position as an American visiting scientist at the National Institutes of Health, in the National Institute of Neurological Diseases and Blindness, under Dr. Richard Masland, wherein I could nurture my diverse interests in a selfstyled Study of Child Growth and Development and Disease Patterns in Primitive Cultures. Our Laboratory of Slow, Latent and Temperate Virus Infections grew out of the elucidation of one of our "disease patterns", kuru, and blossomed into a new field of medicine. For about two decades I have enjoyed at the National Institutes of Health the base and haven for our diverse studies in remote parts of the world together with a small group of students and coworkers and many visiting colleagues who have formed the strong team of our endeavor. Here, Marion Poms, Joe Gibbs, Paul Brown, Vin Zigas, Michael Alpers, David Asher and Nancy Rogers have shared these adventures with me through almost two decades.

My boyhood reading, first in Homer, Virgil, and Plutarch, on which we were nurtured by our Classicist-Romanticist Hungarian mother, led, upon the instigation of my poet brother, to my more thorough return to the classics as a young, too-ardent scientist-cum-physician, and to the modern literature of European authors and philosophers, which I had missed in my university days devoted too exclusively to mathematics and the sciences. This reading changed greatly my way of thinking. Particularly, I would have to credit Dostoevsky, Chekhov and Tolstoy; Montaigne, Baudelaire, Rimbaud, Valery and Gide; Shakespeare, Wordsworth, Yeats and Lawrence; Poe,

Whitman and Melville; Ibsen; Goethe, Schiller, Kant, Nietzsche, Kafka and Mann; Saadi and Hafiz.

In 1954 I took off for Australia to work as a visiting investigator with Frank Burnet at the Walter and Eliza Hall Institute of Medical Research in Melbourne from where, between periods of bench work in immunology and virology, I launched studies on child development and disease patterns with Australian aboriginal and New Guinean populations.

In eighteen volumes of some five thousand pages of published personal journals on my explorations and expeditions to primitive cultures, I have told far more about myself and my work since 1957, when I first saw kuru, under the guidance of Vincent Zigas, than one should in a lifetime . . I do not see how I can précis that here.

UNCONVENTIONAL VIRUSES AND THE ORIGIN AND DISAPPEARANCE OF KURU

Nobel Lecture, December 13, 1976
by D. CARLETON GAJDUSEK
National Institutes of Health, Bethesda, Maryland, USA

Kuru was the first chronic degenerative disease of man shown to be a slow virus infection, with incubation periods measured in years and with a progressive accumulative pathology always leading to death. This established that virus infections of man could, after long delay, produce chronic degenerative disease and disease with apparent heredofamilial patterns of occurrence, and with none of the inflammatory responses regularly associated with viral infections. Soon thereafter, several other progressive degenerative diseases of the brain were likewise attributed to slow virus infections (see Tables 1 and 2). These include delayed and slow measles encephalitis, now usually called subacute sclerosing panencephalitis (SSPE), progressive multifocal leuko-encephalopathy (PML), and transmissible virus dementias usually of the Creutzfeldt-Jakob disease (CJD) type. Thus, slow virus infections, first recognized in animals, became recognized as a real problem in human medicine.

Kuru has led us, however, to a more exciting frontier in microbiology than only the demonstration of a new mechanism of pathogenesis of infectious disease, namely the recognition of a new group of viruses possessing unconventional physical and chemical properties and biological behavior far different from those of any other group of microorganisms. However, these viruses still demonstrate sufficiently classical behavior of other infectious microbial agents for us to retain, perhaps with misgivings, the title of "viruses". It is about these unconventional viruses that I would further elaborate.

The group consists of viruses causing four known natural diseases: two of man, kuru and CJD, and two of animals, scrapie in sheep and goats, and transmissible mink encephalopathy (TME) (Table 1). The remarkable unconventional properties of these viruses are summarized in Tables 3 and 4. Because only primate hosts have been available as indicators for the viruses

Table 1. Naturally-occurring slow virus infections caused by unconventional viruses (subacute spongiform virus encephalopathies)

In man:	In animals:
Kuru	Scrapie
Transmissible virus dementia	In sheep
Creutzfeldt-Jakob disease	In goats
Sporadic	Transmissible mink encephalopathy
Familial	
Familial Alzheimer's disease	

Table 2. Slow infections of man caused by conventional viruses

Disease	Virus
Subacute post-measles leukoencephalitis	Paramyxovirus—defective measles
Subacute sclerosing panencephalitis (SSPE)	Paramyxovirus—defective measles
Subacute encephalitis	Herpetovirus—Herpes-simplex
	Adenovirus—Adeno-types 7 and 32
Progressive congenital rubella	Togavirus—rubella
Progressive panencephalitis as a late sequela following congenital rubella	Togavirus—defective rubella
Progressive multifocal leukoencephalopathy (PML)	Papovavirus—JC; SV-40
Cytomegalovirus brain infection	Herpetovirus—cytomegalovirus
Epilepsia partialis continua (Kozhevnikov's epilepsy) and progressive bulbar palsy in USSR	Togavirus—RSSE and other tick-borne encephalitis viruses
Chronic meningoencephalitis in immunodeficient patients	Picornaviruses—poliomyelitis, ECHO virus
Crohn's disease	Unclassified—RNA virus
Homologous serum jaundice	Unclassified—Hepatitis B, Dane particle
Infectious hepatitis	Parvovirus—Hepatitis A
	Unclassified—Hepatitis B, Dane particle
	Unclassified—Hepatitis C

Table 3. Atypical physical and chemical properties of the unconventional viruses

1. Resistant to formaldehyde
2. Resistant to β-propiolactone
3. Resistant to ethylenediamine tetraacetic acid (EDTA)
4. Resistant to proteases (trypsin, pepsin)
5. Resistant to nucleases (RNase A and III, DNase I)
6. Resistant to heat (80° C); incompletely inactivated at 100° C
7. Resistant to ultraviolet radiation: 2540 Å
8. Resistant to ionizing radiation (γ rays): equivalent target 150,000 daltons
9. Resistant to ultrasonic energy
10. Atypical UV action spectrum: 2370 Å inactivation $= 6 \times 2540$ Å inactivation
11. Invisible as recognizable virion by electron microscopy (only plasma membranes, no core and coat)
12. No non-host proteins demonstrated

causing human disease (or, more recently, cats (24) and guinea pigs (48) for CJD and mink for kuru (24), but with long incubation periods), it has been impossible to characterize these agents well; knowledge of the properties of unconventional viruses is based mostly on the study of the scrapie virus adapted to mice (39, 60) and hamsters (42, 49, 57). The unusual resistance of the viruses to various chemical and physical agents (items 1 to 9 in Table 3), separate this group of viruses from all other microorganisms. In fact, their resistance to ultraviolet (UV) and ionizing radiation, the atypical UV action spectrum for inactivation, and the failure to contain any demonstrable non-host protein, make these infectious particles unique in the biology of replicating infectious agents, and it is only to the newly-described viroids causing six natural plant diseases [potato spindle tuber disease (7—10, 34), chrysanthemum stunt disease, citrus exocortis disease (57, 58), Cadang-Cadang disease of coconut palms (55), cherry chloratic mottle, and cucumber pale fruit disease] that we must turn for analogy (see Figures 1a, 1b).

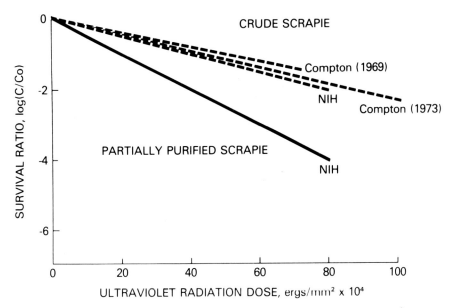

Figure 1. Scrapie virus is unusually resistant to UV inactivation at 2534 to 2540 Å (45,46). This has been interpreted as an indication that it contains no nucleic acid. Recent data from Diener (7,8), however, indicate that the smallest plant virus (potato spindle tuber viroid: PSTV), which is a naked single-stranded RNA of 120,000 daltons, is 90 times more resistant to such UV inactivation than are conventional plant viruses. Since the small infectious nucleic acid of tobacco ring spot virus satellite virus (single-stranded RNA of 75,000 daltons) is 70 times as resistant as are conventional viruses, this high resistance of the two plant viruses is probably because of their small size. The small RNA of PSTV is apparently single-stranded with a circular structure and of such small size that it could code for only about 25 amino acids. Inactivation of scrapie virus by ionizing radiation yields a target size for inactivation equivalent to molecular weight of 150,000 (45). These data, taken with the association of scrapie virus with smooth vesicular membrane during purification and the absence of recognizable virions on electron microscopic study of highly infectious preparations, suggest that the virus is a replicating membrane subunit. It may contain its genetic information in a small nucleic acid moiety incorporated into the plasma membrane. The membrane appears to be the host membrane without altered antigenicity.

1a. Scrapie virus in crude suspensions of mouse brain has been very resistant to UV inactivation at 2540 Å (36,45,46). These three experiments with crude scrapie are in close agreement: NIH (45); Compton A (36); Compton B (45).
Survival ratio is calculated as log C/C_0:

$$\log_{10} \frac{\text{Infectivity titer after irradiation}}{\text{Infectivity titer before irradiation}}$$

Partially purified scrapie (suspension of scrapie mouse brain clarified by two treatments with Genetron in the cold) is somewhat less resistant to UV inactivation, but still much more resistant than other conventional viruses.

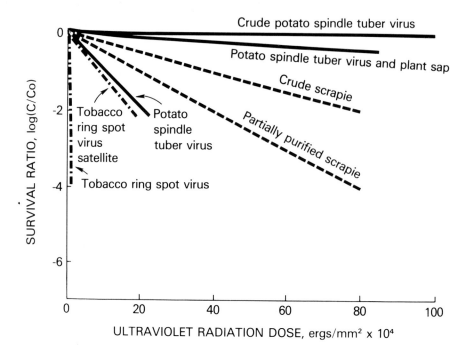

1b. Scrapie inactivation by UV irradiation is compared with that of a conventional plant virus, tobacco ring spot virus, and with the tobacco ring spot virus satellite and potato spindle tuber viroid, both of which contain nucleic acid of molecular weights under 100,000 daltons (7,8). PSTV, as a highly purified nucleic acid, becomes almost totally resistant to UV inactivation (2540 Å) when mixed with clarified normal plant sap, while other viruses placed in this sap are not rendered so resistant. In the crude extract from infected plants the PSTV is almost totally resistant to UV inactivation (7,8). In a second such experiment a different Genetron treated scrapie preparation showed less reduction in UV resistance (45).

UNCONVENTIONAL VIRUSES AS A CAUSE OF THE SUBACUTE SPONGIFORM VIRUS ENCEPHALOPATHIES

Kuru and the transmissible virus dementias have been classified in a group of virus-induced slow infections that we have described as subacute spongiform virus encephalopathies because of the strikingly similar histopathological lesions they induce; and, scrapie and mink encephalopathy appear, both from their histopathology, pathogenesis, and the similarities of their infectious agents, to belong to the same group (Table 1). The basic neurocytological lesion in all of these diseases is a progressive vacuolation in the dendritic and axonal processes and cell bodies of neurons and, to a lesser extent, in astrocytes and oligodendrocytes; an extensive astroglial hypertrophy and proliferation; and, finally, spongiform change or status spongiosus of grey matter (1, 2, 41, 43, 44). These atypical infections differ from other diseases of the human brain which have been subsequently demonstrated to be slow virus infections (Table 2) in that they do not evoke a virus-associated inflammatory response in the brain; they usually show no pleocytosis nor marked rise in protein in the cerebrospinal fluid throughout the course of infection; furthermore, they show

170

no evidence of an immune response to the causative virus and, unlike the situation in the other virus diseases, there are no recognizable virions in electron-microscopic sections of the brain (Table 4).

There are other slow-infections of the central nervous systems which are caused by rumbling nonproductive, even defective, more conventional viruses including measles virus, papovaviruses (JC and SV-40-PML), rubella virus, cytomegalovirus, herpes-simplex virus, adenovirus types 7 and 32, and probably RSSE virus (Table 2). However, unlike these "conventional" viruses the "unconventional" viruses of the spongiform encephalopathies have unusual resistance to ultraviolet radiation and to ionizing radiation (45), to ultrasonication, to heat, proteases and nucleases, and to formaldehyde, β-propiolactone, ethylenediamine tetraacetic acid (EDTA), and sodium desoxycholate (Table 4). They are moderately sensitive to most membrane-disrupting agents such as phenol (90 %), chloroform, ether, urea (6 M), periodate (0.01 M), 2-chloroethanol, alcoholic iodine, acetone, chloroform-butanol, and hypochlorite (0.5—5.0 %) (Table 5). Virions are not recognized on electron microscopic study of infected cells *in vivo* or *in vitro*, nor in highly infectious preparations of virus concentrated by density-gradient banding in the zonal rotor (60). This has led to the speculation that the infectious agents lack a nucleic acid, perhaps are even a self-replicating membrane fragment.

Table 4. Atypical biological properties of the unconventional viruses

1. Long incubation period (months to years; decades)
2. No inflammatory response
3. Chronic progressive pathology (slow infection)
4. No remissions or recoveries: always fatal
5. "Degenerative" histopathology: amyloid plaques, gliosis
6. No visible virion-like structures by electron microscopy
7. No inclusion bodies
8. No interferon production or interference with interferon production by other viruses
9. No interferon sensitivity
10. No virus interference (with over 30 different viruses)
11. No infectious nucleic acid demonstrable
12. No antigenicity
13. No alteration in pathogenesis (incubation period, duration, course) by immuno-suppression or immunopotentiation:
    (a) ACTH, cortisone
    (b) cyclophosphamide
    (c) X-ray
    (d) antilymphocytic serum
    (e) thymectomy/splenectomy
    (f) "nude" athymic mice
    (g) adjuvants
14. Immune "B" cell and "T" cell function intact *in vivo* and *in vitro*
15. No cytopathic effect in infected cells *in vitro*
16. Varying individual susceptibility to high infecting dose in some host species (as with scrapie in sheep)

Table. 5. Methods of inactivating unconventional viruses

1. Autoclaving (121° C at 20 p.s.i.; 30 min.)
2. Hypochlorite ("Clorox"); 0.5—5.0 %
3. Phenol (90 %)
4. Alcoholic iodine solution and organic iodine disinfectants
5. Ether
6. Acetone
7. Chloroform or chloroform-butanol
8. Strong detergents
9. Periodate (0.01 M)
10. 2-chloroethanol
11. Urea (6 M)

A major effort in my laboratory has been and is now being directed toward the molecular biological elucidation of the nature and structure of this group of atypical viruses.

The scrapie virus has been partially purified by fluorocarbon precipitation of proteins and density-gradient banding by zonal rotor ultracentrifugation (60). Other semipurified preparations have been made using ultrafiltration and repeated complete sedimentation and washing of the scrapie virus by means of ultrasonication for resuspension of the virus-containing pellets; such resuspended and washed virus has been banded into peaks of high infectivity using cesium chloride, sucrose, and metrizamide density gradients in the ultracentrifuge by Dr. Paul Brown in my laboratory. Sucrose-saline density-gradient banding of scrapie virus in mouse brains produced wide peaks of scrapie infectivity at densities of 1.14 to 1.23. A second smaller peak of high infectivity at density of 1.26 to 1.28 disappeared on filtration of the crude suspension through 200 nm Nucleopore membranes. On electron microscopic examination, fractions of high infectivity (10^7 to 10^8 LD_{50}/ml) revealed only smooth vesicular membranes with mitochondiral and ribosomal debris and no structures resembling recognizable virions. Lysosomal hydrolases (n-acetyl-β-D-glucosaminidase; β-galactosidase; acid phosphatase) and mitochondrial marker enzyme (INT-succinate reductase) showed most of their activity in fractions of lower density than in the fractions having high scrapie infectivity (60).

We have confirmed the previously noted resistance of scrapie virus to UV inactivation at 254 nm and UV inactivation action spectrum with a six-fold increased sensitivity at 237 nm over that at 254 or 280 nm (45). This should not be taken as proof that no genetic information exists in the scrapie virus as nucleic acid molecules, since work with the smallest RNA viruses, called viroids, indicates a similar resistance to UV inactivation in crude infected plant-sap preparations. Ultraviolet sensitivity also depends greatly on small RNA size, as has been shown by the high resistance of the purified very small tobacco ring spot satellite virus RNA (about 80,000 daltons) (7, 8). Partial purification of scrapie by fluorocarbon only slightly increases UV sensitivity at 254 nm (Figures 1a, 1b) (7, 8, 45). Fluorocarbon-purified scrapie was neither inactivated by RNase A nor III nor by DNase I.

On the other hand, the unconventional viruses possess numerous properties in which they resemble classical viruses, and some of these properties suggest far more complex genetic interaction between virus and host than one might expect for genomes with a molecular weight of only 10^5 daltons (Table 6). They are, moreover, not totally resistant to inactivation nor so dangerous that we cannot work safely with them by using appropriate inactivating agents (Table 5). In spite of very unusual resistance to heat, they are rapidly inactivated by temperatures over 85° C. Autoclaving (120° C/20 psi/45 minutes) completely inactivated scrapie virus in suspensions of mouse brain.

Table 6. Classical virus properties of unconventional viruses

1. Filterable to 25 nm average pore diameter (a.p.d.) (Scrapie, TME); 100 nm a.p.d. (kuru, CJD)
2. Titrate "cleanly" (all individuals succumb to high LD_{50} in most species)
3. Replicate to titers of 10^8/g to 10^{12}/g in brain
4. Eclipse phase
5. Pathogenesis: first replicate in spleen and elsewhere in the reticuloendothelial system, later in brain
6. Specificity of host range
7. "Adaptation" to new host (shortened incubation period)
8. Genetic control of susceptibility in some species (sheep and mice for scrapie)
9. Strains of varying virulence and pathogenicity
10. Clonal (limiting dilution) selection of strains from "wild stock"
11. Interference of slow-growing strain of scrapie with replication of fast-growing strain in mice

CONVENTIONAL VIRUSES CAUSING CHRONIC DISEASE BY DEFECTIVE OR NON-DEFECTIVE REPLICATION

The other chronic diseases of man which have been shown to be slow virus infections are all caused by conventional viruses which in no way tax our imagination (Table 2). They comprise a wide spectrum of chronic and so-called degenerative diseases. Within this group of slow virus infections we find diverse mechanisms of viral replication, various modes of pathogenesis, and different kinds of involvement of the immune system.

In SSPE, the offending measles virus is apparently not present as a fully infectious virion, but instead asynchronous synthesis of virus subunits with defective or incomplete virion assembly occurs; only a portion of the virus genome is expressed, and replication is defective (6, 38, 54, 59). In the case of PML, on the other hand, fully assembled and infectious virus particles are produced (52, 64, 66). In fact, electron microscopically monitored suspensions of the virus particles of the JC papovavirus, density banded from human PML brain, shows that fewer defective particles are being produced than in any known *in vitro* system for cultivating papovaviruses, including the SV-40 virus. Thus, these ordinary viruses are causing slow infections by very different mechanisms. In some cases, as with PML, an immune defect is demonstrated in association with the disease: in this case severe immunosuppression, either from natural primary disease (leukemia, lymphoma, sarcoid, etc.), or an iatrogenic immune suppression, as for renal transplantation or cancer chemotherapy.

The Russian Spring-Summer, or tick-borne encephalitis virus in cases of Kozhevnikov's epilepsy (epilepsia partialis continua) in the Soviet Union, Japan and India, and the rubella virus in adolescents with recrudescence of their congenital rubella infection (60a, 63a) appear also to be proceeding with defective virus replication. In chronic recurrent ECHO virus infection of the central nervous system in children with genetic immune defects, and in subacute brain infection with adenovirus types 7 (47) or 32 (55a), wholly infectious virus, as in the case of PML, seems to be produced.

Kuru and CJD, however, belong to a very different category of virus infections in which no involvement of the immune system has been demonstrable, in which there is no inflammatory response (no pleocytosis in the cerebrospinal fluid and no alteration in CSF protein), and in which the causative virus has defied all conventional attempts at virus taxonomy.

In recent years many other slow virus infections causing chronic diseases in animals have been used as models for various human diseases. Some of these are tabulated in Table 7. In these examples, as for the human diseases, many different mechanisms of virus replication or partial replication are involved in the persistent, latent, chronic, recurrent or slow virus infections. In some of these diseases the host genetic composition is crucial to the type of

Table 7. Slow infections of animals caused by conventional viruses

Disease	Virus
Visna	Retrovirus—Visna
Maedi (Zoegerziekte)	Retrovirus—Maedi
Progressive pneumonia of sheep (PPS; Montana sheep disease)	Retrovirus—PPS-Visna and Maedi related
Motor neurone disease of mice (mouse ALS)	Retrovirus—type "C"
Lymphocytic choriomeningitis	Arenavirus—LCM
Aleutian mink disease	Parvovirus
Hard-pad disease (old-dog distemper)	Paramyxovirus—distemper
Chronic tick-borne encephalitis (RSSE)	Togavirus—RSSE
Pulmonary adenomatosis of sheep (Jaagsiekte)	Unclassified
Mouse cataract disease	Unclassified—mouse cataract virus
Lactic dehydrogenase elevating virus of mice	?Togavirus—LDV
Equine infectious anemia	Unclassified—EIA virus
Rabies	Rhabdovirus—rabies
NZB mouse hemolytic anemia	Retrovirus
Chronic hydrocephalus in hamsters	Paramyxovirus—mumps Orthomyxovirus—influenza
Spontaneous progressive multifocal leukoencephalopathy in rhesus monkeys	Papovavirus—SV-40

pathogenesis that occurs, as is the age of the host at the time of infection, and the immune system may be involved in different ways; immune complex formation is important in some cases and not in others.

The suspicion has been awakened that many other chronic diseases of man may be slow virus infections (see Table 8). Data have gradually accumulated both from the virus laboratory and from epidemiological studies, which suggest that multiple sclerosis and Parkinson's disease, disseminated lupus erythematosis and juvenile diabetes, polymyositis and some forms of chronic arthritis may be slow infections with a masked and possible defective virus as their causes. The study of kuru was carried on simultaneously with a parallel attack on multiple scleroris, amyotrophic lateral sclerosis, and Parkinson's disease; in addition, other degenerative dementias such as Alzheimer's disease, Pick's disease, Huntington's chorea and parkinsonism-dementia were also studied. Chronic encephalitis, epilepsia partialis continua, progressive supranuclear palsy, and degenerative reactions to schizophrenia are among the other diseases under investigation (16, 22, 25, 62). Our attempts at transmission of these diseases to subhuman primate and non-primate laboratory animals have been unsuccessful; no virus has been unmasked from *in vitro* cultivated tissues from the patients, and no virus etiology has been demonstrated for any of these diseases.

Table 8. Chronic diseases of man of suspected slow virus etiology

Multiple Sclerosis	Carcinomatous cerebellar degeneration
Neuromyelitis optica—Devic's syndrome	Tuberous sclerosis
Parkinson's Disease	Ataxia telangiectasia
Amyotrophic Lateral Sclerosis	Progyria
Progressive Supranuclear Palsy	Schizophrenic dementia
Chronic encephalitis with focal epilepsy	Neurofibromatosis
Alzheimer's disease	Disseminated lupus erythematosis
Pick's disease	Chronic arthritis
Huntington's chorea	Dermatomyositis
Parkinsonism-dementia	Scleroderma
Syringomyelia	Ulcerative colitis
Alper's disease	Juvenile diabetes
Polymyositis	Beget's disease
Papulosis atrophicans maligna (Köhlmeier-Degos)	Sjögren's disease

KURU

Kuru is characterized by cerebellar ataxia and a shivering-like tremor that progresses to complete motor incapacity and death in less than one year from onset. It is confined to a number of adjacent valleys in the mountainous interior of New Guinea and occurs in 160 villages with a total population of just over 35,000 (Figures 2—4). *Kuru* means shivering or trembling in the Fore language. In the Fore cultural and linguistic group, among whom over 80 % of the cases occur, it had a yearly incidence rate and prevalence ratio of

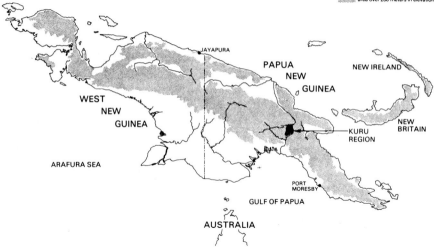

Figure 2. The region in New Guinea from which all kuru patients have come is shown by the irregular black area in the Eastern Highlands Province on the eastern side of the island in Papua New Guinea. It contains more than 35,000 people living in 160 villages (census units) that have experienced kuru. All kuru-affected hamlets lie nestled among rain forest covered mountains from 1,000 to 2,500 m. above sea level.

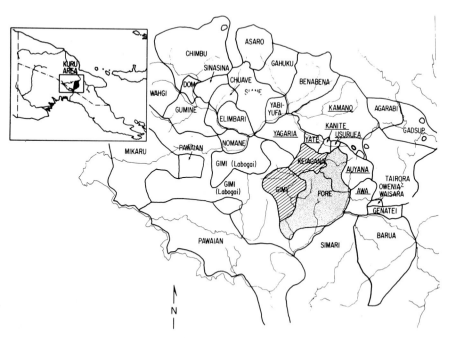

Figure 3. The kuru region in the Eastern Highlands Province of Papua New Guinea showing the cultural and linguistic groups in and surrounding the kuru affected populations.
Inset, upper left: Eastern half of the island of New Guinea showing, in rectangle, area included in the map of larger scale.

176

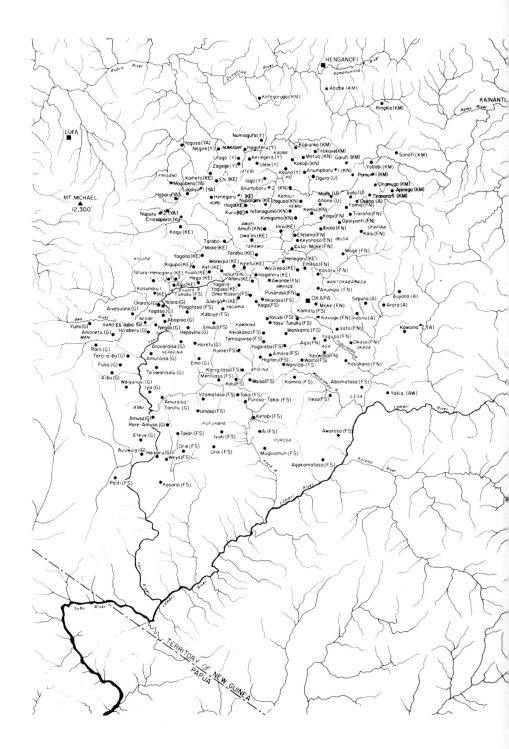

Figure 4. River drainages of the kuru region with superimposed locations of the 160 villages (census units) in which kuru has ever occurred. The cultural and linguistic group of each village is indicated: A Auyana, AW Awa, FN North Fore, FS South Fore, G Gimi, KE Keiagana, KM Kamano, KN Kanite, U Usurufa, Y Yate, YA Yagaria.

about 1 % of the population (Figures 5a, b). During the early years of investigation, after the first description by Gajdusek and Zigas in 1957 (28), it was found to affect all ages beyond infants and toddlers; it was common in male and female children and in adult females, but rare in adult males (Figure 6). This marked excess of deaths of adult females over males has led to a male-to-female ratio of over 3:1 in some villages, and of 2:1 for the whole South Fore group (17, 28, 29, 65).

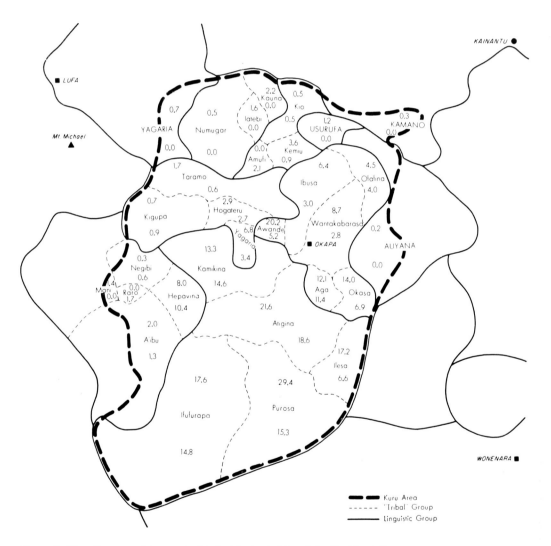

Figure 5. The discovery of kuru coincided with the height of the "epidemic".

5a. Kuru mortality rate in deaths per thousand population per annum in each "tribal" group of the kuru region, 1957—59 and 1961—1963. The numerators of the rates are obtained from the deaths which occurred in the two 3-year periods, the denominators are the populations for 1958 and 1962, respectively. The rates above each name refer to 1957—59, those below to 1961—63.

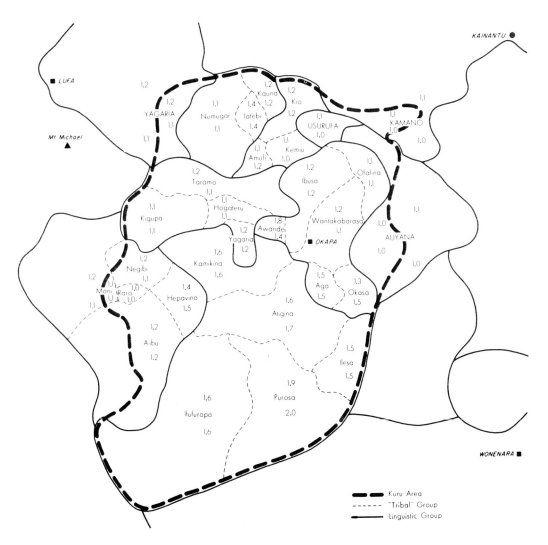

5b. Male: female population ratio in each "tribal" group of the kuru region, 1958 and 1962. The two sets of figures for peripheral groups refer to their portions within and without the kuru region. The ratios above each name refer to 1958, those below to 1962. In these early years of kuru investigation the disease, affecting predominantly females, was causing increasing distortion of the sex ratio.

Kuru has been disappearing gradually during the past 15 years (Figure 7). The incidence of the disease in children has decreased during the past decade, and the disease is no longer seen in either children or adolescents (Figures 8 and 9.) This change in occurrence of kuru appears to result from the cessation of the practice of ritual cannibalism as a rite of mourning and respect for dead kinsmen, with its resulting conjunctival, nasal, and skin contamination with highly infectious brain tissue mostly among women and small children (17).

179

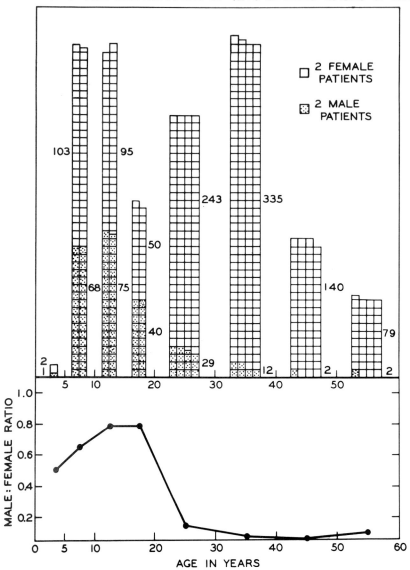

Figure 6. Age and sex distribution of the first 1276 kuru patients studied in the early years of kuru investigations. The youngest patient had onset at 4 years of age, died at 5 years of age.

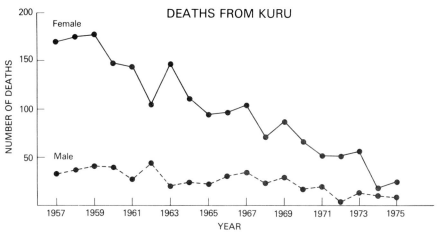

Figure 7. The overall incidence of kuru deaths in male and female patients by year since its discovery in 1957 through 1975. More than 2,500 patients died of kuru in this 17 year period of surveillance, and there has been a slow, irregular decline in the number of patients to one-fifth the number seen in the early years of kuru investigation. The incidence in males has declined significantly only in the last few years, whereas in females it started to decline over a decade earlier. This decline in incidence has occurred during the period of acculturation from a stone age culture in which endocannibalistic consumption of dead kinsmen was practiced as a rite of mourning, to a modern coffee planting society practicing cash economy. Because the brain tissue with which the officiating women contaminated both themselves and all their infants and toddlers contained over 1,000,000 infectious doses per gram, self-inoculation through the eyes, nose, and skin, as well as by mouth, was a certainty whenever a kuru victim was eaten. The decline in incidence of the disease has followed the cessation of cannibalism, which occurred between 1957 and 1962 in various villages.

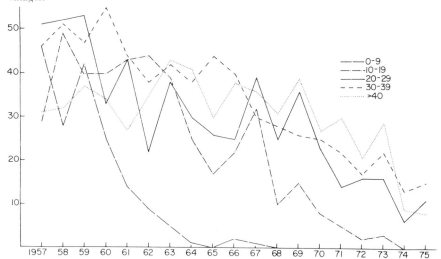

Figure 8. Kuru deaths by age group from 1957 through 1975. The disease has disappeared from the youngest age group (4—9 years) about 5 years before it disappeared in the 10 to 14 year olds, and now it has disappeared in the 15 to 19 year olds. The number of adult patients has declined to less than one-fifth since the early years of investigation. These changes in the pattern of kuru incidence can be explained by the cessation of cannibalism in the late 1950's. No child born since cannibalism ceased in this area has developed the disease.

181

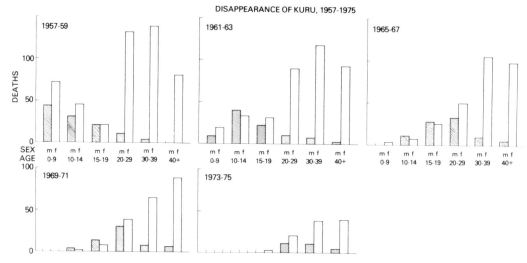

Figure 9. Kuru deaths by age and sex for the years 1957 through 1975 are plotted in 3 year periods, with the exception of those dying in the 1 year intervals between each plot, namely 1960, 1964, 1968, and 1972. These years have been omitted because of irregularities which may have occurred in arbitrarily assigning exact dates of death at the end of the year when dates were not known precisely. The disappearance first in the 4 to 9 year old patients (there were no cases in children under 4 years of age), then in the 10 to 14 year group, and, finally, in the 15 to 19 year group, is clearly shown. No patient under 22 years has died since 1973, and the youngest still-living patient is 24 years old.

The clinical course of kuru is remarkably uniform with cerebellar symptomatology progressing to total incapacitation and death, usually within three to nine months. It starts insidiously without antecedent acute illness and is conveniently divided into three stages: ambulant, sedentary and terminal (Figures 10—15).

For several years all work on the kuru virus was done using chimpanzees, the first species to which the disease was transmitted (Figures 16—18) (22, 25). Eventually, other species of nonhuman primates developed the disease: first, several species of New World monkeys with longer incubation periods than in the chimpanzee; and later, several species of Old World monkeys with yet longer incubation periods (Tables 9 and 10) (23, 32). Very recently, we have transmitted kuru to the mink and ferret, the first nonprimate hosts that have proved to be susceptible, although dozens of other species of laboratory, domestic and wild nonprimate and avian hosts have been inoculated without developing disease after many years of observation. We have now extended the nonprimate host range for the subacute spongiform virus encephalopathies, as shown in Table 11.

The virus has been regularly isolated from the brain tissue of kuru patients. It attains high titers of more than 10^8 infectious doses per gram. In peripheral tissue, namely liver and spleen, it has been found only rarely at the time of death, and in much lower titers. Blood, urine, leukocytes, cerebrospinal fluid, and placenta and embryonal membranes of patients with kuru have not yielded the virus.

Figure 10a. Nine victims of kuru who were assembled one afternoon in 1957 from several villages in the Purosa valley (total population about 600) of the South Fore region. The victims included six adult women, one adolescent girl, one adolescent boy, and a prepubertal boy. All died of their disease within 1 year after this photograph was taken.

10b. Five women and one girl, all victims of kuru, who were still ambulatory, assembled in 1957 in the South Fore village of Pa'iti. The girl shows the spastic strabismus, often transitory, which most children with kuru developed early in the course of the disease. Every patient required support from the others in order to stand without the aid of the sticks they had been asked to discard for the photograph.

Figure 11. Six women with kuru so advanced that they require the use of one or two sticks for support, but are still able to go to garden work on their own. In all cases their disease progressed rapidly to death within less than a year from onset.

12a

12b

12c

Figure 12. Three Fore boys with kuru in 1957; all three were still ambulatory.

12a. The youngest patient with kuru, from Mage village, North Fore, who self-diagnosed the insidious onset of clumsiness in his gait as kuru at 4 years of age, and died at 5 years of age, several years before his mother developed kuru herself.

12b. A South Fore boy from Agakamatasa village, about 8 years of age, who was caught by the camera in an athetoid movement while trying to stand without support, in the early stage of kuru.

12c. A mid-adolescent youth from Anumpa village, North Fore, who demonstrates the difficulty in standing on one foot associated with the early ambulatory stage of kuru.

185

13a

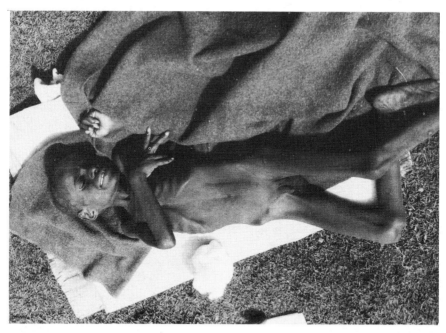

13b

Figure 13. Two Fore children with advanced kuru in 1957. Both had been sedentary for several months and were reaching the terminal stage of the disease.

13a. A girl, about 8 years old, who was no longer able to speak, but who was still alert and intelligent.

13b. A boy, about 8 years of age, who was similary incapacitated after only 3 months of illness.

186

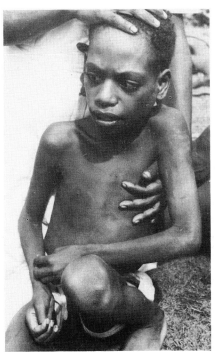

Figure 14. Four preadolescent children, totally incapacitated by kuru in 1957. All had such severe dysarthria that they could no longer communicate by word, but all were still intelligent and alert. All had spastic strabismus. None could stand, sit without support, or even roll over; none had been ill for over six months, and all died within a few months of the time of photography.

15a

15b

15c

Figures 15. Groups of kuru patients in 1957 at the Kuru Research Hospital in Okapa, New Guinea. All died within 1 year of photography. The pictures show many preadolescent child victims of kuru, an age group in which kuru has not occurred in recent years.

15a. Eight kuru patients in the first, or ambulatory, stage of the disease. Five adult women are holding sticks to maintain their balance. Three girls who are still able to walk without the aid of a stick, but with severe ataxia, sit in front of the women.

15b. Eight preadolescent children, four boys and four girls, with kuru. The girl at the far left, in her father's lap, is the same child as that on the left in (a), but is seen 2 months later in the secondary, or sedentary, stage of the disease.

15c. Five children with kuru, two boys in the center, a girl on each side: the adolescent boy supporting the girl on the right is a kuru victim himself, but he is in an earlier stage of the disease. The 4 children requiring support are just passing from the first, or ambulatory, to the second, or sedentary, stage of the disease.

188

Figure 16a. Chimpanzee with a vacant facial expression and a drooping lip, a very early sign of kuru preceding any "hard" neurological signs. Most animals show this sign for weeks or even months before further symptoms of kuru are detectable other than subtle changes in personality.

16b. Three successive views of the face of a chimpanzee with early kuru drawn from cinema frames. Drooping lower lip is an early sign of kuru.

16c. Face of a normal chimpanzee drawn in three successive views from successive cinema views.

189

17a

17b

Figure 17a. Chimpanzee with early experimentally-induced kuru eating from floor without use of prehension. This "vacuum cleaner" form of feeding was a frequent sign in early disease in the chimpanzee when tremor and ataxia were already apparent (*From:* Asher, D. M. et al., In: Nonhuman Primates and Human Diseases, W. Montagna and W. P. McNulty, Jr., eds., Vol. 4, 1973, pp. 43—90).

17b. Range of movement in forelimbs in walking: left, normal chimpanzee; right, chimpanzee in stage 2 of experimental kuru. Quantitative assessment was made by studying individual frames of Research Cinema film (24).

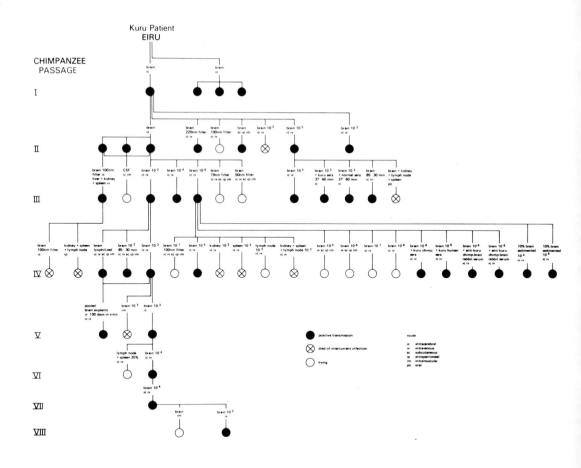

Figure 18. Kuru transmission experiments in chimpanzees, illustrating the early extensive use of this rare and diminishing species and significant curtailment of chimpanzee inoculations after the 4th chimpanzee passage. It was at this time that we discovered that New World monkeys could be used in lieu of the chimpanzee, although they required considerably longer incubation periods. The experiments indicate failure of the agent to pass a 100 nm or smaller filter. They also show the failure of a conventional virus neutralization test, using only 10 infectious doses of kuru virus to neutralize the virus using sera from patients with kuru or from chimpanzees with experimental kuru or antisera made by immunizing rabbits with kuru chimpanzee brain. In these experiments, kidney, spleen and lymph node have not yielded virus, and although chimpanzee brain has had a titer above 10^{-6} by intracerebral inoculation, at 10^{-5} dilutions such brain suspensions inoculated by peripheral routes have not produced disease. In the 3rd passage (on the left), liver, spleen and kidney given intracerebrally, presumably caused disease since 100 nm filtrates of infectious brain have regularly failed to produce the disease; the affected 3rd passage animal had received both inocula.

TRANSMISSIBLE VIRUS DEMENTIAS (CREUTZFELDT-JAKOB DISEASE)

Creutzfeldt-Jacob disease (CJD) is a rare, usually sporadic, presenile dementia found worldwide; it has a familial pattern of inheritance, usually suggestive of autosomal dominant determinations in about 10 % of the cases (Figure 19). The typical clinical picture includes myoclonus, paroxysmal bursts of high voltage slow waves on EEG, and evidence of widespread cerebral dysfunction. The disease is regularly transmissible to chimpanzees (3, 33), New and Old World monkeys (Tables 9 and 10) and the domestic cat (Tables 11 and 12) (23, 32), with pathology in the animal indistinguishable at the cellular level from that in the natural disease or in experimental kuru (Figure 20) (3, 43). We have recently confirmed in our laboratory reports of transmission of CJD from human brain to guinea pigs (48, 48a). In spite of a recent convincing report of transmission of CJD from human brain to mice (5, 5a) we have not yet succeeded in transmitting CJD or kuru to mice.

As we have attempted to define the range of illness caused by the CJD virus, a wide range of clinical syndromes involving dementia in middle and late life have been shown to be such slow virus infections associated with neuronal vacuolation or status spongiosus of gray matter and a reactive astrogliosis.

CJD GENEALOGY CHART

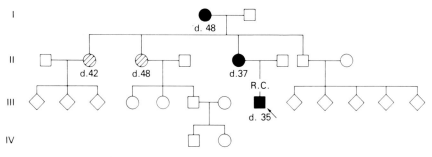

Creutzfeldt-Jakob disease was a rare, almost unknown disease; now cases of transmissible virus dementia are regularly found wherever they are looked for. Better ascertainment of cases, the study of familial aggregations and an unusually high prevalence in Libyan Jews, and the possibility of occupational hazard and transmission through corneal transplant provide promising epidemiological leads to the understanding of the natural history of the disease, and hence to its prevention.

■ Creutzfeldt-Jakob disease confirmed pathologically

▨ Probable Creutzfeldt-Jakob disease

✎ Transmitted to chimpanzee from brain tissue inoculated intracerebrally

Figure 19. Subacute spongiform virus encephalopathy has been transmitted to chimpanzees or New World monkeys from 8 patients with transmissible virus dementias of a familial type. Ten percent of CJD patients have a history of similar disease in kinsmen.

19a. Genealogical chart shows a family with 5 cases of CJD over threee generations, suggesting autosomal dominant inheritance. From patient R. C., the disease has been transmitted to a chimpanzee.

W Family

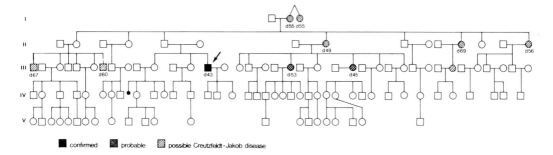

■ confirmed ▨ probable ▨ possible Creutzfeldt-Jakob disease

19b. This family has 11 members suffering from CJD-like disease in three generations. From the brain tissue of patient J. W., obtained at autopsy, the disease has been transmitted to a squirrel monkey.

B FAMILY

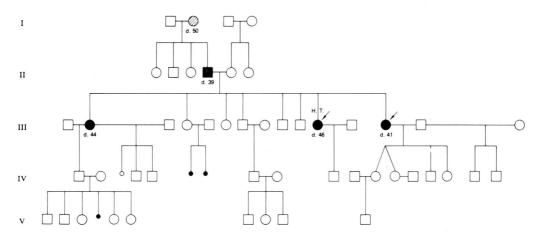

19c. This family has 5 cases of CJD over three generations, again suggesting autosomal dominant inheritance. From the brain tissue of patient H. T., obtained at autopsy, the disease has been transmitted to two squirrel monkeys.

These even include cases that have been correctly diagnosed as brain tumors (glioblastoma, meningioma), brain abscess, Alzheimer's disease, progressive supranuclear palsy, senile dementia, or stroke, or Köhlmeier-Degos disease (27), at some time in their clinical course (51, 62). Hence, the urgent practical problem is to delineate the whole spectrum of subacute and chronic neurological illnesses that are caused by or associated with this established slow virus infection. Because some 14 % of the cases show amyloid plaques akin to those found in kuru, and many show changes similar to those af Alzheimer's disease, in addition to the status spongiosus and astrogliosis of CJD, and because other cases also involve another neurological disease as well as CJD (50, 51, 62), we have started to refer to the transmissible disorder as transmissible virus dementia (TVD).

Since our first transmission of Creutzfeldt-Jakob disease, we have obtained brain biopsy or early postmortem brain tissue on over 200 cases of pathologically confirmed CJD. The clinical, laboratory, and virus investigations of these cases have been summarized in a recent report (62) that extends and updates our earlier report of 35 cases (56). We have been aware of occasional clustering of cases in small population centers, admittedly lacking in natural boundaries, and the unexplained absence of any cases over periods of many years in some large population centers where, at an earlier date, cases were more frequent.

Table 9. Species of laboratory primate susceptible to the subacute spongiform virus encephalopathies

In man	
Kuru	*Apes:* chimpanzee, gibbon
	New World monkeys: capuchin, marmoset, spider, squirrel, woolly
	Old World monkeys: African green, bonnet, cynomolgus macaque, mangabey, rhesus, pig-tailed macaque
Creutzfeldt-Jakob disease	*Apes:* chimpanzee
	New World monkeys: capuchin, marmoset, spider, squirrel, woolly
	Old World monkeys: African green, bushbaby, cynomolgus macaque, mangabey, patas, pig-tailed macaque, rhesus, stump-tailed macaque
In animals	
Scrapie	*New World monkeys:* capuchin, spider, squirrel
	Old World monkeys: cynomolgus macaque, rhesus
Transmissible mink encephalopathy	*New World monkeys:* squirrel
	Old World monkeys: rhesus, stump-tailed macaque

Table 10. Species of laboratory primates susceptible to subacute spongiform encephalopathies

	Incubation periods (in months)			
	Kuru	CJD	Scrapie	TME
Apes				
Chimpanzee (*Pan troglodytes*)	10—82	11—71	(111)	(72+)
Gibbon (*Hylobates lar*)	+(10)	NT	NT	NT
New World monkeys				
Capuchin (*Cebus albifrons*)	10—15	29—34	NT	NT
Capuchin (*Cebus apella*)	11—61	11—47.5	32—35.5	NT
Spider (*Ateles geoffroyi*)	10—85.5	4—50	38	NT
Squirrel (*Saimiri sciureus*)	8—50	5—41	8—63	8—13
Marmoset (*Saguinus sp.*)	1.5—36	18—54	NT	NT
Woolly (*Lagothrix lagothricha*)	33	21	NT	NT
Old World monkeys				
African green (*Cercopithecus aethiops*)	18	33—49.5	(109)	NT
Baboon (*Papia anubis*)	(114)	47.5	NT	NT
Bonnet (*Macaca radiata*)	19—27	(43)	NT	NT
Bushbaby (*Galago senegalensis*)	(104)	16	NT	NT
Cynomolgus macaque (*Macaca fascicularis*)	16	52.5—60	27—72	NT
Patas (*Erythrocebus patas patas*)	(120)	47—60.5	NT	NT
Pig-tailed macaque (*Macaca nemestrina*)	70	+(2)	NT	NT
Rhesus (*Macaca mulatta*)	15—103	43—73	30—37	17—33
Sooty mangabey (*Cercocebus atys*)	+(2)	+(2)—43	NT	NT
Stump-tailed macaque (*Macaca arctoides*)	(120)	60	NT	13
Talapoin (*Cercopithecus talapoin*)	(1+)	64.5	NT	NT

Numbers in parentheses are the number of months elapsed since inoculation, during which the animal remained asymptomatic.

Table 11. Nonprimate hosts for experimental subacute spongiform encephalopathies

In man:	
Kuru	Ferret, mink
Creutzfeldt-Jakob disease	Cat, ferret, guinea pig. ?mouse (5, 5a), hamster (48b)
In animals:	
Scrapie	Gerbil, goat, hamster, mink, mouse, rat, sheep, vole
Transmissible mink encephalopathy	Ferret, goat, hamster, mink, opossum, raccoon, sheep, skunk

Table 12. Creutzfeldt-Jakob disease in cats

Inoculum	Incubation period (months)	Duration (months)
Primary passage		
Human brain	30	2
Serial passage		
Cat brain (passage 1)	19—24	4—5 1/2
Cat brain (passage 2)	18—24	

This geographic and temporal clustering does not apply, however, to a majority of cases and is unexplained by the 10 % of the cases that are familial. Matthews has recently made a similar observation in two clusters in England (50). There are two reports of conjugal disease in which husband and wife died of CJD within a few years of each other (30, 50).

The prevalence of CJD has varied markedly in time and place throughout the United States and Europe, but we have noted a trend toward making the diagnosis more frequently in many neurological clinics in recent years, since attention has been drawn to the syndrome by its transmission to primates (3, 33). For many large population centers of the United States, Europe, Australia, and Asia, we have found a prevalence approaching one per million with an annual incidence and a mortality of about the same magnitude, as the average duration of the disease is 8 to 12 months. Matthews (50) found an annual incidence of 1.3 per million in one of his clusters, which was over 10 times the overall annual incidence for the past decade for England and Wales (0.09 per million). Kahana *et al.* (40) reported the annual incidence of CJD ranging from 0.4 to 1.9 per million in various ethnic groups in Israel. They noted, however, a 30-fold higher incidence of CJD in Jews of Libyan origin above the incidence in Jews of European origin. From recent discussions with our Scandinavian colleagues it is apparent that an annual incidence of at least one per million applies to Sweden and Finland in recent years.

Probable man-to-man transmission of CJD has been reported in a recipient of a corneal graft, which was taken from a donor who was diagnosed retrospectively to have had pathologically confirmed CJD (12). The disease occurred 18 months after the transplant, an incubation period just the average for chimpanzees inoculated with human CJD brain tissue (32, 62). From suspension of brain of the corneal graft recipient we succeeded in transmitting CJD to a chimpanzee although the brain had been at room temperature in 10 % formol-saline for seven months (26a). More recently we learned that two of our confirmed cases of TVD were professional blood donors until shortly before the onset of their symptoms. To date, there have been no transmissions of CJD from blood of either human patients or animals affected with the experimentally transmitted disease. However, we have only transfused two chimpanzees each with more than 300 ml of human whole blood from a different CJD patient

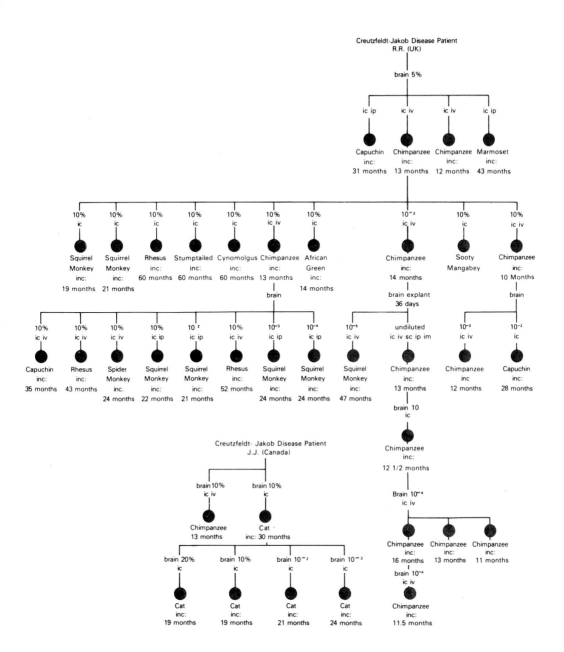

Figure 20. Six serial passages of CJD in chimpanzees, starting with brain tissue from a biopsy of a patient (R. R.) with CJD in the United Kingdom (U. K.). Also shown is transmission of the disease directly from man to the capuchin monkey and marmoset, and from chimpanzee brain to three species of New World monkeys (squirrel, capuchin, spider monkeys), and to six Old World species (rhesus, stumptailed, cynomolgus, African green, pigtailed, and sooty mangabey). Incubation periods in the New World monkeys ranged from 19 to 47 months, and in the Old World monkeys from 43 to 60 months. The pigtailed macaque and the sooty mangabey showed positive CJD pathology when sacrificed without

within the past several months. Finally, the recognition of TVD in a neuro-surgeon (27), and more recently in two physicians, has raised the question of possible occupational infection, particularly in those exposed to infected human brain tissue during surgery, or at postmortem examination (61, 63).

The unexpectedly high incidence of previous craniotomy in CJD patients noted first by Nevin *et al.* (51) and more recently by Matthews (50) and by ourselves (62), raises the possibility of brain surgery either affording a mode of entry for the agent or of precipitating the disease in patients already carrying a latent infection. The former unwelcome possibility now seems to be a reality with the probable transmission of CJD to two young patients with epilepsy from the use of implanted silver electrodes sterilized with 70 % ethanol and formaldehyde vapor after contamination from their use on a patient who had CJD. The patients had undergone such electrode implanta-tion for stereotactic electroencephalographic localization of the epileptic focus at the time of correctional neurosurgery (3a).

Two patients with transmissible virus dementias were not diagnosed clinically or neuropathologically as having CJD, but rather as having Alzheimer's disease (62). In both cases the disease was familial: in one (Figure 21) there were six close family members with the disease in two generations; in the other both the patient's father and sister had died of presenile dementia. The diseases as transmitted to primates were clinically and pathologically typical subacute spongiform virus encephalopathies, and did not have pathological features of Alzheimer's disease in man. More than 30 additional specimens of brain tissue from non-familial Alzheimer's disease have been inoculated into TVD-susceptible primates without producing disease. Therefore, although we

clinical disease. A third passage to the chimpanzee was accomplished using frozen and thawed explanted tissue culture of brain cells that had been growing *in vitro* for 36 days. Using 10^{-3}, 10^{-4}, and 10^{-4} dilutions of brain, respectively, the 4th, 5th, and 6th chimpanzee passages were accomplished. This indicates that the chimpanzee brain contains $\geqslant 50,000$ infectious doses per gram, and that such infectivity is maintained in brain cells cultivated *in vitro* at 37° C for at least one month. The lower left shows transmission of CJD from a second human patient (J. T.) to a cat with a 30 month incubation and serial passage in the cat with 19 to 24 month incubation.

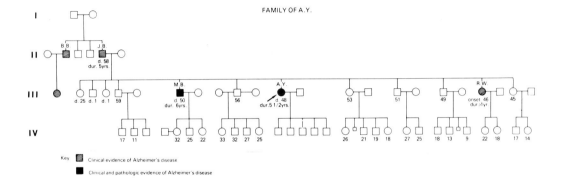

Figure 21a. Y family. Brain tissue obtained from patient A. Y. at biopsy induced subacute spongiform encephalopathy in a squirrel monkey 24 months after intracerebral inoculation. The patient, a 48-year old woman who died after a 68 month course of progressive dementia, quite similar in clinical aspects to the progressive dementia from which her father and brother had died at 54 and 56 years of age, respectively, was diagnosed clinically and neuropathologically as suffering from Alzheimer's disease. Her sister is at present incapacitated by a similar progressive dementia of 4 years' duration. Although the transmitted disease in the squirrel monkey was characterized by severe status spongiosis, none was seen in the patient, although amyloid plaques and neurofibrillary tangles were frequent.

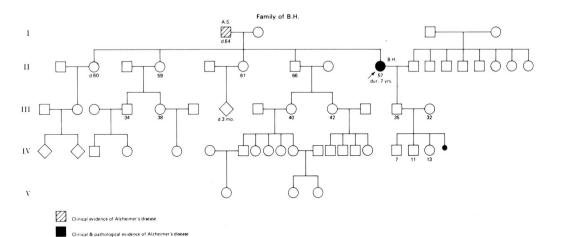

21b. H family. Brain tissue obtained from patient B. H. at surgical biopsy induced subacute spongiform encephalopathy in a squirrel monkey and a capuchin monkey 29 1/2 months and 43 months, respectively, after intracerebral inoculations. The patient, a 57 year old woman, has had slowly progressive dementia and deterioration for the past 7 years. Neuropathological findings revealed abundant neurofibrillary tangles and senile plaques and no evidence of status spongiosis. The patient's father, A. S., had died at age 64 following several years of progressive dementia, behavioral change and memory loss. B. H. is presently alive and institutionalized.

199

cannot claim to have transmitted the classical sporadic Alzheimer's disease to primates, we are confronted with the anomaly that the familial form of Alzheimer's disease has, in these two instances, transmitted as though it were CJD.

The above findings have added impetus to our already extensive studies of Huntington's chorea, Alzheimer's and Pick's diseases, parkinsonism-dementia, senile dementia, and even "dementia praecox", the organic brain disease associated with late uncontrolled schizophrenia.

SCRAPIE

Scrapie is a natural disease of sheep, and occasionally of goats, that has widespread distribution in Europe, America, and Asia. Affected animals show progressive ataxia, wasting, and frequently severe pruritis. The clinical picture and histopathological findings of scrapie closely resemble those of kuru; this permitted Hadlow (35) to suggest that both diseases might have similar etiologies. As early as 1936, Cuillé and Chelle (5b) had transmitted scrapie to the sheep, and its filterable nature and other virus-like properties had been demonstrated two to three decades ago (26). Because scrapie is the only one of the subacute spongiform virus encephalopathies that has been serially transmitted in mice, much more virological information is available about this agent than about the viruses that cause the human diseases.

Although scrapie has been studied longer and more intensely than the other diseases, the mechanism of its spread in nature remains uncertain. It may spread from naturally infected sheep to uninfected sheep and goats, although such lateral transmission has not been observed from experimentally infected sheep or goats. Both sheep and goats, as well as mice, have been experimentally infected by the oral route. It appears to pass from ewes to lambs, even without suckling; the contact of the lamb with the infected ewe at birth appears to be sufficient, because the placenta itself is infectious (39). Transplacental versus oral, nasal, optic, or cutaneous infection in the perinatal period, are unresolved possibilities. Older sheep are infected only after long contact with diseased animals; however, susceptible sheep have developed the disease in pastures previously occupied by scrapied sheep.

Both field studies and experimental work have suggested genetic control of disease occurrence in sheep. In mice, there is evidence of genetic control of length of incubation period and of the anatomic distribution of lesions, which is also dependent on the strain of scrapie agent used. Scrapie has been transmitted in our laboratory to five species of monkeys (Tables 9 and 10) (23, 31, 32), and such transmission has occurred using infected brain from naturally infected sheep and from experimentally infected goats and mice (Figures 22a, b, c). The disease produced is clinically and pathologically indistinguishable from experimental CJD in these species.

200

TRANSMISSION OF U. S. STRAIN (C-506) OF SHEEP SCRAPIE TO MICE AND NON-HUMAN PRIMATES ON PRIMARY AND SERIAL PASSAGE

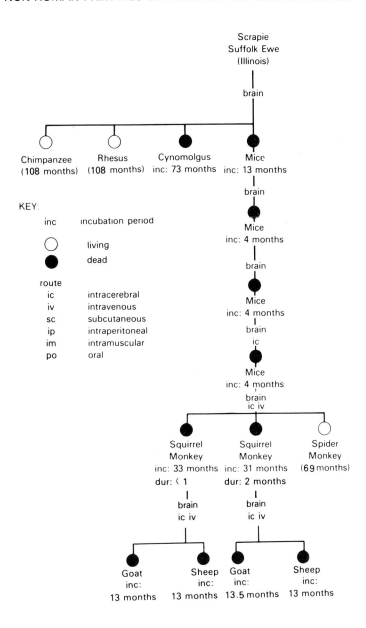

Figure 22. Scrapie has been transmitted to three species of New World monkeys and two species of Old World monkeys (Tables 9, 10).

22a. Transmission of scrapie from the brain of a scrapie-infected Suffolk ewe (C506) in Illinois to a cynomolgus monkey, and from the 4th mouse passage of this strain of scrapie virus to two squirrel monkeys. Incubation period in the cynomolgus was 73 months and in the squirrel monkeys 31 and 33 months. A chimpanzee and a rhesus monkey inoculated 109 months ago with this sheep brain remain well, as does a spider monkey inoculated 70 months ago with brain from the 4th passage of the C506 strain of scrapie in mice.

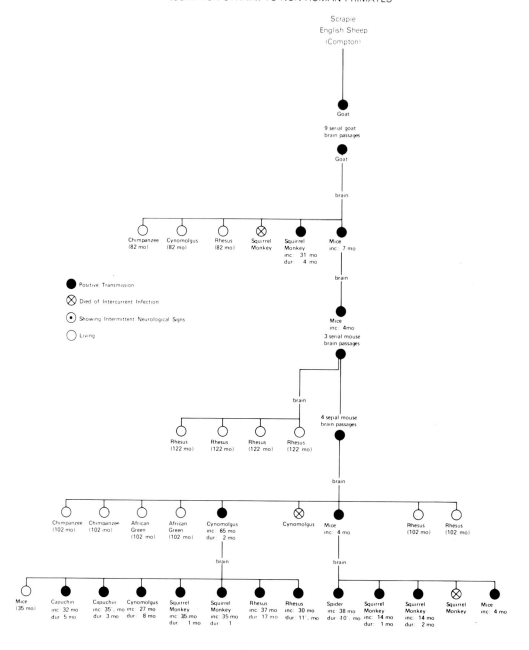

22b. Primary transmission of goat-adapted scrapie (Compton, England strain) to the squirrel monkey and to mice and the transmission of mouse-adapted scrapie to two species of Old World and three species of New World monkeys. Numbers in parentheses are the number of months elapsed since inoculation, during which the animal remained asymptomatic.

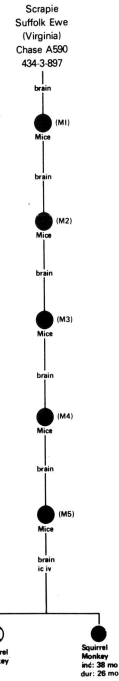

22c. Transmission of mouse-adapted sheep scrapie (U. S. strain 434-3-897) to a squirrel monkey 38 months following intracerebral inoculation with a suspension of scrapie-infected mouse brain containing $10^{7.3}$ infectious units of virus per ml. This animal showed signs of ataxia, tremors and incoordination, and the disease was confirmed histologically. See (b) for an explanation of symbols.

TRANSMISSIBLE MINK ENCEPHALOPATHY

Transmissible mink encephalopathy (TME) is very similar to scrapie both in clinical picture and in pathological lesions. On the ranches on which it developed, the carcasses of scrapie-infected sheep had been fed to the mink; presumably the disease is scrapie. The disease is indistinguishable from that induced in mink by inoculation of sheep or mouse scrapie. Like scrapie, TME has been transmitted by the oral route, but transplacental or perinatal transmission from the mother has not been demonstrated. Physicochemical study of the virus has thus far revealed no differences between TME and the scrapie virus (42, 49).

The disease has been transmitted to the squirrel, rhesus, and stump-tailed monkey (Tables 9 and 10; Figure 13), and to many nonprimate hosts, including the sheep, goat, and ferret, but has not been shown to transmit to mice (Table 11). In monkeys the illness is indistinguishable from experimental CJD in these species.

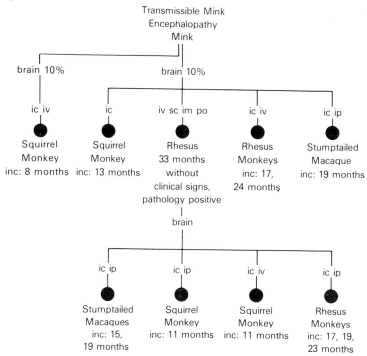

Information from R.F.Marsh, R.J.Eckroade, R.P.Hanson, C.J.Gibbs, and D.C.Gajdusek

Figure 23. Transmissible mink encephalopathy (TME), a rare disease of American ranch mink, is possibly a form of scrapie. The clinical picture and histopathological lesions attendant in the brain, resemble that of scrapie, and scrapie sheep carcasses were fed to mink on ranches on which TME appeared. The disease is transmissible to sheep, goats, certain rodents and New and Old World monkeys. Illustrative data on the primary transmissions of transmissible mink encephalopathy to one species of New World monkey and two species of Old World monkeys, and serial passage of the virus in squirrel, rhesus and stumptailed monkeys are presented in this Figure. Incubation periods are shown in months that elapsed between inoculation and onset of clinical disease. (Figure includes information from our laboratory and from R. F. Marsh, R. J. Eckroade, and R. P. Hanson.)

ORIGIN AND SPREAD OF KURU

Unanswered crucial questions posed by all of these agents are related to their biological origin and mode of survival in nature. The diseases they evoke are not artificial diseases, produced by researchers tampering with cellular macromolecular structures, as some would have it. They are naturally occurring diseases, for none of which do we know the mode of dissemination or maintenance which is adequate to explain their long-term persistence. For kuru we have a full explanation of the unique epidemiological findings and their change over the past two decades: the contamination of close kinsmen within a mourning family group by the opening of the skull of dead victims in a rite of cannibalism, during which all girls, women, babes-in-arms, and toddlers of the kuru victim's family were thoroughly contaminated with the virus (15, 17, 21). The disease is gradually disappearing with the cessation of cannibalism and has already disappeared in children, with progressively increasing age of the youngest victims (Figures 7—9, 24, 26). However, this does not provide us with a satisfactory explanation for the origin of kuru. Was it the unlikely event of a sporadic case of worldwide CJD, which in the unusual cultural setting of New Guinea produced a unique epidemic? We now have the report of a spontaneous case of CJD in a 26 year old native Chimbu New Guinean from the Central Highlands, whose clinical diagnosis was proved by light- and

Figure 24. A Fore mother mourning over the body of her dead daughter, who has just died of kuru. The deep decubitus ulcer below her right hip indicates her chronic debility, which is in contrast to her good nutritional state. Men, and already initiated boys, rarely participated in the mourning rite around the corpse, and even more rarely in the dissection and preparation of the kuru victim's flesh for its ritual endocannibalistic consumption.

Figure 25. All cooking, including that of human flesh from diseased kinsmen, was done in pits with steam made by pouring water over the hot stones, or cooked in bamboo cylinders in the hot ashes. Children participated in both the butchery and the handling of cooked meat, rubbing their soiled hands in their armpits or hair, and elsewhere on their bodies. They rarely or never washed. Infection with the kuru virus was most probably through the cuts and abrasions of the skin, or from nose-picking, eye rubbing, or mucosal injury.

electronmicroscopic examination of a brain biopsy specimen (24, 37a). Serial passage of brain in main in successive cannibalistic rituals might have resulted in a change in the clinical picture of the disease, with modification of the virulence of the original agent.

If such spontaneous CJD is not related to the origin of kuru, another possibility might be that the serial brain passage that occurred in this ritual inoculation of brain from successive victims in multiple sequential passages into their kinsmen yielded a new neurotropic strain of virus from some well-known virus. Finally, in view of what occurs in the defective replication of measles virus in patients with SSPE, we must wonder if a ubiquitous or, at least, a well-known virus may not be modified into a defective, incomplete, or highly integrated or repressed agent *in vivo* in the course of its long masked state in the individual host. Such a new breed of virus may no longer be easily recognizable either antigenically or structurally, because of failure of full synthesis of viral subunits or of their assembly into a known virion. Therefore, we may ask if kuru does not contain some of the subunits of a known agent, modified by its unusual passage history (15, 16, 22).

26a

26b

26c

Figure 26a. An Awa boy just before first stage initiation, while still living in the women's house with his sisters and small pigs. At this age, boys were already well trained in the use of bows and arrows in hunting.

26b. Youthful Awa toxophilite, already a warrior.

26c. Young Awa warriors in their boy's house.

27a

27b

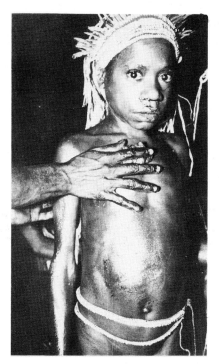

27c

27d

Figure 27. Boys of prepubertal age were removed from the women's houses to enter the *wa'e*, men's house, after elaborate first-stage initiation ceremonies. Thereafter, and for the rest of their lives, they would live, eat, and sleep separately from the women. Married men did not share the houses of their wives, and sexual activity was restricted to daylight in the secluded privacy of the gardens. Three Fore boys are shown in the first stage of initiation in 4 sequences (a—d) during their ceremonial adornment, after having been held in seclusion for several days and having their nasal septa pierced.

27a. Bark strips have been braided into their hair.

27b. Bands of shells of high value to the Fore are fastened to their foreheads.

27c. Their bodies are rubbed with pig grease.

27d. They are given new bark sporans and bows and arrows.

208

CONJECTURAL NATURAL HISTORY OF THE SUBACUTE SPONGI-
FORM VIRUS ENCEPHALOPATHIES: HYPOTHETICAL ORIGIN OF
CREUTZFELDT-JAKOB DISEASE, KURU, AND TRANSMISSIBLE
MINK ENCEPHALOPATHY FROM NATURAL SHEEP SCRAPIE

Scrapie has now been found to cause a disease clinically and neuropathologically indistinguishable from experimental Creutzfeldt-Jakob disease in three
species of New World and two species of Old World monkeys (Tables 9 and 10).
This disease occurs after either intracerebral or peripheral routes of inoculation.
Natural sheep scrapie, as well as experimental goat and mouse scrapie strains
of virus have caused disease in the monkeys. The Compton strain of scrapie
virus, as a result of such passage through primates, develops an altered host
range, for it no longer produces disease in inoculated mice, sheep and goats.
A similar situation has been noted to prevail when scrapie is produced in ferrets
or mink; the mink or ferret brain virus is no longer pathogenic for mice. This
is also true for the virus of natural mink encephalopathy, which, presumably,
had its origin in the feeding of scrapie sheep carcasses to mink on commercial
mink farms.

Creutzfeldt-Jakob disease or kuru viruses may produce, after over two
years of asymptomatic incubation, an acute central nervous disease with death
in a few days in the squirrel monkey; even sudden death without previously
noted clinical disease has been seen. The same strains of kuru or CJD viruses
produce chronic clinical disease in the spider monkey, closely mimicking the
human disease, after incubation periods of two years or more. The time sequence of disease progression also mimics that in man, ranging from several
months to over a year until death. A single strain of kuru or CJD virus may
cause severe status spongiosus lesions in many brain areas, particularly the
cerebral cortex in chimpanzees and spider monkeys with minimal or no
involvement of the brainstem or spinal cord, whereas in the squirrel monkey
this same virus strain may cause extensive brainstem and cord lesions.

From the above findings, it is clear that neither incubation periods nor host
range, nor the distribution or severity of neuropathological lesions, can be
interpreted as having any significance toward unraveling the possible relationships of the four viruses causing the subacute spongiform virus encephalopathies.

As mentioned earlier, we have found that the prevalence of CJD in the
United States and abroad appears to be about one per million whenever
extensive neurological survey for cases is instituted. In a study in Israel, an
overall prevalence in Jews of Libyan origin is 30 times as high as in Jews of
European origin (40). The custom of eating the eyeballs and brains of sheep
in the Jewish households of North African and Middle Eastern origin, as opposed
to Jewish households of European origin, has understandably given rise to the
conjecture that scrapie-infected sheep tissue might be the source of such CJD
infection (37).

Figure 28 presents a conjectural schematic natural history of the subacute
spongiform virus encephalopathies in which the hypothetical origin of CJD,

HYPOTHETICAL ORIGIN OF CREUTZFELDT-JAKOB DISEASE (CJD), KURU, AND TRANSMISSIBLE MINK
ENCEPHALOPATHY (TME) FROM NATURAL SCRAPIE OF SHEEP

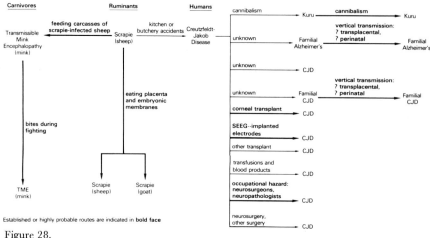

Figure 28.

kuru, and TME from natural scrapie in sheep is proposed with possible routes of transmission indicated. However, such games of armchair speculation provide schemata that cannot yet be tested. They may, nevertheless, have heuristic value. In the absence as yet of proven antigenicity or identified infectious nucleic acid in the agents, neither serological specificity nor nucleic acid homology can be used to answer the compelling question of the relationship between the viruses of kuru, transmissible virus dementia, scrapie, and transmissible mink encephalopathy.

The possibility that the viruses of all four of the subacute spongiform virus encephalopathies are not just closely related agents, but different strains of a single virus which have been modified in different hosts, is easily entertained. The passage of sheep scrapie into other sheep and into goats, at least by the route of feeding of material contaminated with placenta and embryonic membrane (53), and into mink from feeding carcasses of scrapied sheep, are established paths of scrapie transmission. In view of the experimental transmission of scrapie to monkeys, there is serious cause for wonder whether kitchen and butchery accidents involving the contamination of skin and eyes may not be a possible source of CJD in man (36a, 37). We believe that contamination during the cannibalistic ritual was the sole source of transmission of kuru from man to man, and have conjectured above that a spontaneous case of CJD may have given rise to the chain of kuru transmissions (17). The documented case of CJD from corneal transplant (12) suggests that other tissue transplantation may also be a source of infection. It is known that the virus is present in peripheral tissue, as well as in the brain. The case of CJD in a neurosurgeon who had frequently performed autopsies (27), poses a possibility of occupational hazard to the neurosurgeon and neuropathologist (61—63). Finally, the rather frequent report of neurosurgery or other surgery preceding the appearance of CJD, as noted by us (62) and by other workers (50, 51), may indicate that such surgery has been a source of infection, rather than a virus activating incident. This seems to be a real hazard in view of the recent episode of transmission of CJD to two patients from the use of CJD-contaminated electrodes in stereotactic EEG during surgery for epilepsy (3a). The use of formaldehyde for their sterilization was, in view of the resistance of the unconventional viruses to it (26), a very unfortunate choice. The mode of transmission, which at first sight would appear to be vertical in the cases of familial CJD or familial Alzheimer's disease, remains unknown (4, 13, 50, 62). Whether infection is transovarian or occurs in utero or during parturition, or from a milk factor or some other neonatal infection, also remains unknown, although from kuru epidemiological study (i.e., failure to see kuru in children born to kuru-affected mothers since the cessation of cannibalism), we have no evidence for such transmission (17).

PROSPECT

The elucidation of the etiology and epidemiology of a rare, exotic disease restricted to a small population isolate—kuru in New Guinea—has brought us to worldwide considerations that have importance for all of medicine and microbiology. For neurology, specifically, we have considerable new insights into the whole range of presenile dementias and, in particular, to the large problems of Alzheimer's disease and the senile dementias. The implications of vertical transmission of slow virus infections, and of host genetic control of disease expression for all genetic diseases, and the relationship of these slow virus infectious processes to those which may lead to neoplastic transformation, are obvious.

However, the major problems among the degenerative diseases: multiple sclerosis, amyotrophic lateral sclerosis, and parkinsonism remain unsolved, although there are tantalizing laboratory and epidemiological data pointing to the possible role of virus-like agents in these diseases. Perhaps the masked and defective slow infections with conventional viruses such as are seen in PML and SSPE, may provide the best leads for studying these diseases.

The foci of high incidence of amyotrophic lateral sclerosis with associated high incidence of parkinsonism-dementia complex among the Chamorro people on Guam and the Japanese of the Kii Peninsula remain continuing challenges. Our discovery (14) and reevaluation (20) of the very small but very intense focus of such motor neuron disease with associated high incidence of parkinsonism, parkinsonism-dementia, and other peculiar bradykinetic and myoclonic dementia syndromes among the Auyu and Jaqai people in a remote population of West New Guinea, suggests strongly that some common etiological factor may underly the occurrence of all these very different syndromes, as they occur strangely in this one small population and are not found in the much larger surrounding populations.

The models of lysogenicity and of subviral genetically active macromolecular structures from the study of bacterial viruses and bacterial genetics supply ample imaginative framework for an expression of our ideas of possible mechanisms of infectious pathogenesis in man. The unconventional viruses tax even our imagination in relation to molecular biology gained from these studies in bacteria.

For a now-disappearing disease in a small primitive population to have brought us this far is ample reason for pursuing intensively the challenges offered by the still inexplicable high incidence and peculiar profusion of different neurological syndromes, pathologically distinct yet apparently somehow related to each other, which have been discovered in the several small population enclaves (14, 20, 21).

REFERENCES

1. Beck, E., Daniel, P. M., Alpers, M., Gajdusek, D. C., Gibbs, C. J., Jr. and Hassler, R. (1975): Experimental kuru in the spider monkey. Histopathological and ultrastructural studies of the brain during early stages of incubation. Brain 98: 592—620.

2. Beck, E., Daniel, P. M., and Gajdusek, D. C. (1966): A comparison between the neuropathological changes in kuru and scrapie, a system degeneration. In: Proceedings of the Fifth International Congress of Neuropathology, F. Luthy and A. Bischoff, eds., pp. 213—218. Excepta Medica International Congress Series No. 100, Amsterdam.

3. Beck, E., Daniel, P. M., Matthews, W. B., Stevens, D. L., Alpers. M. P., Asher, D. M., Gajdusek, D. C. and Gibbs, C. J., Jr. (1969): Creutzfeldt-Jakob disease: the neuropathology of a transmission experiment. Brain 92: 699—716.

3a. Bernoulli, C., Siegfried, J. Baumgartner, G., Regli, F., Rabinowicz, T., Gajdusek, D. C., and Gibbs, C. J., Jr. (1977): Danger of accidental person-to-person transmission of Creutzfeldt-Jakob disease by surgery. Lancet 1 (8009): 478—479.

4. Bobowick, A., Brody, J. A., Matthews, M. R., Roos, R. and Gajdusek, D. C. (1973): Creutzfeldt-Jakob disease: a case control study. Am. J. Epidemiol 98: 381—394.

5. Brownell, B., Campbell, M. J. and Greenham, L. W. (1975): The experimental transmission of Creutzfeldt-Jakob disease. 51st Annual Meeting, American Association of Neuropathologists, May 30—June 1, New York. Program and Abstracts, #32, p. 46.

5a. Brownell, B., Campbell, M. J., Greenham, L. W. and, Peacock, D. B. (1975): Experimental transmission of Creutzfeldt-Jakob disease. Lancet 2 (7926): 186—187.

5b. Cuillé, J. and Chelle, P.-L. (1936): Pathologie animale la maladie dite tremblante du mouton est-elle inoculable? C. R. Acad. Sci. (D). (Paris) 203: 1552—1554.

6. Dawson, J. R. Jr. (1933): Cellular inclusions in cerebral lesions of lethargic encephalitis. Am. J. Pathol. 9: 7—16.

7. Diener, T. O. (1973): Similarities between the scrapie agent and the agent of potato spindle tuber disease. Ann. Clin. Res. 5: 268—278.

8. Diener, T. O. (1974): Viroids: the smallest known agents of infectious disease. Ann. Rev. Microbiol. 28: 23—29.

9. Diener, T. O. (1976): Towards an understanding of viroid nature and replication. Ann. Microbiol. (Inst. Pasteur) 127A, pp. 7—17.

10. Diener, T. and Hadidi, A. (1977): Viroids. In: Comprehensive Virology, H. Fraenkel-Conrat and R. R. Wagner, eds. Plenum Press, New York. In press.

11. Dubois-Dalcq, M., Rodriguez, M., Reese, T. S., Gibbs, C. J., Jr. and Gajdusek, D. C. (1977): Search for a specific marker in the neural membranes of scrapie mice (a freeze-fracture study). Lab. Invest. 36: 547—553.

12. Duffy, P., Wolf, J., Collins, G., DeVoe, A. G., Steeten, B. and Cowen, D. (1974): Possible person-to-person transmission of Creutzfeldt-Jakob disease. New Engl. J. Med. 299: 692—693.

13. Ferber, R. A., Wiesenfeld, S. L., Roos, R. P., Bobowick, A. R., Gibbs, C. J., Jr. and Gajdusek, D. C. (1974): Familial Creutzfeldt-Jakob disease: transmission of the familial disease to primates. In: Proceedings of the X International Congress of Neurology, A. Subirana, J. M. Espadaler and E. H. Burrows, eds., September 8—15, 1973, Barcelona, pp. 358—380. Excerpta Medica International Congress Series No. 296, Amsterdam.

14. Gajdusek, D. C. (1963): Motor-neuron disease in natives of New Guinea. New Engl. J. Med. 268: 474—476.

15. Gajdusek, D. C. (1972): Spongiform virus encephalopathies. In: Host Virus Reactions with Special Reference to Persistent Agents, G. Dick, ed. J. Clin. Pathol. (Suppl.) 25: 78—83.

16. Gajdusek, D. C. (1973): Kuru and Creutzfeldt-Jakob disease. Experimental models of noninflammatory degenerative slow virus diseases of the central nervous system. Ann. Clin. Res. 5: 254—261.

17. Gajdusek, D. C. (1973): Kuru in the New Guinea Highlands. In: Tropical Neurology, J. D. Spillane, ed., pp. 376—383. Oxford Press, New York.

18. Gajdusek, D. C., ed. (1976): Correspondence on the Discovery and Original Investigations of Kuru. Smadel-Gajdusek Correspondence 1956—1959. National Institutes of Health, Bethesda, Maryland.

19. Gajdusek, D. C. (1977): Urgent opportunistic observations: the study of changing, transient, and disappearing phenomena of medical interest in disrupted primitive human communities. In: Health and Disease in Isolated and Tribal Societies, Julie Whelan, ed. Ciba Foundation Monograph 49 pp. 69—102.

20. Gajdusek, D. C. (1977): Focus of high incidence of motor neuron disease associated with high incidence of Parkinsonism and dementia syndromes in a small population of Awyu New Guineans. New Engl. J. Med. In preparation.

21. Gajdusek, D. C. (1959—1977): Journals 1956—1976, 21 volumes, published in limited edition. National Institutes of Health, Bethesda, Maryland.

22. Gajdusek, D. C. and Gibbs, C. J., Jr. (1973): Subacute and chronic diseases caused by atypical infections with unconventional viruses in aberrant hosts. In: Perspectives in Virology, 8, M. Pollard, ed., pp. 279—311. Academic Press, New York.

23. Gajdusek, D. C. and Gibbs, C. J., Jr. (1975): Familial and sporadic chronic neurological degenerative disorders transmitted from man to primates. In: Primate Models of Neurological Disorders, B. S. Meldrum and C. D. Marsden. eds. Adv. Neurol. 10: 291—317. Raven Press, New York.

24. Gajdusek, D. C. and Gibbs, C. J., Jr. (1975): Slow virus infections of the nervous system and the Laboratories of Slow, Latent and Temperate Virus Infections. In: The Nervous System, D. B. Tower, ed., Vol. 2, The Clinical Neurosciences, T. N. Chase, ed., pp. 113—135.

25. Gajdusek, D. C., Gibbs, C. J., Jr. and Alpers, M. (1966): Experimental transmission of a kuru-like syndrome in chimpanzees. Nature 209: 794—796.

26. Gajdusek, D. C., Gibbs, C. J., Jr. and Alpers, M., eds. (1965): Slow, Latent and Temperate Virus Infections. NINDB Monograph No. 2, National Institutes of Health. PHS Publication No. 1378, U. S. Govt. Printing Office, Washington, D. C., 489 pp.

26a. Gajdusek, D. C., Gibbs, C. J., Jr., Collins, G. and Traub, R. (1976): Survival of Creutzfeldt-Jakob disease virus in formol-fixed brain tissue. New Engl. J. Med. 294: 553.

27. Gajdusek, D. C., Gibbs, C. J., Jr., Earle, K., Dammin, C. J., Schoene, W. and Tyler, H. R. (1974): Transmission of subacute spongiform encephalopathy to the chimpanzee and squirrel monkey from a patient with papulosis atrophicans maligna of Köhlmeier-Degos. In: Proceedings of the X International Congress of Neurology, A. Subirana, J. M. Espadaler and E. H. Burrows, eds., September 8—15, 1973, Barcelona, pp. 390—392. Excerpta Medica International Congress Series No. 319, Amsterdam.

28. Gajdusek, D. C. and Zigas, V. (1957): Degenerative disease of the central nervous system in New Guinea. The endemic occurrence of "kuru" in the native population. New Engl. J. Med. 257: 974—978.

29. Gajdusek, D. C. and Zigas, V. (1959): Kuru: clinical, pathological and epidemiological study of an acute progressive degenerative disease of the central nervous system among natives of the Eastern Highlands of New Guinea. Am. J. Med. 26: 442—469.

30. Garzuly, F., Jellinger, K. and Pilz, P. (1971): Subakute spongiose encephalopathie (Jakob-Creutzfeldt-Syndrom). Klinische-morphologische Analyse von 9 fällen. Arch. Psychiatr. Nervenkr. 214: 207—227.

31. Gibbs, C. J., Jr. and Gajdusek, D. C. (1972): Transmission of scrapie to the cynomolgus monkey (Macaca fascicularis). Nature 236: 73—74.

32. Gibbs, C. J., Jr. and Gajdusek, D. C. (1976): Studies on the viruses of subacute spongiform encephalopathies using primates, their only available indicator. First Inter-American Conference on Conservation and Utilization of American Nonhuman Pri-

mates in Biomedical Research, Lima, Peru, June 2—4. PAHO Scientific Publication No. 317, pp. 83—109. Washington, D. C.

33. Gibbs, C. J., Jr., Gajdusek, D. C., Asher, D. M., Alpers, M. P., Beck, E., Daniel, P. M. and Matthews, W. B. (1968): Creutzfeldt-Jakob disease (subacute spongiform encephalopathy): transmission to the chimpanzee. Science 161: 388—389.

34. Hadidi, A., Jones, D. M., Gillespie, D. H., Wong-Staal, S. and Diener, T. O. (1976): Hybridization of potato spindle tuber viroid to cellular DNA of normal plants. Proc. Nat. Acad. Sci. (USA) 73: 2453—2457.

35. Hadlow, W. J. (1959): Scrapie and kuru. Lancet 2: 289—290.

36. Haig, D. C., Clarke, M. C., Blum, E. and Alper, T. (1969): Further studies on the inactivation of the scrapie agent by ultraviolet light. J. Gen. Virol. 5: 455—457.

36a. Harris, R. A. (1977): A reporter at large: a nice place to live. New Yorker (April 25): 48—91 (citation from page 53).

37. Herzberg, L., Herzberg, B. N., Gibbs, C. J., Jr., Sullivan, W., Amyx, H. and Gajdusek, D. C. (1974): Creutzfeldt-Jakob disease: hypothesis for high incidence in Libyan Jews in Israel. Science 186: 848.

37a. Hornabrook, R. W., and Wagner, F. (1975): Creutzfeldt-Jakob disease. Papua New Guinea Medical Journal 18:226—228.

38. Horta-Barbosa, L., Fuccillo, D. A., London, W. T., Jabbour, J. T., Zeman, W. and Sever, J. L. (1969): Isolation of measles virus from brain cell cultures of two patients with subacute sclerosing panencephalitis. Proc. Soc. Exp. Biol. Med. 132: 272—277.

39. Hunter, G. D., Collis, S. C., Millson, G. C. and Kimberlin, R. H. (1976): Search for scrapie-specific RNA and attempts to detect an infectious DNA or RNA. J. Gen. Virol. 32: 157—162.

40. Kahana, E., Alter, M., Braham, J. and Sofer, D. (1974): Creutzfeldt-Jakob disease: focus among Libyan Jews in Israel. Science 183: 90—91.

41. Klatzo, I., Gajdusek, D. C. and Zigas, V. (1959): Pathology of kuru. Lab. invest. 8: 799—847.

42. Kimberlin, R. H. and Marsh, R. F. (1975): Comparison of scrapie and transmissible mink encephalopathy in hamsters. I. Biochemical studies of brain during development of disease. J. Infect. Dis. 131: 97—103.

43. Lampert, P. W., Gajdusek, D. C. and Gibbs, C. J., Jr. (1972): Subacute spongiform virus encephalopathies. Scrapie, kuru and Creutzfeldt-Jakob disease. Am. J. Pathol. 68: 626—646.

44. Lampert, P., Hooks, J., Gibbs, C. J., Jr. and Gajdusek, D. C. (1971): Altered plasma membranes in experimental scrapie. Acta Neuropathol. (Berlin) 19: 80—93.

45. Latarjet, R., Gajdusek, D. C. and Gibbs, C. J., Jr. (1977): Unusual resistance to UV and ionizing radiation of kuru and scrapie by ionizing radiation. In preparation.

46. Latarjet, R., Muel, B., Haig, D. A., Clarke, M. C. and Alper, T. (1970): Inactivation of the scrapie agent by near-monochromatic ultraviolet light. Nature 227: 1341—1343.

47. Lord, Ann, Sutton, R. N. P. and Corsellis, J. A. N. (1975): Recovery of adenovirus type 7 from human brain cell cultures. J. Neurol. Neurosurg. Psychiat. 38: 710—712.

48. Manuelidis, E. E. (1975): Transmission of Creutzfeldt-Jakob disease from man to the guinea pig. Science 190: 571—572.

48a. Manuelidis, E. E., Kim, J., Angelo, J. N., and Manuelidis, L. (1976): Serial propagation of Creutzfeldt-Jakob disease in guinea pigs. Proc. Nat. Acad. Sci. (USA) 73:223—227.

48b. Manuelidis, E. E., Angelo, J. N., Gorgacz, E. J., and Manuelidis, L. (1977): Transmission of Creutzfeldt-Jakob disease to Syrian hamster. Lancet 1 (8009): 479.

49. Marsh, R. F. and Kimberlin, R. H. (1975): Comparison of scrapie and transmissible mink encephalopathy in hamsters. II. Clinical signs, pathology, and pathogenesis. J. Infect. Dis. 131: 104—110.

50. Matthews, W. B. (1975): Epidemiology of Creutzfeldt-Jakob disease in England and Wales. J. Neurol. Neurosurg. Psychiat. 38: 210—213.

51. Nevin, S., McMenemy, W. H., Behrman, D. and Jones, D. P. (1960): Subacute

spongiform encephalopathy. A subacute form of encephalopathy attributable to vascular dysfunction (spongiform cerebral atrophy). Brain 83: 519—564.

52. Padgett, B. L., ZuRhein, G. M., Walker, D. L., Eckroade, R. J. and Dessel, B. H. (1971): Cultivation of papova-like virus from human brain with progressive multifocal leucoencephalopathy. Lancet 1(7712): 1257—1260.

53. Pattison, I. H., Hoare, M. N., Jebbett, J. N. and Watson, W. A. (1972): Spread of scrapie to sheep and goats by oral dosing with fetal membranes from scrapie affected sheep. Vet. Rec. 99: 465—467.

54. Payne, F. E., Baublis, J. V. and Itabashi, H. H. (1969): Isolation of measles virus from a patient with subacute sclerosing panencephalitis. New Eng. J. Med. 281: 585—589.

55. Randles, J. W., Rillo, E. P. and Diener, T. O. (1976): The viroidlike structure and cellular location of anomalous RNA associated with the Cadang-Cadang disease. Virology 74: 128—129.

55a. Roos, R., Chou, S. M., Rogers, N. G., Basnight, M. and Gajdusek, D. C. (1972): Isolation of an adenovirus 32 strain from human brain in a case of subacute encephalitis. Proc. Soc. Exper. Biol. Med. 139: 73—74.

56. Roos, R., Gajdusek, D. C. and Gibbs, C. J., Jr. (1973): The clinical characteristics of transmissible Creutzfeldt-Jakob disease. Brain 96: 441—462.

57. Semancik, J. S., Marsh, R. F., Geelen, J. L. M. C. and Hanson, R. P. (1977): Properties of the scrapie agent-endomembrane complex from hamster brain. J. Virol. In press.

58. Semancik, J. S. and Vanderwonde, W. J. (1976): Exocortis disease: cytopathic effect on the plasma membrane in association with the pathogenic RNA. Virology 69(2): 719—726.

59. Sever, J. L. and Zeman, W., eds. (1968): Conference on Measles Virus and Subacute Sclerosing Panencephalitis. Neurology 18: 1(Pt. 2), 192 pp.

60. Siakotos, A. N., Bucana, C., Gajdusek, D. C., Gibbs, C. J., Jr. and Traub, R. D. (1976): Partial purification of the scrapie agent from mouse brain by pressure disruption and zonal centrifugation in a sucrose-sodium chloride gradient. Virology 70: 230—237.

60a. Townsend, J. J., Baringer, J. R., Wolinsky, J. S., Malamud, N., Mednick, J. P., Panitch, H. S., Scott, R. A. T., Oshiro, L. S. and Cremer, N. E. (1975): Progressive rubella panencephalitis. Late onset after congenital rubella. New Eng. J. Med. 292: 990—993.

61. Traub, R. D., Gajdusek, D. C. and Gibbs, C. J., Jr. (1974): Precautions in conducting biopsies and autopsies on patients with presenile dementia. J. Neurosurg. 41: 394—395.

62. Traub, R., Gajdusek, D. C. and Gibbs, C. J., Jr. (1977): Transmissible virus dementias. The relation of transmissible spongiform encephalopathy to Creutzfeldt-Jakob disease. In: Aging and Dementia, M. Kinsbourne and L. Smith, eds., pp. 91—146. Spectrum Publishing Inc., Flushing, New York.

63. Traub, R. D., Gajdusek, D. C. and Gibbs, C. J., Jr. (1975): Precautions in autopsies on Creutzfeldt-Jakob disease. Am. J. Clin. Pathol. 64: 417.

63a. Weil, M. L., Itabashi, H. H., Cremer, N. E., Oshiro, L. S., Lennette, E. H. and Carnay, L. (1975): Chronic progressive panencephalitis due to rubella virus simulating subacute sclerosing panencephalitis. New Eng. J. Med. 292: 994—998.

64. Weiner, L. P., Herndon, R. M., Narayan, O., Johnson, R. T., Shah, K., Rubinstein, L. J., Preziosi, T. J. and Conley, F. K. (1972): Isolation of virus related to SV40 from patients with progressive multifocal leucoencephalopathy. New Eng. J. Med. 286: 385—390.

65. Zigas, V. and Gajdusek, D. C. (1957); Kuru: clinical study of a new syndrome resembling paralysis agitans in natives of the Eastern Highlands of Australian New Guinea. Med. J. Australia 2: 745—754.

66. ZuRhein, G. M. and Chou, S. (1968): Papovavirus in progressive multifocal leuko-encephalopathy. In: Infections of the Nervous System, H. M. Zimmerman, editor. Research Publication of the Association for Nervous and Mental Diseases, 44: 254—280. Williams and Wilkins, Baltimore, Maryland.

Saul Bellow

SAUL BELLOW

Saul Bellow was born in Lachine, Quebec, a suburb of Montreal, in 1915, and was raised in Chicago. He attended the University of Chicago, received his Bachelor's degree from Northwestern University in 1937, with honors in sociology and anthropology, did graduate work at the University of Wisconsin, and served in the Merchant Marine during World War II.

Mr. Bellow's first novel, DANGLING MAN, was published in 1944, and his second, THE VICTIM, in 1947. In 1948 he was awarded a Guggenheim Fellowship and spent two years in Paris and traveling in Europe, where he began THE ADVENTURES OF AUGIE MARCH, which won the National Book Award for fiction in 1954. Later books include SEIZE THE DAY (1956) HENDERSON THE RAIN KING (1959), HERZOG (1964), MOSBY'S MEMOIRS AND OTHER STORIES (1968), and MR. SAMMLER'S PLANET (1970). His most recent work of fiction, HUMBOLDT'S GIFT (1975), was awarded the Pulitzer Prize. Both HERZOG and MR. SAMM-LER'S PLANET were awarded the National Book Award for fiction. Mr. Bellow's first non-fiction work, TO JERUSALEM AND BACK: *A Personal Account*, published on October 25, 1976, is his personal and literary record of his sojourn in Israel during several months in 1975.

In 1965 Mr. Bellow was awarded the International Literary Prize for HERZOG, becoming the first American to receive the prize. In January 1968 the Republic of France awarded him the Croix de Chevalier des Arts et Lettres, the highest literary distinction awarded by that nation to non-citizens and in March 1968 he received the B'nai B'rith Jewish Heritage Award for "excellence in Jewish literature", and in November 1976 he is to be awarded the America's Democratic Legacy Award of the Anti-Defamation League of B'nai B'rith, the first time this award has been made to a literary personage.

A playwright as well as a novelist, Saul Bellow is the author of *The Last Analysis* and of three short plays, collectively entitled *Under the Weather*, which were produced on Broadway in 1966. He has contributed fiction to *Partisan Review, Playboy, Harper's Bazaar, The New Yorker, Esquire*, and to literary quarterlies. His criticism has appeared in *The New York Times Book Review, Horizon, Encounter, The New Republic, The New Leader*, and elsewhere. During the 1967 Arab-Israeli conflict, he served as a war correspondent for *Newsday*. He has taught at Bard College, Princeton University, and the University of Minnesota, and is a member of the Committee on Social Thought at the University of Chicago.

Nobel Lecture, December 12, 1976

by SAUL BELLOW
USA

I was a very contrary undergraduate more than 40 years ago. It was my habit to register for a course and then to do most of my reading in another field of study. So that when I should have been grinding away at "Money and Banking" I was reading the novels of Joseph Conrad. I have never had reason to regret this. Perhaps Conrad appealed to me because he was like an American—he was an uprooted Pole sailing exotic seas, speaking French and writing English with extraordinary power and beauty. Nothing could be more natural to me, the child of immigrants who grew up in one of Chicago's immigrant neighborhoods of course!—a Slav who was a British sea captain and knew his way around Marseilles and wrote an Oriental sort of English. But Conrad's *real* life had little oddity in it. His themes were straightforward— fidelity, command, the traditions of the sea, hierarchy, the fragile rules sailors follow when they are struck by a typhoon. He believed in the strength of these fragile-seeming rules, and in his art. His views on art were simply stated in the preface to *The Nigger of the Narcissus*. There he said that art was an attempt to render the highest justice to the visible universe: that it tried to find in that universe, in matter as well as in the facts of life, what was fundamental, enduring, essential. The writer's method of attaining the essential was different from that of the thinker or the scientist. These, said Conrad, knew the world by systematic examination. To begin with the artist had only himself; he descended within himself and in the lonely regions to which he descended he found "the terms of his appeal". He appealed, said Conrad, "to that part of our being which is a gift, not an acquisition, to the capacity for delight and wonder . . . our sense of pity and pain, to the latent feeling of fellowship with all creation—and to the subtle but invincible conviction of solidarity that knits together the loneliness of innumerable hearts . . . which binds together all humanity—the dead to the living and the living to the unborn."

This fervent statement was written some 80 years ago and we may want to take it with a few grains of contemporary salt. I belong to a generation of readers that knew the long list of noble or noble-sounding words, words like "invincible conviction" or "humanity" rejected by writers like Ernest Hemingway. Hemingway spoke for the soliders who fought in the First World War under the inspiration of Woodrow Wilson and other orotund statesmen whose big words had to be measured against the frozen corpses of young men paving the trenches. Hemingway's youthful readers were convinced that the horrors of the 20th century had sicknened and killed humanistic beliefs with their deadly radiations. I told myself therefore that Conrad's rhetoric must be resisted. But I never thought him mistaken. He spoke directly to me. The feeling individual appeared weak—he felt nothing but his own weakness. But if he accepted his weakness and his separateness and descended into himself intensifying his loneliness, he discovered his solidarity with other isolated creatures.

I feel no need now to sprinkle Conrad's sentences with skeptical salt. But there are writers for whom the Conradian novel—all novels of that sort—are gone forever. Finished. There is, for instance, M. Alain Robbe-Grillet, one of the leaders of French literature, a spokesman for "thingism"—*choseisme*. He writes that in great contemporary works, Sartre's *Nausea*, Camus' *The Stranger*, or Kafka's *The Castle*, there are no characters; you find in such books not individuals but—well, entities. "The novel of characters," he says, "belongs entirely in the past. It describes a period: that which marked the apogee of the individual." This is not necessarily an improvement; that Robbe-Grillet admits. But it is the truth. Individuals have been wiped out. "The present period is rather one of administrative numbers. The world's destiny has ceased, for us, to be identified with the rise and fall of certain men of certain families." He goes on to say that in the days of Balzac's bourgeoisie it was important to have a name and a character; character was a weapon in the struggle for survival and success. In that time, "It was something to have a face in a universe where personality represented both the means and the end of all exploration." But our world, he concludes, is more modest. It has renounced the omnipotence of the person. But it is more ambitious as well, "since it looks beyond. The exclusive cult of the 'human' has given way to a larger consciousness, one that is less anthropocentric." However, he comforts us, a new course and the promise of new discoveries lie before us.

On an occasion like this I have no appetite for polemics. We all know what it is to be tired of "characters". Human types have become false and boring. D. H. Lawrence put it early in this century that we human beings, our instincts damaged by Puritanism, no longer care for, were physically repulsive to one another. "The sympathetic heart is broken," he said. He went further, "We stink in each other's nostrils." Besides, in Europe the power of the classics has for centuries been so great that every country has its "identifiable personalities" derived from Moliere, Racine, Dickens or Balzac. An awful phenomenon. Perhaps this is connected with the wonderful French saying, "*S'il y a un caractère, il est mauvais.*" It leads one to think that the unoriginal human race tends to borrow what it needs from convenient sources, much as new cities have often been made out of the rubble of old ones. Then, too, the psychoanalytic conception of character is that it is an ugly rigid formation—something we must resign ourselves to, not a thing we can embrace with joy. Totalitarian ideologies, too, have attacked bourgeois individualism, sometimes identifying character with property. There is a hint of this in M. Robbe-Grillet's argument. Dislike of personality, bad masks, false being has had political results.

But I am interested here in the question of the artist's priorities. Is it necessary, or good, that he should begin with historical analyses, with ideas or systems? Proust speaks in *Time Regained* of a growing preference among young and intelligent readers for works of an elevated analytical, moral or sociological tendency. He says that they prefer to Bergotte (the novelist in *Remembrance of Things Past*) writers who seem to them more profound. "But," says Proust, "from the moment that works of art are judged by reasoning, nothing is stable or certain, one can prove anything one likes."

The message of Robbe-Grillet is not new. It tells us that we must purge ourselves of bourgeois anthropocentrism and do the classy things that our advanced culture requires. Character? "Fifty years of disease, the death notice signed many times over by the serious essayists," says Robbe-Grillet, "yet nothing has managed to knock it off the pedestal on which the 19th century had placed it. It is a mummy now, but one still enthroned with the same—phony—majesty, among the values revered by traditional criticism."

The title of Robbe-Grillet's essay is "On Several Obsolete Notions." I myself am tired of obsolete notions and of mummies of all kinds but I never tire of reading the master novelists. And what is one to do about the characters in their books? Is it necessary to discontinue the investigation of character? Can anything so vivid in them now be utterly dead? Can it be that human beings are at a dead end? Is individuality really so dependent on historical and cultural conditions? Can we accept the account of those conditions we are so "authoritatively" given? I suggest that it is not in the intrinsic interest of human beings but in these ideas and accounts that the problem lies. The staleness, the inadequacy of these repels us. To find the source of trouble we must look into our own heads.

The fact that the death notice of character "has been signed by the most serious essayists" means only that another group of mummies, the most respectable leaders of the intellectual community, has laid down the law. It amuses me that these serious essayists should be allowed to sign the death notices of literary forms. Should art follow culture? Something has gone wrong.

There is no reason why a novelist should not drop "character" if the strategy stimulates him. But it is nonsense to do it on the theoretical ground that the period which marked the apogee of the individual, etc., is ended. We must not make bosses of our intellectuals. And we do them no good by letting them run the arts. Should they, when they read novels, find nothing in them but the endorsement of their own opinions? Are we here on earth to play such games?

Characters, Elizabeth Bowen once said, are not created by writers. They pre-exist and they have to be *found*. If we do not find them, if we fail to represent them, the fault is ours. It must be admitted, however, that finding them is not easy. The condition of human beings has perhaps never been more difficult to define. Those who tell us that we are in an early stage of universal history must be right. We are being lavishly poured together and seem to be experiencing the anguish of new states of consciousness. In America many millions of people have in the last forty years received a "higher education"—in many cases a dubious blessing. In the upheavals of the Sixties we felt for the first time the effects of up-to-date teachings, concepts, sensitivities, the pervasiveness of psychological, pedagogical, political ideas.

Every year we see scores of books and articles which tell the Americans what a state they are in—which make intelligent or simpleminded or extravagant or lurid or demented statements. All reflect the crises we are in while telling us what we must do about them; these analysts are produced by the very disorder and confusion they prescribe for. It is as a writer that I am considering their extreme moral sensitivity, their desire for perfection, their intolerance of the defects of society, the touching, the comical boundlessness of their demands, their anxiety, their irritability, their sensitivity, their tender-mindedness, their goodness, their convulsiveness, the recklessness with which they experiment with drugs and touch-therapies and bombs. The ex-Jesuit Malachi Martin in his book on the Church compares the modern American to Michelangelo's sculpture, *The Captive*. He sees "an unfinished struggle to emerge whole" from a block of matter. The American "captive" is beset in his struggle by "interpretations, admonitions, forewarnings and descriptions of himself by the self-appointed prophets, priests, judges and prefabricators of his travail," says Martin.

Let me take a little time to look more closely at this travail. In private life, disorder or near-panic. In families—for husbands, wives, parents, children— confusion; in civic behavior, in personal loyalties, in sexual practices (I will not recite the whole list; we are tired of hearing it)—further confusion. And with this private disorder goes public bewilderment. In the papers we read what used to amuse us in science fiction—*The New York Times* speaks of death rays and of Russian and American satellites at war in space. In the November *Encounter* so sober and responsible an economist as my colleague, Milton Friedman, declares that Great Britain by its public spending will soon go the way of poor countries like Chile. He is appalled by his own forecast. What — the source of that noble tradition of freedom and democratic rights that began with Magna Carta ending in dictatorship? "It is almost impossible for anyone brought up in that tradition to utter the word that Britain is in danger of losing freedom and democracy; and yet it is a fact!"

It is with these facts that knock us to the ground that we try to live. If I were debating with Professor Friedman I might ask him to take into account the resistance of institutions, the cultural differences between Great Britain and Chile, differences in national character and traditions, but my purpose is not to get into debates I can't win but to direct your attention to the terrible predictions we have to live with, the background of disorder, the visions of ruin.

You would think that one such article would be enough for a single number of a magazine but on another page of *Encounter* Professor Hugh Seton-Watson discusses George Kennan's recent survey of American degeneracy and its dire meaning for the world. Describing America's failure, Kennan speaks of crime, urban decay, drug-addiction, pornography, friviolity, deteriorated educational standards and concludes that our immense power counts for nothing. We cannot lead the world and, undermined by sinfulness, we may not be able to defend ourselves. Professor Seton-Watson writes, "Nothing can defend a society if its upper 100,000 men and women, both the decision-makers and those who help to mould the thinking of the decision-makers, are resolved to capitulate."

So much for the capitalist superpower. Now what about its ideological adversaries? I turn the pages of *Encounter* to a short study by Mr. George Watson, Lecturer in English at Cambridge, on the racialism of the Left. He tells us that Hyndman, the founder of the Social Democratic Federation, called the South African war the Jews' war; that the Webbs at times expressed racialist views (as did Ruskin, Carlyle and T. H. Huxley before them); he relates that Engels denounced the smaller Slav peoples of Eastern Europe as counter-revolutionary ethnic trash; and Mr. Watson in conclusion cites a public statement by Ulrike Meinhof of the West German "Red Army Faction" made at a judicial hearing in 1972 approving of "revolutionary extermination". For her, German anti-semitism of the Hitler period was essentially anti-capitalist. "Auschwitz," she is quoted as saying, "meant that six million Jews were killed and thrown on the waste heap of Europe for what they were: money Jews (Geldjuden)."

I mention these racialists of the Left to show that for us there is no simple choice between the children of light and the children of darkness. Good and evil are not symmetrically distributed along political lines. But I have made my point; we stand open to all anxieties. The decline and fall of everything is our daily dread, we are agitated in private life and tormented by public questions.

And art and literature—what of them? Well, there is a violent uproar but we are not absolutely dominated by it. We are still able to think, to discriminate, and to feel. The purer, subtler, higher activities have not succumbed to fury or to nonsense. Not yet. Books continue to be written and read. It may be more difficult to reach the whirling mind of a modern reader but it is possible to cut through the noise and reach the quiet zone. In the quiet zone we may find that he is devoutly waiting for us. When complications increase, the desire for essentials increases too. The unending cycle of crises that began with the First World War has formed a kind of person, one who has lived through terrible, strange things, and in whom there is an observable shrinkage of prejudices, a casting off of disappointing ideologies, an ability to live with many kinds of madness, an immense desire for certain durable human goods—truth, for instance, or freedom, or wisdom. I don't think I am exaggerating; there is plenty of evidence for this. Disintegration? Well, yes. Much is disintegrating but we are experiencing also an odd kind of refining process. And this has been going on for a long time. Looking into Proust's *Time Regained* I find that he was clearly aware of it. His novel, describing French society during the Great War, tests the strength of his art. Without art, he insists, shirking no personal or collective horrors, we do not know ourselves or anyone else. Only art penetrates what pride, passion, intelligence and habit erect on all sides—the seeming realities of this world. There is another reality, the genuine one, which we lose sight of. This other reality is always sending us hints, which, without art, we can't receive. Proust calls these hints our "true impressions." The true impressions, our persistent intuitions, will, without art, be hidden from us and we will be left with nothing but a "terminology for practical ends which we falsely call life." Tolstoi put the matter in much the same way. A book like his *Ivan Ilyitch* also describes these same "practical ends" which

224

conceal both life and death from us. In his final sufferings Ivan Ilyitch becomes an individual, a "character", by tearing down the concealments, by seeing through the "practical ends."

Proust was still able to keep a balance between art and destruction, insisting that art was a necessity of life, a great independent reality, a magical power. But for a long time art has not been connected, as it was in the past, with the main enterprise. The historian Edgar Wind tells us in *Art and Anarchy* that Hegel long ago observed that art no longer engaged the central energies of man. These energies were now engaged by science—a "relentless spirit of rational inquiry." Art had moved to the margins. There it formed "a wide and splendidly varied horizon." In an age of science people still painted and wrote poetry but, said Hegel; however splendid the gods looked in modern works of art and whatever dignity and perfection we might find "in the images of God the Father and the Virgin Mary" it was of no use: we no longer bent our knees. It is a long time since the knees were bent in piety. Ingenuity, daring exploration, freshness of invention replaced the art of "direct relevance." The most significant achievement of this pure art, in Hegel's view, was that, freed from its former responsibilities, it was no longer "serious." Instead it raised the soul through the "serenity of form above any painful involvement in the limitations of reality." I don't know who would make such a claim today for an art that raises the soul above painful involvements with reality. Nor am I sure that at this moment, it is the spirit of rational inquiry in pure science that engages the central energies of man. The center seems (temporarily perhaps) to be filled up with the crises I have been describing.

There were European writers in the 19th century who would not give up the connection of literature with the main human enterprise. The very suggestion would have shocked Tolstoi and Dostoevski. But in the West a separation between great artists and the general public took place. They developed a marked contempt for the average reader and the bourgeois mass. The best of them saw clearly enough what sort of civilization Europe had produced, brilliant but unstable, vulnerable, fated to be overtaken by catastrophe, the historian Erich Auerbach tells us. Some of these writers, he says, produced "strange and vaguely terrifying works, or shocked the public by paradoxical and extreme opinions. Many of them took no trouble to facilitate the understanding of what they wrote—whether out of contempt for the public, the cult of their own inspiration, or a certain tragic weakness which prevented them from being at once simple and true."

In the 20th century theirs is still the main influence, for despite a show of radicalism and innovation our contemporaries are really very conservative. They follow their 19th century leaders and hold to the old standard, interpreting history and society much as they were interpreted in the last century. What would writers do today if it would occur to them that literature might once again engage those "central energies", if they were to recognize that an immense desire had arisen for a return from the periphery, for what was simple and true?

Of course we can't come back to the center simply because we want to; but the fact that we are wanted might matter to us and the force of the crisis is so great that it may summon us back to such a center. But prescriptions are futile. One can't tell writers what to do. The imagination must find its own path. But one can fervently wish that they—that we—would come back from the periphery. We do not, we writers, represent mankind adquately. What account do Americans give of themselves, what accounts of them are given by psychologists, sociologists, historians, journalists, and writers? In a kind of contractual daylight they see themselves in the ways with which we are so desperately familiar. These images of contractual daylight, so boring to Robbe-Grillet and to me, originate in the contemporary world view: We put into our books the consumer, civil servant, football fan, lover, television viewer. And in the contractual daylight version their life is a kind of death. There is another life coming from an insistent sense of what we are which denies these daylight formulations and the false life—the death in life—they make for us. For it is false, and we know it, and our secret and incoherent resistance to it cannot stop, for that resistance arises from persistent intuitions. Perhaps humankind cannot bear too much reality, but neither can it bear too much unreality, too much abuse of the truth.

We do not think well of ourselves; we do not think amply about what we are. Our collective achievements have so greatly "exceeded" us that we "justify" ourselves by pointing to them. It is the jet plane in which we commonplace human beings have crossed the Atlantic in four hours that embodies such value as we can claim. Then we hear that this is closing time in the gardens of the West, that the end of our capitalist civilization is at hand. Some years ago Cyril Connolly wrote that we were about to undergo "a complete mutation, not merely to be defined as the collapse of the capitalist system, but such a sea-change in the nature of reality as could not have been envisaged by Karl Marx or Sigmund Freud." This means that we are not yet sufficiently shrunken; we must prepare to be smaller still. I am not sure whether this should be called intellectual analysis or analysis by an intellectual. The disasters are disasters. It would be worse than stupid to call them victories as some statesmen have tried to do. But I am drawing attention to the fact that there is in the intellectual community a sizable inventory of attitudes that have become respectable— notions about society, human nature, class, politics, sex, about mind, about the physical universe, the evolution of life. Few writers, ever among the best, have taken the trouble to re-examine these attitudes or orthodoxies. Such attitudes only glow more powerfully in Joyce or D. H. Lawrence than in the books of lesser men; they are everywhere and no one challenges them seriously. Since the Twenties, how many novelists have taken a second look at D. H. Lawrence, or argued a different view of sexual potency or the effects of industrial civilization on the instincts? Literature has for nearly a century used the same stock of ideas, myths, strategies. "The most serious essayists of the last fifty years," says Robbe-Grillet. Yes, indeed. Essay after essay, book after book, confirm the most serious thoughts—Baudelairian, Nietzschean, Marxian, Psychoanalytic, etcetera, etcetera—of these most serious essayists. What Robbe-Grillet says about character can be said also about these ideas, maintaining all the usual things about mass society, dehumanization and the rest. How weary we are of them. How poorly they represent us. The pictures they offer no more resemble us than we resemble the reconstructed reptiles and other monsters in a museum of paleontology. We are much more limber, versatile, better articulated, there is much more to us, we all feel it.

What is at the center now? At the moment, neither art nor science but mankind determining, in confusion and obscurity, whether it will endure or go under. The whole species—everybody—has gotten into the act. At such a time it is essential to lighten ourselves, to dump encumbrances, including the encumbrances of education and all organized platitudes, to make judgments of our own, to perform acts of our own. Conrad was right to appeal to that part of our being which is a gift. We must hunt for that under the wreckage of many systems. The failure of those systems may bring a blessed and necessary release from formulations, from an over-defined and misleading consciousness. With increasing frequency I dismiss as merely respectable opinions I have long held—or thought I held—and try to discern what I have really lived by, and what others live by. As for Hegel's art freed from "seriousness" and glowing on the margins, raising the soul above painful involvement in the limitations of reality through the serenity of form, that can exist nowhere now, during this struggle for survival. However, it is not as though the people who engaged in this struggle had only a rudimentary humanity, without culture, and knew nothing of art. Our very vices, our mutilations, show how rich we are in thought and culture. How much we know. How much we even feel. The struggle that convulses us makes us want to simplify, to reconsider, to eliminate the tragic weakness which prevented writers—and readers—from being at once simple and true.

Writers are greatly respected. The intelligent public is wonderfully patient with them, continues to read them and endures disappointment after disappointment, waiting to hear from art what it does not hear from theology, philosophy, social theory, and what it cannot hear from pure science. Out of the struggle at the center has come an immense, painful longing for a broader, more flexible, fuller, more coherent, more comprehensive account of what we human beings are, who we are, and what this life is for. At the center mankind struggles with collective powers for its freedom, the individual struggles with dehumanization for the possession of his soul. If writers do not come again into the center it will not be because the center is pre-empted. It is not. They are free to enter. If they so wish.

The essence of our real condition, the complexity, the confusion, the pain of it is shown to us in glimpses, in what Proust and Tolstoi thought of as "true impressions". This essence reveals, and then conceals itself. When it goes away it leaves us again in doubt. But we never seem to lose our connection with the depths from which these glimpses come. The sense of our real powers, powers we seem to derive from the universe itself, also comes and goes. We are reluctant to talk about this because there is nothing we can prove, because our language is inadequate and because few people are willing to risk talking about it. They would have to say, "There is a spirit" and that is taboo. So almost

227

everyone keeps quiet about it, although almost everyone is aware of it.

The value of literature lies in these intermittent "true impressions". A novel moves back and forth between the world of objects, of actions, of appearances, and that other world from which these "true impressions" come and which moves us to believe that the good we hang onto so tenaciously—in the face of evil, so obstinately—is no illusion.

No one who has spent years in the writing of novels can be unaware of this. The novel can't be compared to the epic, or to the monuments of poetic drama. But it is the best we can do just now. It is a sort of latter-day lean-to, a hovel in which the spirit takes shelter. A novel is balanced between a few true impressions and the multitude of false ones that make up most of what we call life. It tells us that for every human being there is a diversity of existences, that the single existence is itself an illusion in part, that these many existences signify something, tend to something, fulfill something; it promises us meaning, harmony and even justice. What Conrad said was true, art attempts to find in the universe, in matter as well as in the facts of life, what is fundamental, enduring, essential.

LE PRIX
EN MÉMOIRE
D'ALFRED NOBEL

EN 1976

INSTITUTION

Lors de son tricentenaire en 1968, LA BANQUE DE SUÈDE fit une donation à la FONDATION NOBEL pour décerner, par l'intermédiaire de L'ACADÉMIE ROYALE DES SCIENCES, un *Prix de sciences économiques en mémoire d'Alfred Nobel.*

Les statuts de la distribution du prix sont, mutatis mutandis, les mêmes que pour les Prix Nobel. La remise du prix doit avoir lieu à la cérémonie Nobel le 10 décembre en même temps que celle des Prix Nobel.

Le montant du prix correspond à celui du Prix Nobel de l'année. Un diplôme particulier ainsi qu'une médaille d'or sont remis à cette occasion.

En 1976, le Comité chargé de préparer les affaires était composé des membres suivants:

MM. E. Lundberg, professeur de sciences économiques, *président du Comité;* H. WOLD, professeur de statistique; A. LINDBECK, professeur de sciences économiques et bancaires; S. CARLSON, professeur de gestion des entreprises; *secrétaire du Comité:* M. R. BENTZEL, professeur de sciences économiques.

ATTRIBUTION DU PRIX

L'ACADÉMIE ROYALE DES SCIENCES
a décidé, le 14 octobre 1976, d'attribuer le Prix de sciences économiques institué en mémoire d'Alfred Nobel à

MILTON FRIEDMAN
de l'Université de Chicago, Illinois, États-Unis

pour sa contribution à l'analyse de la consommation, à l'histoire et à la théorie monétaires ainsi que ses éclaircissements sur la complexité de la politique de stabilisation.

Le nombre de propositions statutaires de candidatures s'est monté à 37.

LES INSIGNES ET LE MONTANT DU PRIX

Les lauréats ont reçu un *diplôme*, une *médaille* et un *document* indiquant le montant du prix.

Le montant du prix en mémoire d'Alfred Nobel comme celui des Prix Nobel s'élève à 681 000 couronnes suédoises.

Le diplôme au lauréat de sciences économiques en mémoire d'Alfred Nobel, M. M. Friedman, est exécuté par l'artiste peintre suédois M. Tage Hedqvist.

Commentaires aux images du diplôme :

Milton Friedman
Le motif s'inspire de la recherche accomplie par le lauréat dans le domaine de l'histoire monétaire, et du lien intemporel qui existe entre la monnaie et le commerce.

Milton Friedman

THE PRIZE FOR ECONOMIC SCIENCE, IN MEMORY OF ALFRED NOBEL

Speech by Professor ERIK LUNDBERG of the Royal Academy of Sciences
Translation from the Swedish text

Your Majesties, Your Royal Highnesses, Ladies and Gentlemen,

To a considerable extent, economists are concerned with questions of economic policy; how and why governments, in their efforts to solve crises, constantly create new complications inside and between countries. For the analysis and interpretation of all the different lines of development, demands are made on the methodology and model construction of the economist. Unfortunately the social sciences—despite high ambitions—can never reach the hoped for exactitude. The enormous capabilities of people and governments to create new complications, new contradictions and conflicts, are inexhaustible and go far above and beyond the economists' powers to bring order into the system.

This year's prize-winner in Economics is *Milton Friedman*. His research is in fact aimed precisely at bringing about clarity and system in our economic thoughts in a whole range of areas, which, apart from economic policy, includes economic history, economic theory and methodological questions.

Perhaps Friedman's most characteristic feature is his unique propensity and ability to effectively influence and disturb current notions and previously established knowledge. One can claim that without Friedman's provocative contribution in a series of areas, the development of economic research would have been different, or, possibly only later taken its present course. Friedman's ability to influence the course of research and debate on economic policy reminds one to some extent of Keynes. Against a background of effective, often powerfully simplified, criticism of current doctrines, Friedman has presented a different point of view, an alternative theory, most often with the support of empirical analysis.

Friedman's name is primarily associated with the renaissance of the idea of the importance of money in the explanation of inflation and the concomitant revived understanding of, and belief in, the possibilities of monetary policy. Through him we have acquired the slogan "money matters" or even "only money matters" in connection with the appearance of monetarism as a Chicago School. This marked emphasis on the role of money should be seen in the light of how economists—often successors to Keynes—over a long period of time almost totally neglected money and monetary policy in the analysis of the course of business cycles and inflation. From the beginning of the 1950s Friedman has pioneered a justified reaction against the earlier post-Keynesian bias. The intensive debate around Friedman's theories and theses also brought about a reconsideration of the monetary policies of the central banks—primarily in the U.S.A. and West Germany. It is rare indeed that an economist has gained such direct and indirect influence as Friedman has, not only on the course of scientific research, but also on actual policies.

Friedman's studies on lags in all types of economic policies should be recognized as one of his most fruitful contributions. It is Friedman who coined the expressions observation-, decision- and effect-lags as terms for previously rather neglected but fundamental difficulties in obtaining a correct timing for stabilization policies during the course of business cycles. Friedman has shown how the long and varying lags pertaining to changes in the supply of money, can work in a destabilizing way. His intensively discussed economic-political conclusions drawn from these observations are that monetary policy should be simplified and be less ambitious implying the goal of keeping a stable long-term rate of development for money supply. During recent years this point of view has been accepted, to some extent, by some leading central banks.

Friedman has left his mark on yet another area of the scientific debate on the causes of inflation. This concerns the course of diffusion of wage and price rises. Friedman was the first to show that the prevalent assumption of a simple "trade-off" between unemployment and the rate of inflation only held temporarily as a transient phenomenon; in the long run (more than five years) there is no such "trade-off". According to Friedman's theory, a level of unemployment which is held below a structural equilibrium level leads to a cumulative rate of price and wage increase, primarily because of the destabilizing role that expectations play. Presentday formulations of wage and price determination are, in important respects, built on Friedman's hypotheses about the importance of inflationary expectations.

A large part of Friedman's conclusions about the possibilities of economic policy is based on his liberal belief in the positive, built-in properties of a functioning market economy. Out of this derives his negative view of the ability of governmental authorities to intervene in market mechanisms, through financial and regulatory policies to reach full employment or prevent too large imports. But it is not only a question of philosophical and liberal-political belief. On several points Friedman has made stringent analyses of how a competitive market system works. At the beginning of the 1950s Friedman was the pioneer among proposers of a new order for the international currency system based on free exchange rates. He studied the problem theoretically but also looked for empirical evidence in order to judge how such a system would function. As a matter of fact, Friedman was one of the first to perceive—and to explain—why the Bretton Woods system, with relatively fixed exchange rates, must sooner or later break down.

From a purely scientific viewpoint, one of Friedman's most important contributions is his reshaping of consumption theory with the help of the hypotheses about "the permanent income", in place of current annual income, as a decisive factor in determining total consumption expenditure. Here an extremely fruitful distinction is made between households' temporary income and more permanent income; Friedman shows that a substantially larger part of the former income is saved than of the latter. Friedman has carefully tested this theory on comprehensive statistical material and gained interesting results. Friedman's version of the consumption function has had a lasting effect both on theory and on empirical research.

The large work "A Monetary History of the United States 1867—1960" should be seen as one of Friedman's most solid and at the same time pioneering contributions. Here Friedman has collaborated with an economic historian. The detailed analysis of the comprehensive historical-statistical material to a large extent bears Friedman's stamp. It is seldom that one experiences, as one does in this work, such a fine combination of a detailed historical account over the whole range of developmental phases, institutional changes, the multitude of personal contributions made by leading politicians and bankers, critical evaluation of the source material as well as a perspicacious and balanced economic analysis of the complicated material in question. Perhaps one notices especially his imaginative and energetically accomplished investigation of the strategic role played by the policy of the Federal Reserve System in setting off the 1929 crisis and in deepening and prolonging the following depression.

Professor Milton Friedman is awarded the 1976 Nobel Memorial Prize in Economics for his contribution to consumption analysis and to monetary history and theory, including his observations of the complexity of stabilization policy.

Professor Friedman,
On behalf of the Royal Academy of Sciences I ask you to receive your prize from the hands of His Majesty the King.

CONFÉRENCE

LE LAURÉAT
NOTICE BIOGRAPHIQUE

MILTON FRIEDMAN

I was born July 31, 1912, in Brooklyn, N.Y., the fourth and last child and first son of Sarah Ethel (Landau) and Jeno Saul Friedman. My parents were born in Carpatho-Ruthenia (then a province of Austria-Hungary; later, part of inter-war Czechoslovakia, and, currently, of the Soviet Union). They emigrated to the U.S. in their teens, meeting in New York. When I was a year old, my parents moved to Rahway, N.J., a small town about 20 miles from New York City. There, my mother ran a small retail "dry goods" store, while my father engaged in a succession of mostly unsuccessful "jobbing" ventures. The family income was small and highly uncertain; financial crisis was a constant companion. Yet there was always enough to eat, and the family atmosphere was warm and supportive.

Along with my sisters, I attended public elementary and secondary schools, graduating from Rahway High School in 1928, just before my 16th birthday. My father died during my senior year in high school, leaving my mother plus two older sisters to support the family. Nonetheless, it was taken for granted that I would attend college, though, also, that I would have to finance myself.

I was awarded a competitive scholarship to Rutgers University (then a relatively small and predominantly private university receiving limited financial assistance from the State of New Jersey, mostly in the form of such scholarship awards). I was graduated from Rutgers in 1932, financing the rest of my college expenses by the usual mixture of waiting on tables, clerking in a retail store, occasional entrepreneurial ventures, and summer earnings. Initially, I specialized in mathematics, intending to become an actuary, and went so far as to take actuarial examinations, passing several but also failing several. Shortly, however, I became interested in economics, and eventually ended with the equivalent of a major in both fields.

In economics, I had the good fortune to be exposed to two remarkable men: Arthur F. Burns, then teaching at Rutgers while completing his doctoral dissertation for Columbia; and Homer Jones, teaching between spells of graduate work at the University of Chicago. Arthur Burns shaped my understanding of economic research, introduced me to the highest scientific standards, and became a guiding influence on my subsequent career. Homer Jones introduced me to rigorous economic theory, made economics exciting and relevant, and encouraged me to go on to graduate work. On his recommendation, the Chicago economics department offered me a tuition shcolarship. As it happened, I was also offered a scholarship by Brown University in applied mathematics, but by that time I had definitely transferred my primary allegiance to economics. Arthur Burns and Homer Jones remain today among my closest and most valued friends.

Though 1932—33, my first year at Chicago, was financially my most difficult year, intellectually it opened new worlds. Jacob Viner, Frank Knight, Henry Schultz, Lloyd Mints, Henry Simons and, equally important, a brilliant group of graduate students from all over the world exposed me to a cosmopolitan and vibrant intellectual atmosphere of a kind that I had never dreamed existed. I have never recovered.

Personally, the most important event of that year was meeting a shy, withdrawn, lovely, and extremely bright fellow economics student, Rose Director. We were married six years later, when our depression fears of where our livelihood would come from had been dissipated, and, in the words of the fairy tale, have lived happily ever after. Rose has been an active partner in all my professional work since that time.

Thanks to Henry Schultz' friendship with Harold Hotelling, I was offered an attractive fellowship at Columbia for the next year. The year at Columbia widened my horizons still further. Harold Hotelling did for mathematical statistics what Jacob Viner had done for economic theory: revealed it to be an integrated logical whole, not a set of cook-book recipes. He also introduced me to rigorous mathematical economics. Wesley C. Mitchell, John M. Clark and others exposed me to an institutional and empirical approach and a view of economic theory that differed sharply from the Chicago view. Here, too, an exceptional group of fellow students were the most effective teachers.

After the year at Columbia, I returned to Chicago, spending a year as research assistant to Henry Schultz, who was then completing his classic, *The Theory and Measurement of Demand*. Equally important, I formed a lifelong friendship with two fellow students, George J. Stigler and W. Allen Wallis.

Allen went first to New Deal Washington. Largely through his efforts, I followed in the summer of 1935, working at the National Resources Committee on the design of a large consumer budget study then under way. This was one of the two principal components of my later *Theory of the Consumption Function*.

The other came from my next job—at the National Bureau of Economic Research, where I went in the fall of 1937 to assist Simon Kuznets in his studies of professional income. The end result was our jointly published *Incomes from Independent Professional Practice*, which also served as my doctoral dissertation at Columbia. That book was finished by 1940, but its publication was delayed until after the War because of controversy among some Bureau directors about our conclusion that the medical profession's monopoly powers had raised substantially the incomes of physicians relative to that of dentists. More important scientifically, that book introduced the concepts of permanent and transitory income.

The catalyst in combining my earlier consumption work with the income analysis in Professional Incomes into the permanent income hypothesis was a series of fireside conversations at our summer cottage in New Hampshire with my wife and two of our friends, Dorothy S. Brady and Margaret Reid, all of whom were at the time working on consumption.

I spent 1941 to 1943 at the U.S. Treasury Department, working on wartime tax policy, and 1943—45 at Columbia University in a group headed by Harold Hotelling and W. Allen Wallis, working as a mathematical statistician on problems of weapon design, military tactics, and metallurgical experiments. My capacity as a mathematical statistician undoubtedly reached its zenith on V. E. Day, 1945.

In 1945, I joined George Stigler at the University of Minnesota, from which he had been on leave. After one year there, I accepted on offer from the University of Chicago to teach economic theory, a position opened up by Jacob Viner's departure for Princeton. Chicago has been my intellectual home ever since. At about the same time, Arthur Burns, then director of research at the National Bureau, persuaded me to rejoin the Bureau's staff and take responsibility for their study of the role of money in the business cycle.

The combination of Chicago and the Bureau has been highly productive. At Chicago, I established a Workshop in Money and Banking, which has enabled our monetary studies to be a cumulative body of work to which many have contributed, rather than a one-man project. I have been fortunate in its participants, who include, I am proud to say, a large fraction of all the leading contributors to the revival in monetary studies that has been such a striking development in our science in the past two decades. At the Bureau, I was supported by Anna J. Schwartz, who brought an economic historian's skill, and an incredible capacity for painstaking attention to detail, to supplement my theoretical propensities. Our work on monetary history and statistics has been enriched and supplemented by both the empirical studies and the theoretical developments that have grown out of the Chicago Workshop.

In the fall of 1950, I spent a quarter in Paris as a consultant to the U.S. governmental agency administering the Marshall Plan. My major assignment was to study the Schuman plan, the precursor of the common market. This was the origin of my interest in floating exchange rates, since I concluded that a common market would inevitably founder without floating exchange rates. My essay, "The Case for Flexible Exchange Rates", was one product.

During the academic year 1953—54, I was a Fulbright visiting professor at Gonville & Caius College, Cambridge University. Because my liberal policy views were "extreme" by any Cambridge standards, I was acceptable to, and able greatly to profit from, both groups into which Cambridge economics was tragically and very deeply divided: D. H. Robertson and the "anti-Keynesians"; Joan Robinson, Richard Kahn and the Keynesian majority.

Beginning in the early 1960's, I was increasingly drawn into the public arena, serving in 1964 as an economic adviser to Senator Goldwater in his unsuccessful quest for the presidency and, in 1968, as one of a committee of economic advisers during Richard Nixon's successful quest. In 1966, I began to write a triweekly column on current affairs for Newsweek magazine, alternating with Paul Samuelson and Henry Wallich. However, these public activities have remained a minor avocation—I have consistently refused offers of full-time positions in Washington. My primary interest continues to be my scientific work.

In 1977, I retire from active teaching at the University of Chicago, though retaining a link with the Department and its research activities. Thereafter, I shall continue to spend spring and summer months at our second home in Vermont, where I have ready access to the library at Dartmouth College—and autumn and winter months as a Senior Research Fellow at the Hoover Institution of Stanford University.

INFLATION AND UNEMPLOYMENT

Nobel Memorial Lecture, December 13, 1976
by MILTON FRIEDMAN
The University of Chicago, Illinois, USA

When the Bank of Sweden established the prize for Economic Science in memory of Alfred Nobel (1968), there doubtless was—as there doubtless still remains—widespread skepticism among both scientists and the broader public about the appropriateness of treating economics as parallel to physics, chemistry, and medicine. These are regarded as "exact sciences" in which objective, cumulative, definitive knowledge is possible. Economics, and its fellow social sciences, are regarded more nearly as branches of philosophy than of science properly defined, enmeshed with values at the outset because they deal with human behavior. Do not the social sciences, in which scholars are analyzing the behavior of themselves and their fellow men, who are in turn observing and reacting to what the scholars say, require fundamentally different methods of investigation than the physical and biological sciences? Should they not be judged by different criteria?

1. SOCIAL AND NATURAL SCIENCES

I have never myself accepted this view. I believe that it reflects a misunderstanding not so much of the character and possibilities of social science as of the character and possibilities of natural science. In both, there is no "certain" substantive knowledge; only tentative hypotheses that can never be "proved", but can only fail to be rejected, hypotheses in which we may have more or less confidence, depending on such features as the breadth of experience they encompass relative to their own complexity and relative to alternative hypotheses, and the number of occasions on which they have escaped possible rejection. In both social and natural sciences, the body of positive knowledge grows by the failure of a tentative hypothesis to predict phenomena the hypothesis professes to explain; by the patching up of that hypothesis until someone suggests a new hypothesis that more elegantly or simply embodies the troublesome phenomena, and so on ad infinitum. In both, experiment is sometimes possible, sometimes not (witness meteorology). In both, no experiment is ever completely controlled, and experience often offers evidence that is the equivalent of controlled experiment. In both, there is no way to have a self-contained closed system or to avoid interaction between the observer and the observed. The Gödel theorem in mathematics, the Heisenberg uncertainty principle in physics, the self-fulfilling or self-defeating prophecy in the social sciences all exemplify these limitations.

Of course, the different sciences deal with different subject matter, have different bodies of evidence to draw on (for example, introspection is a more important source of evidence for social than for natural sciences), find different techniques of analysis most useful, and have achieved differential success in predicting the phenomena they are studying. But such differences are as great among, say, physics, biology, medicine, and meteorology as between any of them and economics.

Even the difficult problem of separating value judgments from scientific judgments is not unique to the social sciences. I well recall a dinner at a Cambridge University college when I was sitting between a fellow economist and R. A. Fisher, the great mathematical statistician and geneticist. My fellow economist told me about a student he had been tutoring on labor economics, who, in connection with an analysis of the effect of trade unions, remarked, "Well surely, Mr. X (another economist of a different political persuasion) would not agree with that." My colleague regarded this experience as a terrible indictment of economics because it illustrated the impossibility of a value-free positive economic science. I turned to Sir Ronald and asked whether such an experience was indeed unique to social science. His answer was an impassioned "no", and he proceeded to tell one story after another about how accurately he could infer views in genetics from political views.

One of my great teachers, Wesley C. Mitchell, impressed on me the basic reason why scholars have every incentive to pursue a value-free science, whatever their values and however strongly they may wish to spread and promote them. In order to recommend a course of action to achieve an objective, we must first know whether that course of action will in fact promote the objective. Positive scientific knowledge that enables us to predict the consequences of a possible course of action is clearly a prerequisite for the normative judgment whether that course of action is desirable. The Road to Hell is paved with good intentions, precisely because of the neglect of this rather obvious point.

This point is particularly important in economics. Many countries around the world are today experiencing socially destructive inflation, abnormally high unemployment, misuse of economic resources, and, in some cases, the suppression of human freedom not because evil men deliberately sought to achieve these results, nor because of differences in values among their citizens, but because of erroneous judgments about the consequences of government measures: errors that at least in principle are capable of being corrected by the progress of positive economic science.

Rather than pursue these ideas in the abstract [I have discussed the methodological issues more fully in (1)], I shall illustrate the positive scientific character of economics by discussing a particular economic issue that has been a major concern of the economics profession throughout the postwar period; namely, the relation between inflation and unemployment. This issue is an admirable illustration because it has been a controversial political issue throughout the period, yet the drastic change that has occurred in accepted professional views was produced primarily by the scientific response to experience that contradicted a tentatively accepted hypothesis—precisely the classical process for the revision of a scientific hypothesis.

I cannot give here an exhaustive survey of the work that has been done on this issue or of the evidence that has led to the revision of the hypothesis. I shall be able only to skim the surface in the hope of conveying the flavor of that work and that evidence and of indicating the major items requiring further investigation.

Professional controversy about the relation between inflation and unemployment has been intertwined with controversy about the relative role of monetary, fiscal, and other factors in influencing aggregate demand. One issue deals with how a change in aggregate nominal demand, however produced, works itself out through changes in employment and price levels; the other, with the factors accounting for the changes in aggregate nominal demand.

The two issues are closely related. The effects of a change in aggregate nominal demand on employment and price levels may not be independent of the source of the change, and conversely the effect of monetary, fiscal, or other forces on aggregate nominal demand may depend on how employment and price levels react. A full analysis will clearly have to treat the two issues jointly. Yet there is a considerable measure of independence between them. To a first approximation, the effects on employment and price levels may depend only on the magnitude of the change in aggregate nominal demand, not on its source. On both issues, professional opinion today is very different than it was just after World War II because experience contradicted tentatively accepted hypotheses. Either issue could therefore serve to illustrate my main thesis. I have chosen to deal with only one in order to keep this lecture within reasonable bounds. I have chosen to make that one the relation between inflation and unemployment, because recent experience leaves me less satisfied with the adequacy of my earlier work on that issue than with the adequacy of my earlier work on the forces producing changes in aggregate nominal demand.

2. STAGE 1: NEGATIVELY SLOPING PHILLIPS CURVE

Professional analysis of the relation between inflation and unemployment has gone through two stages since the end of World War II and is now entering a third. The first stage was the acceptance of a hypothesis associated with the

Figure 1. Simple Phillips Curve

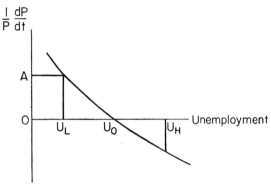

name of A. W. Phillips that there is a stable negative relation between the level of unemployment and the rate of change of wages—high levels of unemployment being accompanied by falling wages, low levels of unemployment by rising wages (24). The wage change in turn was linked to price change by allowing for the secular increase in productivity and treating the excess of price over wage cost as given by a roughly constant mark-up factor.

Figure 1 illustrates this hypothesis, where I have followed the standard practice of relating unemployment directly to price change, short-circuiting the intermediate step through wages.

This relation was widely interpreted as a causal relation that offered a stable trade-off to policy makers. They could choose a low unemployment target, such as U_L. In that case they would have to accept an inflation rate of A. There would remain the problem of choosing the measures (monetary, fiscal, perhaps other) that would produce the level of aggregate nominal demand required to achieve U_L, but if that were done, there need be no concern about maintaining that combination of unemployment and inflation. Alternatively, the policy makers could choose a low inflation rate or even deflation as their target. In that case they would have to reconcile themselves to higher unemployment: U_O for zero inflation, U_H for deflation.

Economists then busied themselves with trying to extract the relation depicted in Figure 1 from evidence for different countries and periods, to eliminate the effect of extraneous disturbances, to clarify the relation between wage change and price change, and so on. In addition, they explored social gains and losses from inflation on the one hand and unemployment on the other, in order to facilitate the choice of the "right" trade-off.

Unfortunately for this hypothesis, additional evidence failed to conform with it. Empirical estimates of the Phillips curve relation were unsatisfactory. More important, the inflation rate that appeared to be consistent with a specified level of unemployment did not remain fixed: in the circumstances of the post-World War II period, when governments everywhere were seeking to promote "full employment", it tended in any one country to rise over time and to vary sharply among countries. Looked at the other way, rates of inflation that had earlier been associated with low levels of unemployment were experienced along with high levels of unemployment. The phenomenon of simultaneous high inflation and high unemployment increasingly forced itself on public and professional notice, receiving the unlovely label of "stagflation".

Some of us were sceptical from the outset about the validity of a stable Phillips curve, primarily on theoretical rather than empirical grounds [(2), (3), (4)]. What mattered for employment, we argued, was not wages in dollars or pounds or kronor but real wages—what the wages would buy in goods and services. Low unemployment would, indeed, mean pressure for a higher real wage—but real wages could be higher even if nominal wages were lower, provided that prices were still lower. Similarly, high unemployment would, indeed, mean pressure for a lower real wage—but real wages could be lower, even if nominal wages were higher, provided prices were still higher.

There is no need to assume a stable Phillips curve in order to explain the apparent tendency for an acceleration of inflation to reduce unemployment. That can be explained by the impact of *unanticipated* changes in nominal demand on markets characterized by (implicit or explicit) long-term commitments with respect to both capital and labor. Long-term labor commitments can be explained by the cost of acquiring information by employers about employees and by employees about alternative employment opportunities plus the specific human capital that makes an employee's value to a particular employer grow over time and exceed his value to other potential employers.

Only surprises matter. If everyone anticipated that prices would rise at, say, 20 percent a year, then this anticipation would be embodied in future wage (and other) contracts, real wages would then behave precisely as they would if everyone anticipated no price rise, and there would be no reason for the 20 percent rate of inflation to be associated with a different level of unemployment than a zero rate. An unanticipated change is very different, especially in the presence of long-term commitments—themselves partly a result of the imperfect knowledge whose effect they enhance and spread over time. Long-term commitments mean, first, that there is not instantaneous market clearing (as in markets for perishable foods) but only a lagged adjustment of both prices and quantity to changes in demand or supply (as in the house-rental market); second, that commitments entered into depend not only on current observable prices, but also on the prices expected to prevail throughout the term of the commitment.

3. STAGE 2: NATURAL RATE HYPOTHESIS

Proceeding along these lines, we [in particular, E. S. Phelps and myself (4), (22), (23)] developed an alternative hypothesis that distinguished between the short-run and long-run effects of unanticipated changes in aggregate nominal demand. Start from some initial stable position and let there be, for example, an unanticipated acceleration of aggregate nominal demand. This will come to each producer as an unexpectedly favorable demand for his product. In an environment in which changes are always occurring in the relative demand for different goods, he will not know whether this change is special to him or pervasive. It will be rational for him to interpret it as at least partly special and to react to it, by seeking to produce more to sell at what he now perceives to be a higher than expected market price for future output. He will be willing to pay higher nominal wages than he had been willing to pay before in order to attract additional workers. The real wage that matters to him is the wage in terms of the price of his product, and he perceives that price as higher than before. A higher nominal wage can therefore mean a lower *real* wage as perceived by him.

To workers, the situation is different: what matters to them is the purchasing power of wages not over the particular good they produce but over all goods in general. Both they and their employers are likely to adjust more slowly their perception of prices in general—because it is more costly to acquire information about that—than their perception of the price of the particular good they

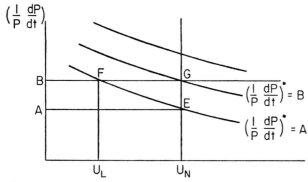

Figure 2. Expectations-adjusted Phillips Curve

produce. As a result, a rise in nominal wages may be perceived by workers as a rise in real wages and hence call forth an increased supply, at the same time that it is perceived by employers as a fall in real wages and hence calls forth an increased offer of jobs. Expressed in terms of the average of perceived future prices, real wages are lower; in terms of the perceived future average price, real wages are higher.

But this situation is temporary: let the higher rate of growth of aggregate nominal demand and of prices continue, and perceptions will adjust to reality. When they do, the initial effect will disappear, and then even be reversed for a time as workers and employers find themselves locked into inappropriate contracts. Ultimately, employment will be back at the level that prevailed before the assumed unanticipated acceleration in aggregate nominal demand.

This alternative hypothesis is depicted in Figure 2. Each negatively sloping curve is a Phillips curve like that in Figure 1 except that it is for a particular anticipated or perceived rate of inflation, defined as the perceived average rate of price change, *not* the average of perceived rates of individual price change (the order of the curves would be reversed for the second concept). Start from point E and let the rate of inflation for whatever reason move from A to B and stay there. Unemployment would initially decline to U_L at point F, moving along the curve defined for an anticipated rate of inflation $\left(\dfrac{1}{P}\dfrac{dP}{dt}\right)^{*}$ of A. As anticipations adjusted, the short-run curve would move upward, ultimately to the curve defined for an anticipated inflation rate of B. Concurrently unemployment would move gradually over from F to G. [For a fuller discussion, see (5).]

This analysis is, of course, oversimplified. It supposes a single unanticipated change, whereas, of course, there is a continuing stream of unanticipated changes; it does not deal explicitly with lags, or with overshooting; or with the process of formation of anticipations. But it does highlight the key points: what matters is not inflation per se, but unanticipated inflation; there is no stable trade-off between inflation and unemployment; there is a "natural rate of unemployment" (U_N), which is consistent with the real forces and with accurate perceptions; unemployment can be kept below that level only by an accelerating inflation; or above it, only by accelerating deflation.

The "natural rate of unemployment", a term I introduced to parallel Knut Wicksell's "natural rate of interest", is not a numerical constant but depends on "real" as opposed to monetary factors—the effectiveness of the labor market, the extent of competition or monopoly, the barriers or encouragements to working in various occupations, and so on.

For example, the natural rate has clearly been rising in the United States for two major reasons. First, women, teenagers, and part-time workers have been constituting a growing fraction of the labor force. These groups are more mobile in employment than other workers, entering and leaving the labor market, shifting more frequently between jobs. As a result, they tend to experience higher average rates of unemployment. Second, unemployment insurance and other forms of assistance to unemployed persons have been made available to more categories of workers, and have become more generous in duration and amount. Workers who lose their jobs are under less pressure to look for other work, will tend to wait longer in the hope, generally fulfilled, of being recalled to their former employment, and can be more selective in the alternatives they consider. Further, the availability of unemployment insurance makes it more attractive to enter the labor force in the first place, and so may itself have stimulated the growth that has occurred in the labor force as a percentage of the population and also its changing composition.

The determinants of the natural rate of unemployment deserve much fuller analysis for both the United States and other countries. So also do the meaning of the recorded unemployment figures and the relation between the recorded figures and the natural rate. These issues are all of the utmost importance for public policy. However, they are side issues for my present limited purpose.

The connection between the state of employment and the level of efficiency or productivity of an economy is another topic that is of fundamental importance for public policy but is a side issue for my present purpose. There is a tendency to take it for granted that a high level of recorded unemployment is evidence of inefficient use of resources and conversely. This view is seriously in error. A low level of unemployment may be a sign of a forced-draft economy that is using its resources inefficiently and is inducing workers to sacrifice leisure for goods that they value less highly than the leisure under the mistaken belief that their real wages will be higher than they prove to be. Or a low natural rate of unemployment may reflect institutional arrangements that inhibit change. A highly static rigid economy may have a fixed place for everyone whereas a dynamic, highly progressive economy, which offers everchanging opportunities and fosters flexibility, may have a high natural rate of unemployment. To illustrate how the same rate may correspond to very different conditions: both Japan and the United Kingdom had low average rates of unemployment from, say, 1950 to 1970, but Japan experienced rapid growth, the U.K., stagnation.

The "natural-rate" or "accelerationist" or "expectations-adjusted Phillips curve" hypothesis—as it has been variously designated—is by now widely accepted by economists, though by no means universally. A few still cling to the original Phillips curve; more recognize the difference between short-run and long-run curves but regard even the long-run curve as negatively sloped, though more steeply so than the short-run curves; some substitute a stable relation between the acceleration of inflation and unemployment for a stable relation between inflation and unemployment—aware of but not concerned about the possibility that the same logic that drove them to a second derivative will drive them to ever higher derivatives.

Much current economic research is devoted to exploring various aspects of this second stage—the dynamics of the process, the formation of expectations, and the kind of systematic policy, if any, that can have a predictable effect on real magnitudes. We can expect rapid progress on these issues. (Special mention should be made of the work on "rational expectations", especially the seminal contributions of John Muth, Robert Lucas, and Thomas Sargent.) [Gordon (9).]

4. STAGE 3: A POSITIVELY SLOPED PHILLIPS CURVE?

Although the second stage is far from having been fully explored, let alone fully absorbed into the economic literature, the course of events is already producing a move to a third stage. In recent years, higher inflation has often been accompanied by higher not lower unemployment, especially for periods of several years in length. A simple statistical Phillips curve for such periods seems to be positively sloped, not vertical. The third stage is directed at accommodating this apparent empirical phenomenon. To do so, I suspect that it will have to include in the analysis the interdependence of economic experience and political developments. It will have to treat at least some political phenomena not as independent variables—as exogenous variables in econometric jargon—but as themselves determined by economic events—as endogenous variables [Gordon (8)]. The second stage was greatly influenced by two major developments in economic theory of the past few decades—one, the analysis of imperfect information and of the cost of acquiring information, pioneered by George Stigler; the other, the role of human capital in determining the form of labor contracts, pioneered by Gary Becker. The third stage will, I believe, be greatly influenced by a third major development—the application of economic analysis to political behavior, a field in which pioneering work has also been done by Stigler and Becker as well as by Kenneth Arrow, Duncan Black, Anthony Downs, James Buchanan, Gordon Tullock, and others.

The apparent positive relation between inflation and unemployment has been a source of great concern to government policy makers. Let me quote from a recent speech by Prime Minister Callaghan of Great Britain:

"We used to think that you could just spend your way out of a recession and increase employment by cutting taxes and boosting Government spending. I tell you, in all candour, that that option no longer exists, and that insofar as it ever did exist, it only worked by injecting bigger doses of inflation into the

250

economy followed by higher levels of unemployment as the next step. That is the history of the past 20 years" (speech to Labour Party Conference, 28 September 1976).

The same view is expressed in a Canadian government white paper: "Continuing inflation, particularly in North America, has been accompanied by an increase in measured unemployment rates" ("The Way Ahead: A Framework for Discussion," Government of Canada Working Paper, October 1976).

These are remarkable statements, running as they do directly counter to the policies adopted by almost every Western government throughout the postwar period.

a. *Some evidence*

More systematic evidence for the past two decades is given in Table 1 and Figures 3 and 4, which show the rates of inflation and unemployment in seven industrialized countries over the past two decades. According to the five-year averages in Table 1, the rate of inflation and the level of unemployment moved in opposite directions—the expected simple Phillips curve outcome—in five out of seven countries between the first two quinquennia (1956—60, 1961—65); in only four out of seven countries between the second and third quinquennia (1961—65 and 1966—70); and in only one out of seven countries between the final two quinquennia (1966—70 and 1970—75). And even the one exception—Italy—is not a real exception. True, unemployment averaged a shade lower from 1971 to 1975 than in the prior five years, despite a more than tripling of the rate of inflation. However, since 1973, both inflation and unemployment have risen sharply.

The averages for all seven countries plotted in Figure 3 bring out even more

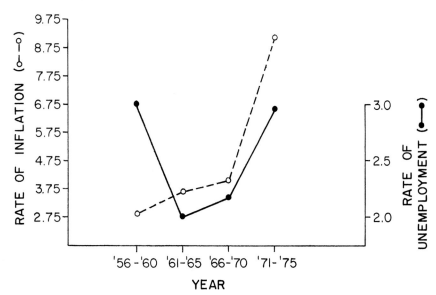

Figure 3. Rates of Unemployment and Inflation, 1956 to 1975, by Quinquennia; Unweighted Average for Seven Countries

251

clearly the shift from a negatively sloped simple Phillips curve to a positively sloped one. The two curves move in opposite directions between the first two quinquennia; in the same direction thereafter.

Table 1. Inflation and unemployment in seven countries, 1956 to 1975: Average values for successive quinquennia

DP = Rate of price change, percent per year
U = Unemployement, percentage of labor force

	France		Ger-many		Italy		Japan		Sweden		United Kingdom		United States		Un-weight-ed Aver-age Seven Count-ries	
	DP	U	DP	U	DP	U	DP	U	DP	U	DP	U	DP	U	DP	U
1956 through 1960	5.6	1.1	1.8	2.9	1.9	6.7	1.9	1.4	3.7	1.9	2.6	1.5	2.0	5.2	2.8	3.0
1961 through 1965	3.7	1.2	2.8	0.7	4.9	3.1	6.2	0.9	3.6	1.2	3.5	1.6	1.3	5.5	3.7	2.0
1966 through 1970	4.4	1.7	2.4	1.2	3.0	3.5	5.4	1.1	4.6	1.6	4.6	2.1	4.2	3.9	4.1	2.2
1971 through 1975	8.8	2.5	6.1	2.1	11.3	3.3	11.4	1.4	7.9	1.8	13.0	3.2	6.7	6.1	9.3	2.9

Note: DP is rate of change of consumer prices compounded annually from calendar year 1955 to 1960; 1960 to 1965; 1965 to 1970; 1970 to 1975. U is average unemployment during five indicated calendar years. As a result, DP is dated one-half year prior to associated U.

The annual data in Figure 4 tell a similar, though more confused, story. In the early years, there is wide variation in the relation between prices and unemployment, varying from essentially no relation, as in Italy, to a fairly clear-cut year-to-year negative relation, as in the U.K. and the U.S. In recent years, however, France, the U.S., the U.K., Germany and Japan all show a clearly marked rise in both inflation and unemployment—though for Japan, the rise in unemployment is much smaller relative to the rise in inflation than in the other countries, reflecting the different meaning of unemployment in the different institutional environment of Japan. Only Sweden and Italy fail to conform to the general pattern.

Of course, these data are at most suggestive. We do not really have seven independent bodies of data. Common international influences affect all countries so that multiplying the number of countries does not multiply propor-

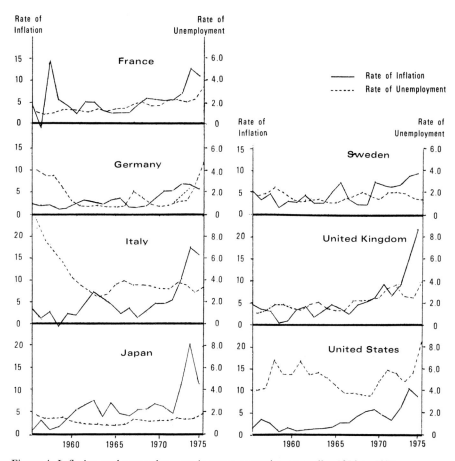

Figure 4. Inflation and unemployment in seven countries, annually, 1956 to 1975

tionately the amount of evidence. In particular, the oil crisis hit all seven countries at the same time. Whatever effect the crisis had on the rate of inflation, it directly disrupted the productive process and tended to increase unemployment. Any such increases can hardly be attributed to the acceleration of inflation that accompanied them; at most the two could be regarded as at least partly the common result of a third influence [Gordon (7)].

Both the quinquennial and annual data show that the oil crisis cannot wholly explain the phenomenon described so graphically by Mr. Callaghan. Already before the quadrupling of oil prices in 1973, most countries show a clearly marked association of rising inflation and rising unemployment. But this too may reflect independent forces rather than the influence of inflation on unemployment. For example, the same forces that have been raising the natural rate of unemployment in the U.S. may have been operating in other countries and may account for their rising trend of unemployment, independently of the consequences of inflation.

Despite these qualifications, the data strongly suggest that, at least in some countries, of which Britain, Canada, and Italy may be the best examples, rising inflation and rising unemployment have been mutually reinforcing, rather than the separate effects of separate causes. The data are not inconsistent with the stronger statement that, in all industrialized countries, higher rates of inflation have some effects that, at least for a time, make for higher unemployment. The rest of this paper is devoted to a preliminary exploration of what some of these effects may be.

b. A tentative hypothesis

I conjecture that a modest elaboration of the natural-rate hypothesis is all that is required to account for a positive relation between inflation and unemployment, though of course such a positive relation may also occur for other reasons. Just as the natural-rate hypothesis explains a negatively sloped Phillips curve over short periods as a temporary phenomenon that will disappear as economic agents adjust their expectations to reality, so a positively sloped Phillips curve over somewhat longer periods may occur as a transitional phenomenon that will disappear as economic agents adjust not only their expectations but their institutional and political arrangements to a new reality. When this is achieved, I believe that—as the natural-rate hypothesis suggests—the rate of unemployment will be largely independent of the average rate of inflation, though the efficiency of utilization of resources may not be. High inflation need not mean either abnormally high or abnormally low unemployment. However, the institutional and political arrangements that accompany it, either as relics of earlier history or as products of the inflation itself, are likely to prove antithetical to the most productive use of employed resources—a special case of the distinction between the state of employment and the productivity of an economy referred to earlier.

Experience in many Latin American countries that have adjusted to chronically high inflation rates—experience that has been analyzed most perceptively by some of my colleagues, particularly Arnold Harberger and Larry Sjaastad [(12), (25)]—is consistent, I believe, with this view.

In the version of the natural-rate hypothesis summarized in Figure 2, the vertical curve is for alternative rates of fully anticipated inflation. Whatever that rate—be it negative, zero or positive—it can be built into every decision if it is fully anticipated. At an anticipated 20 percent per year inflation, for example, long-term wage contracts would provide for a wage in each year that would rise relative to the zero-inflation wage by just 20 percent per year; long-term loans would bear an interest rate 20 percentage points higher than the zero-inflation rate, or a principal that would be raised by 20 percent a year; and so on—in short, the equivalent of a full indexing of all contracts. The high rate of inflation would have some real effects, by altering desired cash balances, for example, but it need not alter the efficiency of labor markets, or the length or terms of labor contracts, and hence, it need not change the natural rate of unemployment.

This analysis implicitly supposes, first, that inflation is steady or at least no more variable at a high rate than at a low—otherwise, it is unlikely that inflation would be as fully anticipated at high as at low rates of inflation; second, that the inflation is, or can be, open, with all prices free to adjust to the higher rate, so that relative price adjustments are the same with a 20 percent inflation as with a zero inflation; third, really a variant of the second point, that there are no obstacles to indexing of contracts.

Ultimately, if inflation at an average rate of 20 percent per year were to prevail for many decades, these requirements could come fairly close to being met, which is why I am inclined to retain the long-long-run vertical Phillips curve. But when a country initially moves to higher rates of inflation, these requirements will be systematically departed from. And such a transitional period may well extend over decades.

Consider, in particular, the U.S. and the U.K. For two centuries before World War II for the U.K., and a century and a half for the U.S., prices varied about a roughly constant level, showing substantial increases in time of war, then postwar declines to roughly prewar levels. The concept of a "normal" price level was deeply imbedded in the financial and other institutions of the two countries and in the habits and attitudes of their citizens.

In the immediate post-World War II period, prior experience was widely expected to recur. The fact was postwar inflation superimposed on wartime inflation; yet the expectation in both the U.S. and the U.K. was deflation. It took a long time for the fear of postwar deflation to dissipate—if it still has—and still longer before expectations started to adjust to the fundamental change in the monetary system. That adjustment is still far from complete [Klein (16)].

Indeed, we do not know what a complete adjustment will consist of. We cannot know now whether the industrialized countries will return to the pre-World War II pattern of a long-term stable price level, or will move toward the Latin American pattern of chronically high inflation rates—with every now and then an acute outbreak of super- or hyperinflation, as occurred recently in Chile and Argentina [Harberger (11)]—or will undergo more radical economic and political change leading to a still different resolution of the present ambiguous situation.

This uncertainty—or more precisely, the circumstances producing this uncertainty—leads to systematic departures from the conditions required for a vertical Phillips curve.

The most fundamental departure is that a high inflation rate is not likely to be steady during the transition decades. Rather, the higher the rate, the more variable it is likely to be. That has been empirically true of differences among countries in the past several decades [Jaffe and Kleiman (14); Logue and Willett (17)]. It is also highly plausible on theoretical grounds—both about actual inflation and, even more clearly, the anticipations of economic agents with respect to inflation. Governments have not produced high inflation as a deliberate announced policy but as a consequence of other policies—in particular, policies of full employment and welfare state policies raising government spending. They all proclaim their adherence to the goal of stable prices. They do so in response to their constituents, who may welcome many of the side effects of inflation, but are still wedded to the concept of stable money. A burst of inflation produces strong pressure to counter it. Policy goes from one

direction to the other, encouraging wide variation in the actual and anticipated rate of inflation. And, of course, in such an environment, no one has
single-valued anticipations. Everyone recognizes that there is great uncertainty
about what actual inflation will turn out to be over any specific future interval
[Jaffe and Kleiman (14); Meiselman (20)].

The tendency for inflation that is high on the average to be highly variable
is reinforced by the effect of inflation on the political cohesiveness of a country
in which institutional arrangements and financial contracts have been adjusted
to a long-term "normal" price level. Some groups gain (e.g., home owners);
others lose (e.g., owners of savings accounts and fixed interest securities).
"Prudent" behavior becomes in fact reckless, and "reckless" behavior in fact
prudent. The society is polarized; one group is set against another. Political
unrest increases. The capacity of any government to govern is reduced at the
same time that the pressure for strong action grows.

An increased variability of actual or anticipated inflation may raise the
natural rate of unemployment in two rather different ways.

First, increased volatility shortens the optimum length of unindexed commitments and renders indexing more advantageous [Gray (10)]. But it takes
time for actual practice to adjust. In the meantime, prior arrangements introduce rigidities that reduce the effectiveness of markets. An additional element
of uncertainty is, as it were, added to every market arrangement. In addition,
indexing is, even at best, an imperfect substitute for stability of the inflation
rate. Price indexes are imperfect; they are available only with a lag, and
generally are applied to contract terms only with a further lag.

These developments clearly lower economic efficiency. It is less clear what
their effect is on recorded unemployment. High average inventories of all
kinds is one way to meet increased rigidity and uncertainty. But that may
mean labor-hoarding by enterprises and low unemployment or a larger force
of workers between jobs and so high unemployment. Shorter commitments may
mean more rapid adjustment of employment to changed conditions and so low
unemployment, or the delay in adjusting the length of commitments may lead
to less satisfactory adjustment and so high unemployment. Clearly, much
additional research is necessary in this area to clarify the relative importance
of the various effects. About all one can say now is that the slow adjustment of
commitments and the imperfections of indexing may contribute to the recorded
increase in unemployment.

A second related effect of increased volatility of inflation is to render market
prices a less efficient system for coordinating economic activity. A fundamental
function of a price system, as Hayek (13) emphasized so brilliantly, is to transmit compactly, efficiently, and at low cost the information that economic
agents need in order to decide what to produce and how to produce it, or how
to employ owned resources. The relevant information is about *relative* prices—
of one product relative to another, of the services of one factor of production
relative to another, of products relative to factor services, of prices now
relative to prices in the future. But the information in practice is transmitted
in the form of *absolute* prices—prices in dollars or pounds or kronor. If the

price level is on the average stable or changing at a steady rate, it is relatively easy to extract the signal about relative prices from the observed absolute prices. The more volatile the rate of general inflation, the harder it becomes to extract the signal about relative prices from the absolute prices: the broadcast about relative prices is as it were being jammed by the noise coming from the inflation broadcast [Lucas (18), (19); Harberger (11)]. At the extreme, the system of absolute prices becomes nearly useless, and economic agents resort either to an alternative currency, or to barter, with disastrous effects on productivity.

Again, the effect on economic efficiency is clear, on unemployment less so. But, again, it seems plausible that the average level of unemployment would be raised by the increased amount of noise in market signals, at least during the period when institutional arrangements are not yet adapted to the new situation.

These effects of increased volatility of inflation would occur even if prices were legally free to adjust—if, in that sense, the inflation were open. In practice, the distorting effects of uncertainty, rigidity of voluntary long-term contracts, and the contamination of price signals will almost certainly be reinforced by legal restrictions on price change. In the modern world, governments are themselves producers of services sold on the market: from postal services to a wide range of other items. Other prices are regulated by government, and require government approval for change: from air fares to taxicab fares to charges for electricity. In these cases, governments cannot avoid being involved in the price-fixing process. In addition, the social and political forces unleashed by volatile inflation rates will lead governments to try to repress inflation in still other areas: by explicit price and wage control, or by pressuring private businesses or unions "voluntarily" to exercise "restraint", or by speculating in foreign exchange in order to alter the exchange rate.

The details will vary from time to time and from country to country, but the general result is the same: reduction in the capacity of the price system to guide economic activity; distortions in relative prices because of the introduction of greater friction, as it were, in all markets; and, very likely, a higher recorded rate of unemployment [(5)].

The forces I have just described may render the political and economic system dynamically unstable and produce hyperinflation and radical political change—as in many defeated countries after World War I, or in Chile and Argentina more recently. At the other extreme, before any such catastrophe occurs, policies may be adopted that will achieve a relatively low and stable rate of inflation and lead to the dismantling of many of the interferences with the price system. That would re-establish the preconditions for the straightforward natural-rate hypothesis and enable that hypothesis to be used to predict the course of the transition.

An intermediate possibility is that the system will reach stability at a fairly constant though high average rate of inflation. In that case, unemployment should also settle down to a fairly constant level decidedly lower than during the transition. As the preceding discussion emphasizes, *increasing* volatility and *increasing* government intervention with the price system are the major

257

factors that seem likely to raise unemployment, not *high* volatility or a *high* level of intervention.

Ways of coping with both volatility and intervention will develop: through indexing and similar arrangements for coping with volatility of inflation; through the development of indirect ways of altering prices and wages for avoiding government controls.

Under these circumstances, the long-run Phillips curve would again be vertical, and we would be back at the natural-rate hypothesis, though perhaps for a different range of inflation rates than that for which it was first suggested.

Because the phenomenon to be explained is the coexistence of high inflation and high unemployment, I have stressed the effect of institutional changes produced by a transition from a monetary system in which there was a "normal" price level to a monetary system consistent with long periods of high, and possibly highly variable, inflation. It should be noted that once these institutional changes were made, and economic agents had adjusted their practices and anticipations to them, a reversal to the earlier monetary framework or even the adoption in the new monetary framework of a successful policy of low inflation would in its turn require new adjustments, and these might have many of the same adverse transitional effects on the level of employment. There would appear to be an intermediate-run negatively sloped Phillips curve instead of the positively sloped one I have tried to rationalize.

5. CONCLUSION

One consequence of the Keynesian revolution of the 1930's was the acceptance of a rigid absolute wage level, and a nearly rigid absolute price level, as a starting point for analyzing short-term economic change. It came to be taken for granted that these were essentially institutional data and were so regarded by economic agents, so that changes in aggregate nominal demand would be reflected almost entirely in output and hardly at all in prices. The age-old confusion between absolute prices and relative prices gained a new lease on life.

In this intellectual atmosphere it was understandable that economists would analyze the relation between unemployment and *nominal* rather than *real* wages and would implicitly regard changes in anticipated *nominal* wages as equal to changes in anticipated *real* wages. Moreover, the empirical evidence that initially suggested a stable relation between the level of unemployment and the rate of change of nominal wages was drawn from a period when, despite sharp short-period fluctuations in prices, there was a relatively stable long-run price level and when the expectation of continued stability was widely shared. Hence these data flashed no warning signals about the special character of the assumptions.

The hypothesis that there is a stable relation between the level of unemployment and the rate of inflation was adopted by the economics profession with alacrity. It filled a gap in Keynes' theoretical structure. It seemed to be the "one equation" that Keynes himself had said "we are . . . short" (15). In addition, it seemed to provide a reliable tool for economic policy, enabling the economist to inform the policy maker about the alternatives available to him.

As in any science, so long as experience seemed to be consistent with the reigning hypothesis, it continued to be accepted, although as always, a few dissenters questioned its validity.

But as the '50's turned into the '60's, and the '60's into the '70's, it became increasingly difficult to accept the hypothesis in its simple form. It seemed to take larger and larger doses of inflation to keep down the level of unemployment. Stagflation reared its ugly head.

Many attempts were made to patch up the hypothesis by allowing for special factors such as the strength of trade unions. But experience stubbornly refused to conform to the patched up version.

A more radical revision was required. It took the form of stressing the importance of surprises—of differences between actual and anticipated magnitudes. It restored the primacy of the distinction between "real" and "nominal" magnitudes. There is a "natural rate of unemployment" at any time determined by real factors. This natural rate will tend to be attained when expectations are on the average realized. The same real situation is consistent with any absolute level of prices or of price change, provided allowance is made for the effect of price change on the real cost of holding money balances. In this respect, money is neutral. On the other hand, unanticipated changes in aggregate nominal demand and in inflation will cause systematic errors of perception on the part of employers and employees alike that will initially lead unemployment to deviate in the opposite direction from its natural rate. In this respect, money is not neutral. However, such deviations are transitory, though it may take a long chronological time before they are reversed and finally eliminated as anticipations adjust.

The natural-rate hypothesis contains the original Phillips curve hypothesis as a special case and rationalizes a far broader range of experience, in particular the phenomenon of stagflation. It has by now been widely though not universally accepted.

However, the natural-rate hypothesis in its present form has not proved rich enough to explain a more recent development—a move from stagflation to slumpflation. In recent years, higher inflation has often been accompanied by higher unemployment—not lower unemployment, as the simple Phillips curve would suggest, nor the same unemployment, as the natural-rate hypothesis would suggest.

This recent association of higher inflation with higher unemployment may reflect the common impact of such events as the oil crisis, or independent forces that have imparted a common upward trend to inflation and unemployment.

However, a major factor in some countries and a contributing factor in others may be that they are in a transitional period—this time to be measured by quinquennia or decades not years. The public has not adapted its attitudes or its institutions to a new monetary environment. Inflation tends not only to be higher but also increasingly volatile and to be accompanied by widening government intervention into the setting of prices. The growing volatility of

259

inflation and the growing departure of relative prices from the values that market forces alone would set combine to render the economic system less efficient, to introduce frictions in all markets, and, very likely, to raise the recorded rate of unemployment.

On this analysis, the present situation cannot last. It will either degenerate into hyperinflation and radical change; or institutions will adjust to a situation of chronic inflation; or governments will adopt policies that will produce a low rate of inflation and less government intervention into the fixing of prices.

I have told a perfectly standard story of how scientific theories are revised. Yet it is a story that has far-reaching importance.

Government policy about inflation and unemployment has been at the center of political controversy. Ideological war has raged over these matters. Yet the drastic change that has occurred in economic theory has not been a result of ideological warfare. It has not resulted from divergent political beliefs or aims It has responded almost entirely to the force of events: brute experience proved far more potent than the strongest of political or ideological preferences.

The importance for humanity of a correct understanding of positive economic science is vividly brought out by a statement made nearly two hundred years ago by Pierre S. du Pont, a Deputy from Nemours to the French National Assembly, speaking, appropriately enough, on a proposal to issue additional assignats—the fiat money of the French Revolution:

"Gentlemen, it is a disagreeable custom to which one is too easily led by the harshness of the discussions, to assume evil intentions. It is necessary to be gracious as to intentions; one should believe them good, and apparently they are; but we do not have to be gracious at all to inconsistent logic or to absurd reasoning. Bad logicians have committed more involuntary crimes than bad men have done intentionally" (25 September 1790).

ACKNOWLEDGMENTS

I am much indebted for helpful comments on the first draft of this paper to Gary Becker, Karl Brunner, Phillip Cagan, Robert Gordon, Arnold Harberger, Harry G. Johnson, S. Y. Lee, James Lothian, Robert E. Lucas, David Meiselman, Allan Meltzer, José Scheinkman, Theodore W. Schultz, Anna J. Schwartz, Larry Sjaastad, George J. Stigler, Sven-Ivan Sundqvist, and participants in the Money and Banking Workshop of the University of Chicago.

I am deeply indebted also to my wife, Rose Director Friedman, who took part in every stage of the preparation of the paper, and to my secretarial assistant, Gloria Valentine, for performance above and beyond the call of duty.

REFERENCES

(1) Friedman, Milton, "The Methodology of Positive Economics," *Essays in Positive Economics* (Chicago: University of Chicago Press, 1953).

(2) —, "What Price Guideposts?" In G. P. Shultz and R. Z. Aliber, eds., *Guidelines: Informal Contracts and the Market Place* (Chicago: University of Chicago Press, 1966), pp. 17—39 and 55—61.

(3) —, "An Inflationary Recession," *Newsweek*, October 17, 1966.

(4) —, "The Role of Monetary Policy," *American Economic Review* 58 (March 1968): 1—17.

(5) —, *Price Theory* (Chicago: Aldine Publishing Co., 1976), ch. 12.

(6) —, *Inflation: Causes and Consequences* (Bombay: Asia Publishing House, 1963), reprinted in *Dollars and Deficits* (Englewood Cliffs, N. J.: Prentice-Hall, 1968), pp. 21—71.

(7) Gordon, Robert J., "Alternative Responses of Policy to External Supply Shocks," *Brookings Papers on Economic Activity*, no. 1 (1975), pp. 183—206.

(8) —, "The Demand and Supply of Inflation," *Journal of Law and Economics* 18 (December 1975): 807—836.

(9) —, "Recent Developments in the Theory of Inflation and Unemployment," *Journal of Monetary Economics* 2 (1976:) 185—219.

(10) Gray, Jo Anna, "Essays on Wage Indexation." Unpublished Ph.D. dissertation, University of Chicago, 1976.

(11) Harberger, Arnold C., "Inflation," *The Great Ideas Today, 1976* (Chicago: Encyclopaedia Britannica, Inc., 1976), pp. 95—106.

(12) —, "The Inflation Problem in Latin America," a report prepared for the Buenos Aires (March 1966) meeting of the Inter-American Committee of the Alliance for Progress, published in Spanish as "El problema de la inflación en América Latina," in Centro de Estudios Monetarios Latinoamericanos, *Boletin Mensual*, June 1966, pp. 253—269. Reprinted in Economic Development Institute, *Trabajos sobre desarrollo económico* Washington, D. C.: IBRD, 1967).

(13) Hayek, F. A., "The Use of Knowledge in Society," *American Economic Review* 35 (September 1945): 519—530.

(14) Jaffe, Dwight and Kleiman, Ephraim, "The Welfare Implications of Uneven Inflation." Seminar paper no. 50, Institute for International Economic Studies, University of Stockholm, November 1975.

(15) Keynes, J. M., *General Theory of Employment, Interest, and Money* (London: Macmillan, 1936), p. 276.

(16) Klein, Benjamin, "Our New Monetary Standard: The Measurement and Effects of Price Uncertainty, 1880—1973," *Economic Inquiry*, December 1975, pp. 461—483.

(17) Logue, Dennis E. and Willett, Thomas D., "A Note on the Relation between the Rate and Variability of Inflation," *Economica*, May 1976, pp. 151—158.

(18) Lucas, Robert E., "Some International Evidence on Output-Inflation Tradeoffs," *American Economic Review* 63 (June 1973): 326—334.

(19) —, "An Equilibrium Model of the Business Cycle," *Journal of Political Economy* 83 (December 1975): 1113—1144.

(20) Meiselman, David, "Capital Formation, Monetary and Financial Adjustments," *Proceedings* 27th National Conference of Tax Foundation, 1976, pp. 9—15.

(21) Muth, John, "Rational Expectations and the Theory of Price Movements," *Econometrica* 29 (July 1961): 315—333.

(22) Phelps, E. S., "Phillips Curve, Expectations of Inflation and Optimal Unemployment Over Time," *Economica* (N. S.) 34 (August 1967): 254—281.

(23) —, "Money Wage Dynamics and Labor Market Equilibrium." In E. S. Phelps, ed., *Microeconomic Foundations of Employment and Inflation Theory* (New York: Norton, 1970).

(24) Phillips, A. W., "The Relationship between Unemployment and the Rate of Change of Money Wage Rates in the United Kingdom, 1861—1957," *Economica*, November 1958, pp. 283—299.

(25) Sjaastad, Larry A., "Monetary Policy and Suppressed Inflation in Latin America." In R. Z. Aliber, ed., *National Monetary Policies and the International Financial System* (Chicago: University of Chicago Press, 1974), pp. 127—138.